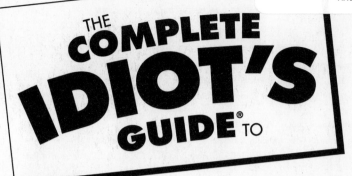

Mary Magdalene

by Lesa Bellevie

ALPHA

A member of Penguin Group (USA) Inc.

Dedicated to Chris, Nicholas, and Zinn.

ALPHA BOOKS

Published by the Penguin Group

Penguin Group (USA) Inc., 375 Hudson Street, New York, New York 10014, U.S.A.

Penguin Group (Canada), 10 Alcorn Avenue, Toronto, Ontario, Canada M4V 3B2 (a division of Pearson Penguin Canada Inc.)

Penguin Books Ltd, 80 Strand, London WC2R 0RL, England

Penguin Ireland, 25 St Stephen's Green, Dublin 2, Ireland (a division of Penguin Books Ltd)

Penguin Group (Australia), 250 Camberwell Road, Camberwell, Victoria 3124, Australia (a division of Pearson Australia Group Pty Ltd)

Penguin Books India Pvt Ltd, 11 Community Centre, Panchsheel Park, New Delhi—110 017, India

Penguin Group (NZ), cnr Airborne and Rosedale Roads, Albany, Auckland 1310, New Zealand (a division of Pearson New Zealand Ltd)

Penguin Books (South Africa) (Pty) Ltd, 24 Sturdee Avenue, Rosebank, Johannesburg 2196, South Africa

Penguin Books Ltd, Registered Offices: 80 Strand, London WC2R 0RL, England

Copyright © 2005 by Lesa Bellevie

International Standard Book Number: 1-59257-345-2
Library of Congress Catalog Card Number: 2004115797

07 06 05   8 7 6 5 4 3 2 1

Interpretation of the printing code: The rightmost number of the first series of numbers is the year of the book's printing; the rightmost number of the second series of numbers is the number of the book's printing. For example, a printing code of 05-1 shows that the first printing occurred in 2005.

Printed in the United States of America

Note: This publication contains the opinions and ideas of its author. It is intended to provide helpful and informative material on the subject matter covered. It is sold with the understanding that the author and publisher are not engaged in rendering professional services in the book. If the reader requires personal assistance or advice, a competent professional should be consulted.

The author and publisher specifically disclaim any responsibility for any liability, loss, or risk, personal or otherwise, which is incurred as a consequence, directly or indirectly, of the use and application of any of the contents of this book.

Most Alpha books are available at special quantity discounts for bulk purchases for sales promotions, premiums, fund-raising, or educational use. Special books, or book excerpts, can also be created to fit specific needs.

For details, write: Special Markets, Alpha Books, 375 Hudson Street, New York, NY 10014.

Publisher: *Marie Butler-Knight*
Product Manager: *Phil Kitchel*
Senior Managing Editor: *Jennifer Bowles*
Senior Acquisitions Editor: *Randy Ladenheim-Gil*
Development Editor: *Lynn Northrup*
Production Editor: *Megan Douglass*

Copy Editor: *Keith Cline*
Cartoonist: *Richard King*
Cover/Book Designer: *Trina Wurst*
Indexer: *Julie Bess*
Layout: *Ayanna Lacey*
Proofreading: *John Etchison*

Contents at a Glance

Contents

7   The Seven Demons   87

8   The Crucifixion   99

Foreword

The figure of Mary Magdalene has fascinated many throughout the centuries, including artists, sermonizers, playwrights, poets, scholars, church reformers, and people who pray. In the New Testament she is mentioned as a follower of Jesus and as a witness to his crucifixion. She (alone or with other women) finds the tomb of Jesus empty, and in two Gospels (Matthew and John), she receives the first appearance of the risen Jesus.

Legends sprang up concerning Mary Magdalene, emphasizing a past life of sexual sin, conversion by Jesus, and repentance. The legend-making was accomplished by conflating the texts that do mention Mary Magdalene, with stories of anonymous women in the Gospels. Most important among the latter are the stories of the "woman of the city, a sinner" who crashes a party, anoints the feet of Jesus, and is forgiven for her sins (Luke 7); the woman caught in adultery, saved by Jesus from the punishment of stoning (John 8); and the Samaritan woman who had many men but no husband (John 4). Mary Magdalene thus acquired her still-dominant—and undeserved—reputation as a prostitute. We can still find her depicted thus in the movies (for example, Mel Gibson's *The Passion of the Christ*) and plays (*Jesus Christ, Superstar*). Sometimes she is portrayed as Jesus' love interest and even wife (for example, Kazanstakis's *The Last Temptation of Christ* and Dan Brown's *The Da Vinci Code*).

Recent scholarship has attempted to peel away the legend, analyze the ancient texts, and get down to the Gospel memories of the first-century Jewish woman associated with the initial moments of Christian faith in the resurrection of Jesus. This has meant uncovering the memory of her as an apostle and leader in the early church. New and more complex understandings of Christian origins are being proposed.

In the twentieth and twenty-first centuries interest in her has been kindled because of several significant developments: New Testament historical-critical scholarship, which notes how the four Gospels differ from one another, and develops methods and perspectives to reconstruct possible historical events; the recent discovery of ancient apocryphal manuscripts that do not depict Mary as a sinner but as a leader of superior understanding, loved by Jesus; women's studies programs in colleges and universities, in which feminist scholarship—dedicated to the proposition that women are and always were fully human—is brought to bear on every field of knowledge, including Religious Studies; the women's movement which promotes the leadership of women, and attention to so-called "women's issues" and to human sexuality; and deep changes in organized religions.

Lesa Bellevie has done an amazing job of drawing together a tremendous amount of information on Mary Magdalene. Bellevie's judgment is trustworthy concerning the spectacular aspects, such as the Grail Legend. Bravo! After you have read her book I hope you ask the questions that help you process all this data: Why was Mary Magdalene's image so powerful and so distorted? What is its meaning for the present and future?

Dr. Jane D. Schaberg (Ph.D., Union Theological Seminary/Columbia University NYC)

Dr. Schaberg is professor of Religious Studies and Women's Studies at the University of Detroit Mercy. Among her publications are *The Resurrection of Mary Magdalene: Legends, Apocrypha and Christian Testament* (Continuum, 2002); *The Illegitimacy of Jesus: A Feminist Theological Interpretation of the New Testament Infancy Narratives* (Sheffield Press, 1992); and numerous scholarly articles and poems. She lectures widely, and is now at work on a memoir of her experience as a foster mother. She can be contacted at JaneDSchaberg@cs.com.

Introduction

What is the power and attraction of one woman? Mary Magdalene stands as a testament to the draw of a paradox on human imagination, whether religious and devotional or secular and poetic. For 2,000 years, people have been speculating about who she may have been, and today we still search for meaning in the subtleties of her legend and fragments of deteriorating papyrus. Are we any closer to an answer?

Mary Magdalene is a woman without much of a story, but because her name has appeared in so many places at so many times, it was inevitable that stories would be created for her. We know that she was close to Jesus, but we don't know how close, and we don't know in what way. We know that she followed him, that she stood resolute in the midst of danger and sorrow, and we know that she was ultimately rewarded for her perseverance. We know that the earliest Christians honored her for the role she played in the unfolding of what has been called "the greatest story ever told."

What we'll find is that the part she played in the Christian story is only the beginning of our fascination with Mary Magdalene. It only served as a launching point from which her legends would take on lives of their own. There are many different Mary Magdalenes to know, and it is only by considering them together that we can begin to get a complete picture of this wonderfully mysterious and complex woman. She is every bit as complicated as we are, and indeed, one of her primary functions seems to have been as a mirror, reflecting back to us the way that we think about ourselves.

But in case you're wondering, I haven't waxed philosophical to such a degree in the pages that follow. My aim in writing *The Complete Idiot's Guide to Mary Magdalene* has been to present everything you need to know to understand why Mary Magdalene has had such phenomenal staying power, and why we continue to be fascinated by her. Whereas other books about Mary Magdalene focus on one particular perspective, or are written for an academic audience, this one contains a wide array of information in an easy-to-understand format.

What You'll Find in This Book

To present such a wild diversity of material in an orderly fashion, this book is divided into six main parts:

Part 1, "Mary Magdalene: A Complicated Woman," introduces you to Mary Magdalene and establishes a foundation on which you'll be able to build as you learn more about her many legends. I fill you in on how she became confused with other women in the Gospels and go over some of the most popular misconceptions.

Part 2, "The Biblical Mary Magdalene," is all about Mary Magdalene in Christianity, which is the most traditional view that we have of her. We examine exactly what the Gospels say about her and go over what life may have been like for her in first-century Palestine. We also see how Jesus treated women in general, which can help us understand what her experience may have been of the man whom she followed so faithfully.

Part 3, "The Legendary Mary Magdalene," takes a look at how her legends really got a foothold in the Middle Ages, and how some of the most important figures in Christianity were influenced by her. We also see some of the different ways that Mary Magdalene is remembered around the world today as a result of her medieval popularity.

Part 4, "The Gnostic Mary Magdalene," helps you understand what all of this Gnosticism business is about. I guide you through the complicated world of Gnostic Christianity and introduce you to the texts that have recently been discovered. Then we look at why it's impossible to talk about Mary Magdalene without mentioning her importance to the Gnostics.

Part 5, "Thoroughly Modern Magdalene," examines the many ideas currently circulating about Mary Magdalene. There are a few perspectives that are prevalent, and no other resource helps sort them from one another. After you read this section, you'll have a good grasp of all the different things people are saying about Mary Magdalene today.

Part 6, "Exploring Mary Magdalene," shows you how to spot Mary Magdalene in the many works of art that depict her, and recommends some other resources for further study. If you'd like to do something special to incorporate a devotion to Mary Magdalene into your life, I included some ideas for ways to express this. You'll also find some tasty suggestions for celebrating her feast day on July 22.

I also include four appendixes—a quick lookup of Mary Magdalene references, a list of resources, a chronology, and a glossary—to help you learn more about Mary Magdalene.

Extras

To call some additional details to your attention, I placed certain bits of information into special boxes. Because of Mary Magdalene's unique importance during the Middle Ages, I tried to choose names for the boxes that bring to mind the dusty old texts that tell us so much about her.

Illuminations

Just as illuminated manuscripts give color and depth to a text, these boxes help embellish certain points.

Lingua Magda

In these boxes, you find definitions for terms that help tell Mary Magdalene's many stories.

It Is Written

Sometimes, the best way to add clarity to a subject is by quoting someone else. These boxes contain words from someone else's pen.

Quite Contrary

Look out! These boxes alert you to the presence of a commonly held misconception.

A Note About Bible Versions

Throughout the book, passages from the Bible are taken from the Revised Standard Version, which corrects many of the mistranslations present in the King James Version. The only exception to my use of the RSV is in Chapter 6, in which I do quote from the King James Version. The reason I've decided to do so is that the King James Version of the Bible is the version by which people have been learning about Mary Magdalene since 1611.

Acknowledgments

For several years I've known that I wanted to write an introductory book about Mary Magdalene for the general reader. I was never precisely sure how it would happen, so when I was approached about writing this book, I was ecstatic. My husband, Chris, shared in my joy and responded by working hard to organize our lives around the writing of the manuscript. I never would have been able to juggle as many obligations as I had during the writing of this book if not for his love and support, and his acknowledgement of Mary Magdalene's importance to me. This book is dedicated to him, first and foremost.

I must also thank Nicholas, for being exceptionally patient and understanding even though I was, in essence, working two or three jobs all summer; and Zinn, with his uniquely toddler *joie de vivre* that fills our home with laughter. I love you both more than words, and dedicate this book to you also.

To Professor Mark Strauss, the technical reviewer for this book: I appreciate your critical eye and your willingness to undertake this project; the book is better as a result of your involvement. Thank you so much.

Thanks also to Diane Herr, for her valuable research into Mary Magdalene in music; Aron Wolf, for always being willing to help me with Greek; Carl Hood Jr., for bouncing ideas around with me; Brandy Williams, for her kind encouragement; Stephan Hoeller, whose lecture on *The Gospel of Mary* brought the text to life for me; Margaret Starbird, who has always been willing to answer my many questions; Quintus' Latin Translation Service; the members of the Magdalene.org e-mail list, who continue to give me insight into how Mary Magdalene is being appreciated in our culture; and finally, to Dawn, without whose help I never would have been able to manage such an incredibly busy time: "For now she is mourned, and her self rejoices."

Special Thanks to the Technical Reviewer

The Complete Idiot's Guide to Mary Magdalene was reviewed by an expert who double-checked the accuracy of what you'll learn here, to help us ensure that this book gives you everything you need to know about this fascinating woman. Special thanks are extended to Professor Mark L. Strauss, Ph.D.

Dr. Strauss is Professor of New Testament at Bethel Seminary San Diego. He is the author of *The Davidic Messiah in Luke—Acts* (Sheffield Academic Press, 1995); *Distorting Scripture? The Challenge of Bible Translation and Gender Accuracy* (Inter-Varsity, 1998); "The Gospel of Luke" in *Zondervan Illustrated Bible Background Commentary* (Zondervan, 2002); and other books and articles.

Trademarks

Part 1

Mary Magdalene: A Complicated Woman

To say that women are complicated creatures is a pretty outdated notion, but when it comes to Mary Magdalene, it couldn't be more true. She's a beauty, she's a hag; she's an apostle, she's a harlot; she's faithful, she's fickle; she's fallen, she's redeemed. Where can we even begin to unravel the mystique that surrounds this baffling woman?

We start at the beginning, of course, in the Gospels. And from there, we take a quick trip through the past 2,000 years to see where certain ideas about her first popped up. After we've done that, you have a basic understanding of how everything fits together, allowing us to dig deeper in later sections. Don't worry if you aren't a history buff, we sail through the different periods in a breeze, stopping to take a look at only the most important events as they relate to Mary Magdalene.

Chapter 1

Mary *Who?*

In This Chapter

- Galilee: the backdrop for Jesus' ministry
- Questions behind the name "Mary Magdalene"
- How is it possible to be sinful *and* holy?
- A woman for all ages: Mary Magdalene's enduring legacy

Beauty. Vanity. Sensuality. Love. Pain. Sorrow. If these characteristics were colors, they would be crucial hues for painting a picture of the Mary Magdalene we've come to know. She is a haunting image of seduction and exotic perfumes to some, and a pious example of the most fervent religious devotion to others. It would be entirely fair, if not a bit of an understatement, to say that Mary Magdalene is a complicated woman.

Her story starts two thousand years ago, and is still inspiring people today. As you can well imagine, a lot of things can happen in the space of two thousand years (that's 20 centuries!), so we'll need some kind of overview before we can dig deeper into the details. Here we start by remembering her place in the Christian story, and then move on to a discussion of how she got her name. Because not everyone in the Gospels came to be such a famous personality, we also spend some time looking at the main reasons why her legend has endured as long as it has.

A Long Time Ago, in Galilee ...

We begin our search for Mary Magdalene in a small area called Galilee, against the backdrop of first-century Palestine. At the time, Palestine was part of the Roman Empire. A large region encompassing the territory from roughly the modern border of Syria in the north to the southern end of the Dead Sea, Palestine was a rich cultural ferment of Greek and Roman influence as well as Jewish tradition. It was in this setting that one of the most significant men in history started his career as a public speaker.

A Man Named Jesus

Before meeting Mary Magdalene, we should take a look at the man who was responsible for bringing her to our attention: Jesus. If it weren't for Jesus, after all, would we know of a woman named Mary Magdalene? Would her name have endured for two *thousand* years? Almost certainly not. Mary Magdalene is, first and foremost, a Christian figure, and it's important for us to back up and get a little bit of perspective on where she fits into the Christian story before moving forward into the dazzling world of legend she has inspired.

Jesus was, of course, the man on whom the entire Christian religion is based. He was called "Christ," which means "the anointed one," to indicate that his followers thought he was the Jewish Messiah whose coming had been prophesied. The Gospels tell of his miraculous birth to the young virgin girl, Mary of Nazareth, his uncanny knowledge of scripture, and his ministry of teaching that "the kingdom of God is at hand." His message was met by political and religious opposition, which led to his eventual arrest, trial, and public execution by crucifixion, a death by hanging on a cross. Christians worldwide believe that he rose from the dead and then ascended into heaven.

Illuminations

The first use of the word "Christian" in the New Testament appears in the book of Acts. (Acts 26:28) There are more than 1,000 different Christian sects in North America alone.

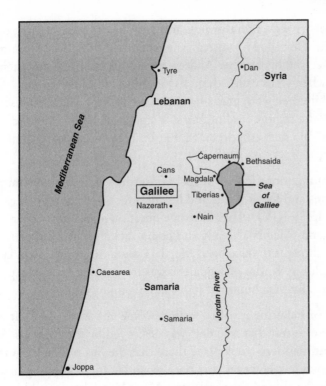

Map of Galilee in first-century Palestine.

Nestled in a region of Palestine known as Galilee was Jesus' hometown, Nazareth. A first-century Jewish historian named Flavius Josephus wrote that Galilee's borders were on the Mediterranean to the west, the Jordan River to the east, Samaria to the south, and roughly along the modern border between Israel and Lebanon to the north. Galilee was the lushest area in the region, and was known for its incredible fertility. From the fish pulled out of the Sea of Galilee to the olive groves and fruit orchards, it is little wonder that anyone who grew up in such an idyllic setting, as Jesus had, would make use of seed imagery in his stories, as in this passage from the Gospel of Matthew:

> Another parable he put before them, saying, "The kingdom of heaven is like a grain of mustard seed which a man took and sowed in his field; it is the smallest of all seeds, but when it has grown it is the greatest of shrubs and becomes a tree, so that the birds of the air come and make nests in its branches." (Matthew 13:31–32 KJV)

Although Jesus' ministry took him throughout Palestine, he spent a great deal of time in the Galilee region. He called his disciples from among those he encountered in the area. Simon Peter and his brother Andrew were fishermen, casting their nets on the Sea of Galilee, when Jesus called them to join him. He called James and John, the sons of Zebedee, while they were mending their fishing nets. With his disciples, Jesus traveled throughout the region, healing the sick and speaking to gathered crowds. It was probably during one such stop to teach that Jesus would have encountered a woman named Mary.

The New Testament mentions in the Gospel of Matthew that after the miracle of multiplying the loaves and fishes, Jesus and his followers went to a town called Magdala (Matthew 15:39 KJV). (There is some question about how accurate the translation of the name "Magdala" really is; I come back to that a little later in the chapter.) The place thought to have been Magdala was a maritime town, known for fisheries and shipbuilding. If Mary Magdalene was from Magdala, this is probably where she would have first encountered Jesus and his followers.

In 66 C.E., the Jews of Palestine revolted against Rome and war ensued. It was during this time of chaos and unrest that Magdala was destroyed by the Romans. Josephus wrote that such great massacres took place there that the Sea of Galilee was red with blood. Magdala rebounded, however, and once again became a thriving maritime town. It was destroyed a second time well after Mary Magdalene would have lived there, and there is very little now to mark the places where she may have walked.

Illuminations

For many years, a small village called el-Mejdel sat on the site believed to have once been Magdala. Today, a small agricultural settlement, again called Magdala, occupies the area. Recently a ship known as "the Jesus boat" was discovered about a mile north of ancient Magdala; the ship had been preserved in mud and dates back to the first century. Archaeologists have also discovered a ship mosaic in the ruins of a villa, and a synagogue that may also date back to the time of Christ.

A Ministry Open to All

Jesus' ministry was special in innumerable ways, but one of the most surprising was that he included people who were usually excluded from fully participating in Jewish society. According to Jesus, *Gentiles*, sinners, the sick, the poor, and women were all welcome in the kingdom of God. Not only do many of the stories of Jesus' actions and miracles include women, but the *parables* he told often featured female characters that women could relate to.

Perhaps because Jesus knew that women had spiritual concerns also, he attracted a following of women. It would have been considered unusual—even scandalous—to the more con-servative Jews of the time to see women traveling with men who weren't their hus-bands or family members. Like all societies, first-century Palestine was made up of some people who obeyed the laws and some who took a more liberal approach, but generally, women were accorded much less status in the culture than men. The fact that Jesus would even speak to women in public was a break with tradition, so teach-ing female students as a rabbi was downright revolutionary!

Lingua Magda

A **Gentile** is a non-Jewish person. A story that con-veys a teaching is a **parable**.

The Gospels say that his female followers provided for him and his ministry, so they probably had funds of their own to spend on food, shelter, and the other essentials for living. Mary Magdalene was one of the women included in the list of those who provided for Jesus. We come back to the subject of Jesus and women in Chapter 5.

Not Even Her Name Is Simple

Most people who write about Mary Magdalene take her name for granted. Mary Magdalene was Mary Magdalene. Simple, right? Well, not really. Although most scholars accept the name "Magdalene" as a reference to her hometown, Magdala, the truth is that there are some big questions involved.

Did Magdala Really Exist?

If you have a King James Version of the New Testament handy, you can open it to the Gospel of Matthew, chapter 15, verse 39. There you will see this passage: "And he sent away the multitude, and took ship, and came into the coasts of Magdala."

Where *is* Magdala?

The earliest evidence of Magdala comes in a book called the *Talmud*, which was written after Magdala was destroyed. The Talmud is a collection of writings begun as early as the second century C.E. to record all of the laws, stories, rituals, and other information about Jewish life that was previously passed through oral tradition.

As you can probably imagine, it is a very large book, and there are even two different versions: the Palestinian and the Babylonian. Here's a summary of what you need to know:

- There are two towns called Magdala mentioned in the Talmud: Magdala Gadar and Magdala Nunayya.

- Magdala Nunayya means "tower of the fishes," probably because it contained fisheries and was situated on the Sea of Galilee.

- The two versions of the Talmud disagree on the distance from Magdala Nunayya to another town called Tiberius.

- The Talmud mentions that the Romans destroyed Magdala Nunayya.

What we learn about Magdala from the Talmud is interesting, but it isn't enough to figure out whether one or the other of the Magdalas is *the* Magdala we're looking for. So to strengthen the argument for a town called Magdala during the first century, we need to turn again to the historian Josephus. Josephus was a witness to the Jewish rebellion against Rome, and his writings are extremely valuable documents of what took place. It is from him that we learn more about one little town on the Sea of Galilee that was destroyed during the war:

- Josephus mentions a town called Taricheae, which means a "place of pickling houses," probably related to the preservation of fish.

- Taricheae matches the more reliable distance from Tiberius given for Magdala Nunayya that's given in the Talmud.

- Taricheae was destroyed by the Romans during the rebellion.

From these details, scholars have decided that Taricheae was probably the same town as Magdala Nunayya, and that it was probably known as Magdala during Jesus and Mary Magdalene's lifetime. But what about the Gospel accounts of Magdala? Are they translated correctly?

Probably not.

Depending on which translation of the New Testament you happen to pick up, you may or may not find Magdala. The discrepancy comes from the fact that the earlier and more reliable Greek manuscripts used by modern translations do not mention "Magdala." They do mention two other towns: Magedan (Matthew 15:39) and Dalmanutha (Mark 8:10). Perhaps it isn't terribly difficult to see how "Magedan" could have been rendered as "Magdala," but how in the world could we go from "Dalmanutha" to "Magdala"?

Two reasons have been suggested why scribes may have changed "Dalmanutha" to "Magedan":

- The location of Dalmanutha was a total mystery.

- "Dalmanutha" could appear similar to "Magedan" when written in Greek.

From the word "Magedan," it is only a short trip to "Magdala."

I'm betting that you understand now why the questions about Magdala don't really have clear answers. What does this mean for Mary Magdalene? Only that we can't say with absolute certainty that her name reflects her hometown.

> **Illuminations**
>
> In one Greek version of the New Testament called Codex Bezae Cantabrigiensis, which dates from the fifth or sixth century, there are scribal notes in the margin giving instructions to change "Dalmanutha" in Mark 8:10 to "Magdala."

Was It a Nickname?

Another theory about Mary Magdalene's name is that it is an epithet, or nickname. The reason that there even *is* a nickname theory has already been covered: the open questions about whether or not a town called Magdala even existed in the first century C.E.

The names "Magdalene" and "Magdala" derive from a common Hebrew root, *migdal*, which means "tower," "stronghold," or "fortress." This has led to suggestions that perhaps Mary Magdalene's name reflects some quality about her; perhaps she was tall, or forthright, or somehow an example of strength best represented by tower imagery. Nicknames were not entirely unheard of in the Gospels. Jesus called Simon "Peter," which means "rock," and he nicknamed James and John "Boanerges," which means "the sons of thunder." In the early fifth century C.E., St. Jerome wrote in a letter:

> Mary of Magdala received the epithet "fortified with towers" because of her earnestness and strength of faith, and was privileged to see the rising of Christ first before even the apostles.

The nickname idea has picked up momentum during recent years due to the publication of Margaret Starbird's book *The Goddess in the Gospels* (see Appendix B). In addition to the notion that it wouldn't have been terribly unusual for Jesus to have

Quite Contrary _____

As an example of how errors have crept into the New Testament as the result of mis-translations, scribal mistakes, and popular tradition, it has been determined that the person whom Paul praises as "outstanding among the apostles" in Romans 16:7 isn't, in fact, a man named Junius, but a woman named Junia.

given Mary Magdalene a nickname, Starbird theo-rizes that the numerical value of the Greek words for "the Magdalene" is significant enough to suggest the name was chosen with intention rather than by the accident of birth. We return to Margaret Starbird's theories about Mary Magdalene in Chapter 20.

Although this is a fascinating idea, there isn't any solid historical evidence that this is the case. In the centuries between when the Gospels were first com-posed and the first instance of Mary Magdalene's name that still survives, there are plenty of opportu-nities for scribal error to creep in. It is controversial, to say the least, to rely on the spelling or etymology of "the Magdalene" as evidence of its own origin.

Superstar Saint–and Sinner

As everyone knows, a name is not a person. Who is the woman behind the name? What do we know about her?

Mary Magdalene was the female follower of Jesus who was mentioned more fre-quently than any of the others. Her greatest role is that of the first witness of the resurrection, which guarantees a place for her in annual Easter services. This has kept her in Christian minds for two thousand years.

Roman Catholics and Orthodox Christians consider Mary Magdalene a saint, which means that she was an exceptionally holy person who is now in the presence of God, and is able to intercede on behalf of people who pray to her. (In other words, as a saint, Mary Magdalene has access to God's ear and can put in a good word for you.) She has been one of the most commonly adored saints, and at times she eclipsed even the Virgin Mary in popularity. This might be hard to believe; as you browse your local Christian bookstore for items bearing Mary Magdalene's name or image, you are likely to find very little.

This brings us to the next point, which is that Mary Magdalene is also one of the most infamous sinners in history. Because she was incorrectly thought to have been a prostitute before meeting Jesus, she has been called all manner of nasty names. Even though she was thought to have been redeemed by Jesus, she was made into a symbol for female sexuality anyway and heaped with related cultural baggage. This puts Mary

Magdalene at the heart of a paradox: She is, in our minds, at once a prostitute and a holy person. Until very recently, and occasionally still, a person who took Mary Magdalene as their patron saint was often viewed with some disapproval because of her sinfulness, as if it somehow rubs off on those who honor her.

Maybe it is this enormous contradiction that has enraptured us for so long.

A Woman for All Ages

Just who Mary Magdalene is has been malleable, based on the religious and social needs of any given time and place. Regardless, she really did, more or less, spring into existence as a complex figure. Right from the beginning, there was much more to her than met the eye.

Maybe you're wondering how we know anything at all about Mary Magdalene. These are some of the sources of information about her:

- Religious texts, such as the New Testament

- Writings by early Christians

- Paintings, mosaics, and other art forms

- Sermons, homilies, and other religious documents

- Plays, poems, and songs

Of course, the oldest material, and the source of everything known of Mary Magdalene, is in the Gospels. Although the other sources don't tell us about Mary Magdalene herself, they do tell us what people have thought about her and how she has inspired us through the years.

It Is Written

Carl Orff's famous composition, *Carmina Burana,* is based on a thirteenth-century Passion play in which Mary Magdalene was an important character. One section of *Carmina Burana* that retains an unnamed reference to Mary Magdalene is "Chramer, gip die varwe mir" (Shopkeeper, give me color):

"Shopkeeper, give me color
to make my cheeks red,
so that I can make the young men
love me, against their will."

A Refresher on Historical Periods

Because Mary Magdalene appears almost constantly throughout the past two thousand years, and because I refer to different time periods throughout this book, let's take a brief look at how Western history is divided.

Defining the historical periods isn't an easy job because it is usually done as convenient, depending on what is being studied by any given scholar. There are no sharp cut-off dates for the different periods of history; there is always overlap in both directions that could call a specific date into question. So for our purposes, I'm defining the periods of Western history as follows:

♦ 0–500 C.E.: The early Christian era

♦ 501–1300 C.E.: The Middle Ages (the "medieval" period)

♦ 1301–1500 C.E.: The Renaissance

♦ 1501–present: The modern era

When referring to a century rather than an exact year, the century is one number higher than represented in the year. For example, if I refer to the sixth century, I'm talking about the years 500–599 C.E. This is because the years 0–99 C.E. were the first century, years 100–199 C.E. were the second century, and so on.

Early Popularity

Mary Magdalene appeared quietly on the art scene in a third-century baptistery, which shows her in one of her earliest and most important Christian roles: that of a *myrrhophore,* or someone who bears myrrh. Myrrh is a spice with a powerful scent that had many uses, including the preparation of the dead. In the Gospels, the myrrhophores, or myrrh-bearers, were the women who went to Jesus' tomb to anoint his body only to discover that he had risen from the dead. The Gospels don't agree on how many women went to the tomb; in addition to Mary Magdalene, there were one or two other women. The myrrhophore role was meaningful because during the first centuries of Christianity, more emphasis was placed on the miracles of Jesus and the resurrection than on his crucifixion and sacrifice. As witnesses to such a notable event, the myrrhophores were considered to be very holy women. Mary Magdalene would have enjoyed the respect due a myrrhophore before being cast as a sinner in popular imagination.

Also in the third century, Hippolytus of Rome, who was one of the most important theologians and writers during the early Christian era, is believed to have composed a commentary on the *Song of Songs* (sometimes called *Canticle of Canticles*). It is now questioned whether or not it was actually Hippolytus who composed the text, but regardless of who the author was, the commentary remained very important.

The *Song of Songs* is an Old Testament text regarded as a love poem with deeply spiritual significance. In the text, a man and woman exchange passionate and arduous words describing their relationship and love for one another. *Song of Songs* is a beautifully lyrical piece of literature with ancient origins, and Jews viewed it as an allegory for the relationship between God and the nation of Israel. The woman in *Song of Songs* is called a Shulamite, a name that probably indicates her nationality. Parts of the story portray her as a bride in search of her beloved bridegroom.

Illuminations

Ecclesia is Greek for "church" or "assembly" and refers to the entire body of believers in a given religion, particularly Judaism and Christianity. In Christianity, Ecclesia is another word for the collective term "the Church."

Hippolytus made some very interesting observations about *Song of Songs*. First, he compared Mary Magdalene with the Shulamite woman. By doing so, he was making her into a representative of the Church, collectively, in the role of the *Bride of Christ*. Like the Shulamite woman, she was the forlorn bride searching for her bridegroom, just as the Church was seen as Christ's spiritual bride (Eph. 5:25; Rev. 19:7). Hippolytus' Mary Magdalene stood for this relationship in Christianity just as the Shulamite woman had for Judaism.

Another creative idea Hippolytus had was to associate Mary Magdalene with Eve. He called her the *New Eve*. According to the book of Genesis, Eve was the first woman ever created. She and her husband, Adam, lived in the Garden of Eden until she was persuaded by a serpent to taste forbidden fruit. She convinced Adam to taste it, too, and God sent them out into the world as a punishment.

Eve's garden was the Garden of Eden, and according to Hippolytus, Mary Magdalene's garden was outside of Jesus' tomb. Eve's mistake had an effect on all generations that followed her, but Mary Magdalene, by recognizing the power of Jesus' sacrifice and resurrection, showed humanity the path to redemption. This is an identity that would be applied to Jesus' mother in later years.

The last important title Hippolytus bestowed on Mary Magdalene was that of apostle to the apostles, or as it was to later appear in Latin, *apostola apostolorum*. An "apostle" is a messenger, and as the first witness of the resurrection, Mary Magdalene had the task of conveying the news to the other disciples. Later in the book we take a closer look at the modern interest in Mary Magdalene's apostolic role.

The Middle Ages

During the Christian era and early Middle Ages, a great deal of emphasis was placed on the doctrine of the Fall, which refers, of course, to that little episode with Adam, Eve, and the serpent in the Garden of Eden. Because Eve was the first person to disobey God, leading to the Fall itself, she was believed to bear the guilt for bringing sin into the world. As a result, all women, as the "daughters of Eve," came to represent the sinfulness of the flesh. Sexuality, only barely tolerated within the sanctity of marriage, was seen as a dangerous enterprise with eternal implications for the soul.

> **It Is Written**
>
> God's sentence of females lives on today: as does the guilt necessarily persist. You are the devil's gateway; you are the violator of that Tree; you are the first deserter of divine law; you are she by whom Adam, who the devil dared not approach, was convinced; you so easily dashed Man, the image of God; on account of what you deserve—that is, death—even God's son had to die.
>
> —Tertullian, *The Attire of Women* (third century)

By the sixth century C.E., there was much confusion about who was who in the Gospels (something we will return to in the next chapter). This confusion led to Mary Magdalene's most infamous identity, that of a prostitute. In her guise as prostitute, she came up against the Church's growing asceticism with full force; she was the object of scorn for her sinfulness and a lesson in piety and redemption for her faithfulness. She became a useful contradiction for all occasions, and she was used to the fullest advantage.

But the persistence of the idea of Mary Magdalene as prostitute isn't to say that she wasn't appreciated in her other roles, because she was. During the Middle Ages, emphasis was placed on different aspects of her story, real or imagined. Usually, anything said of her was with the understanding that she *had* been a prostitute, which led to her identities as a *penitent* and as a *contemplative*. A penitent is one who feels sorrow or guilt for sins or mistakes, and who may have sincerely set about on a new path in life to make amends. Penitents may perform *penance*, spiritual or moral deeds to make amends for past errors. A contemplative is one who contemplates, or thinks deeply on a subject. Some penitents lived solitary lives, spending time reflecting on their sins and redemption. Some legends tell of Mary Magdalene leading this kind of life.

Great allowances were made because of her close relationship with Jesus. During the high to late Middle Ages, Mary Magdalene was once again being used to fill out narratives of *the Passion*. She appeared again as the symbolic Bride of Christ, as well as the apostle of the apostles. Special emphasis was placed on the fondness that Jesus had for her and her friendship, and as someone who loved and was loved by Jesus, she became an incredibly popular saint.

> **Lingua Magda**
>
> **The Passion** refers to the events during the last day of Jesus' life, culminating with the crucifixion, with an understanding of the suffering he endured for the benefit of humankind.

The Fascination Continues

What has changed about how we think of Mary Magdalene today, compared to what has been said of her in the past? Quite a lot. As Mary, Jesus' mother, became more popular, she was given the title of New Eve to show how her obedience to God had countered Eve's disobedience. As strange as it might seem, the Bride of Christ moniker was placed on the Virgin Mary, too. Although Mary Magdalene was overshadowed by the Virgin Mary as Bride of Christ and the New Eve, and although the apostle identity all but faded away in the furor over female inferiority, she would continue to be associated with all of these titles from time to time.

What did this leave for Mary Magdalene? The repentant prostitute identity, of course. And so she has remained through the modern era until the present day. In spite of this, Mary Magdalene has continued to stir imaginations and inspire reflection on her role in the Gospels.

In the past century, there has been an increasing awareness that there is nothing in the Gospels that says she was a prostitute, and interest in Mary Magdalene has been picking up momentum. During the past 20 years, much has been written about the role she plays in the Gnostic texts. Gnosis is a Greek term for "knowledge," and

Gnosticism refers to an early sect of Christianity that flourished for several hundred years before finally being squeezed out by orthodox Christianity. There were many different schools of Gnostic thought, but they all shared a common theme of salvation through personal spiritual revelation and knowledge. You learn more about Gnosticism in Chapter 13.

Mary Magdalene's role as an apostle has been rediscovered and new innovations on her identity as Bride of Christ have taken place. We spend more time exploring the modern interest in Mary Magdalene in Part 5.

The Least You Need to Know

- ◆ Mary Magdalene's hometown was probably Magdala, a town near the Sea of Galilee.

- ◆ The origins of the name "Magdalene" are unclear.

- ◆ Mary Magdalene was the most frequently mentioned of Jesus' female followers.

- ◆ Mary Magdalene is considered a saint among some Christian traditions.

- ◆ Most of Mary Magdalene's many identities originated very early in Christian history.

- ◆ Although Mary Magdalene's more positive identities have been downplayed or reassigned, our fascination with her continues.

Chapter 2

A Case of Mistaken Identity

In This Chapter

- ◆ Two Marys who helped shape Mary Magdalene
- ◆ Unnamed women in the Gospels connected to Mary
- ◆ An anonymous bad girl? It must be Mary Magdalene!
- ◆ Four anointing scenes, plenty of confusion
- ◆ Pope Gregory the Great weighs in

In Chapter 1, I mentioned how Mary Magdalene came to be known as a prostitute, but there is much more to the story. Now let's take a more detailed look at what led to all the confusion over her identity. We also check out one scene in the Gospels that's at the root of the problem: the anointing of Jesus.

Confusion alone isn't usually enough to create a new myth, so why did the idea that Mary Magdalene was a prostitute stick around, anyway? To answer this question, we need to explore what happened when a very powerful person came into contact with popular misunderstandings. By doing this, we'll see that it's impossible to lay the blame for Mary Magdalene's reputation at any one person's feet (as much as we might want to).

Mary, Mary ...

Anyone who has spent any time at all reading the Bible has probably noticed that Mary must have been a common name. In fact, it *was* a common name. The name Mary appears a whopping 54 times in the New Testament, referring to the following women:

- Mary, mother of Jesus

- Mary Magdalene

- Mary, mother of James and Joses (Mark 15:40; 16:10; Matt. 27:56; Luke 24:10)

- Mary of Bethany (Luke 10:39; John 11:1)

- Mary, wife of Cleophas (John 19:25). Spelled Clopas in most modern versions (from the Greek)

- Mary, the mother of Mark (Acts 12:12)

- Mary, unspecified (Romans 16:6)

- "the other Mary" (Matt. 27:61; 28:1)

Illuminations

Depending on whom you ask, the name "Mary" means either "bitter" or "the perfect one." The vast gulf in etymology comes from a disagreement about how to approach the older Hebrew name, "Miryam," (or Miriam) from which "Mary" is derived.

Who are these women? It's beyond the scope of this book to go into detail about each of these Marys, but we do take a look at two who have had major impact on how Mary Magdalene has been viewed.

The Virgin Mary

As strange as it might seem, I receive many letters from people asking whether Mary Magdalene was Jesus' mother.

What!?

Chances are that *you* know Mary Magdalene wasn't his mother, and in fact, you might find it appalling that anyone would think such a thing. It goes to show, though, how muddled the Marys in the Gospels can get. I can't tell you how many times I've seen an auction item labeled with Mary Magdalene's name in spite of the fact that it's clearly Jesus' mother. It happens quite often; so if you make any purchases of Mary Magdalene merchandise, buyer beware!

Jesus' mother was, of course, the woman commonly called the Virgin Mary. She is called "virgin" to reflect the Roman Catholic belief in her continuing virginity after Jesus was born. Many Protestant denominations don't teach that she was forever virgin, so they refer to her as "Mary, mother of Jesus." Throughout the book, I refer to Jesus' mother as "the Virgin Mary," "Jesus' mother," or, as she is sometimes also known, "Mary of Nazareth."

In early Christianity, the Virgin Mary wasn't usually confused with Mary Magdalene; they were seen as two very different women. There are examples of non-Biblical texts, however, in which she replaced Mary Magdalene as first witness to the resurrection. This was most likely *not* the result of confusion. Some early Christians thought it would be more appropriate that someone as pure as the Virgin Mary should be the first witness.

As I mentioned in Chapter 1, the Virgin Mary was to become recognized as the New Eve and as the Bride of Christ. In both of these roles, she would become the predominant example, edging out Mary Magdalene in popularity as time went on.

As the New Eve, the emphasis was a little different than with Mary Magdalene. Where Mary Magdalene provided an almost mirror image of Eve's fall from grace, the Virgin Mary showed an example of how obedience toward God brought redemption into the world. When the angel Gabriel appeared to her and told her that she would bear a child to God, her words "Behold the handmaid of the Lord; be it done unto me according to thy word" served as a pivotal moment in the Biblical story of humankind. By choosing to do what was asked of her, the Virgin Mary did correctly what Eve had done incorrectly: she was obedient.

It may seem mysterious to contemplate Jesus' mother as the Bride of Christ, but this is a mystical title. No one said that she was *literally* the Bride of Christ, just as no one had said that Mary Magdalene was *literally* his wife. The Virgin Mary fulfilled the role of Bride of Christ much in the same way that Mary Magdalene had; she became a representative of the Ecclesia, the Church, the bride for whom Jesus was returning. The Church, as bride awaiting the bridegroom, needed to be chaste and faithful. Certainly a tainted sinner like Mary Magdalene couldn't stand for something so pure and righteous!

It Is Written

Paul's words to the believers at Corinth:

"I feel a divine jealousy for you, for I betrothed you to Christ to present you as a pure bride to her one husband."

—2 Corinthians 11:2

Mary of Bethany

During Jesus' ministry, he became friends with a woman named Martha and her sister, Mary, who lived in a town called Bethany. Mary and Martha were the sisters of Lazarus, whom Jesus raised from the dead. The Gospels also say that Jesus loved them. It isn't clear to what extent Mary and Martha of Bethany followed Jesus as he traveled, because the Gospels say he went to their house. If they kept a house, then they were probably not part of his band of traveling followers. Luke 10:38 illustrates this point:

> Now as they went on their way, he entered a village; and a woman named
> Martha received him into her house.

Mary of Bethany is remembered as a woman who anointed Jesus before the crucifixion. Because this scene is so crucial to the Gospel story (it is one of the only scenes that appears in all four Gospels), her role as anointer is one that comes under considerable scrutiny. We come back to that shortly.

In some traditions, Mary Magdalene's identity fully merged with Mary of Bethany; they were believed to be one and the same person. This makes it harder to understand why the name "Magdalene" would point at her hometown, though; was she from Magdala, or from Bethany? Those who believe that "Magdalene" is a nickname say that Bethany is her hometown, so the two women are the same. Still others suggest that Mary Magdalene *must* be Mary of Bethany because there's no way that, being as close to Jesus as Mary of Bethany was, she wouldn't have been at the crucifixion. I find both of these arguments to be unconvincing, and proceed on the assumption that Mary Magdalene and Mary of Bethany were two different people.

Illuminations

The Golden Legend, a book of medieval legends about the lives of the saints, written by Jacobus de Voragine in 1275, demonstrates how creative the explanations were for reconciling Mary Magdalene with Mary of Bethany. In *The Golden Legend,* Mary Magdalene was said to be of noble lineage, and had inherited a castle at Magdala, from which she derived her name. Her brother Lazarus inherited a portion of Jerusalem, and Martha a castle at Bethany. When Mary Magdalene gave herself over to the pleasures of the flesh, and Lazarus entered the knighthood(!), the ever-dependable and practical Martha took over the administration of their estates.

Unnamed Women

The Gospels are full of stories about women who aren't mentioned by name. There was the woman who touched Jesus' hem to be healed (Mark 9:20), there was the widow whose son was healed at Nain (Luke 7:12), there was the Greek woman whose daughter was healed of an "unclean spirit" (Mark 7:26), and the list goes on. Still other unnamed women have been connected to Mary Magdalene so thoroughly that she is likely to forever be associated with them. Let's take a look at who they are.

Luke's Anonymous Sinner

In the Gospel of Luke, Jesus was *anointed* by a woman who is called, simply, a sinner who comes from the city. If we were to imagine the scene taking place, it would go something like this:

Jesus and the Pharisee sit down to dinner. [The Pharisee were one of the powerful sects of Judaism at the time of Christ. They taught strict adherence to the written and oral laws.] *A woman bursts in the door. She kneels at Jesus' feet and cries on them, getting them all wet with her tears. Afterward, she wipes them dry with her hair. Then she kisses his feet and pours ointment on them.*

Simon: You can't be a prophet! If you were, you wouldn't let that low-life touch you!

Lingua Magda

To **anoint** is the act of putting oil or ointment onto someone to indicate their consecration to a purpose. Kings of Israel were anointed in a ritual act of sanctification to the people and to God. In this case, the woman may have anointed Jesus as recognition that he was the Messiah—the Anointed One. Or perhaps it was simply an act of love and veneration.

Jesus: Listen here, Simon, I have a bone to pick with you. Say there was a guy who loaned some money to two people: one owed $500, and one owed $50. Neither of them could pay, so he forgave both debts. So which one loved him more as a result?

Simon: I suppose the one who owed the most.

Jesus: Bingo! Now take a look at this woman. When I came to your house, you didn't offer any water for me to wash my feet, but she came in and washed them with her tears. Then she dried them with her hair, kissed them, and poured sweet-smelling stuff on them. So you see, Simon, her many sins are forgiven because she loves me a lot. The person who isn't forgiven of much doesn't love very much.

Then Jesus forgave the woman for her sins.

For a very long time, Luke's anonymous sinner-woman has been assumed to be a prostitute. Frankly, the evidence for this is pretty weak, but here are some of the reasons why the belief persists:

- The woman's hair was worn loose, in a culture where proper women had their heads covered.

- The woman freely touched Jesus even though, according to Jewish law, it would have made him unclean.

- The shock displayed by Jesus' host shows that she was living in some sort of disgrace.

Perhaps the most convincing evidence is that a woman living outside of the cultural norm was often called a harlot. This didn't mean that she was literally selling her body for money, only that society accorded her about the same amount of respect as if she did. A woman who did her own thing without regard for the rules may as well have been a prostitute for all anyone cared. A woman's place in society, for better or for worse, was always related to the fact that she was a *woman*; her sexuality was always at the forefront. If you take a look at the women in the Bible, you will see that whatever a woman does, right or wrong, it is often somehow related to her sexuality or the very fact that she is a woman.

So if a woman's sins were sexual sins, then to say that the woman in Luke was a "sinner" leads us to a well-founded belief that she had done *something* illicit. It is important to consider the reasons for this woman's reputation because it is from her that Mary Magdalene gets slapped with the prostitute label. Mary Magdalene was introduced for the first time immediately following the anointing scene in Luke, causing many to believe that she must have been the unnamed sinner from the previous scene.

The confusion over Luke's anonymous sinner and Mary Magdalene has always been troubling, and in the Middle Ages some authors tried to combine them. A *harmony* is a text that aims to bring all four Gospels into agreement. As a result, harmonies often contain some "creative" material (i.e., "made up") to reconcile any differences. In at least one medieval harmony, Mary Magdalene's introduction in Luke contains a direct reference to her as the woman who had done the anointing.

The Woman Caught in Adultery

The Gospel of John contains a story about a woman who had been "caught in the very act" of adultery and was brought before Jesus by religious leaders (John 8:3–11). Putting him to a test to see whether he would say something that disagreed with scripture, they pointed out that the law said she was to be stoned for such an offense. Then they asked him what he thought they should do with her. Jesus responded that whoever had lived a life without sin should cast the first stone. Of course, all present realized that they had committed at least some small infraction during their lives, so they left one by one. Jesus then told the woman that he didn't condemn her, and that she should "go and sin no more."

It is a very popular belief that this woman was Mary Magdalene, but the reasons for this are not clear. Usually thought to be a matter of lumping all the sexual sins committed by women in the Gospels onto one convenient figure, Mary Magdalene the prostitute took on yet another erroneous attribute. She was now an adulteress.

> **Quite Contrary**
>
> Portraying Mary Magdalene as the woman caught in adultery is one of the most commonly mistaken scenes in cinematic renditions of Jesus' life. Martin Scorsese's film *The Last Temptation of Christ*, based on the novel by Nikos Kazantzakis, and most recently, Mel Gibson's film *The Passion of the Christ* both perpetuate this legend.

The Woman at the Well

While he was traveling in Samaria, the Gospel of John says that Jesus stopped and sat at Jacob's Well to rest while the disciples were off buying food. A Samaritan woman approached the well to draw water, and Jesus asked her for a drink. Surprised, she asked Jesus why he would bother to ask her for such a thing since Jews and Samaritans didn't mingle. He then told her that he would give her the "living water" and that she should go call her husband. This is where things get interesting.

> **Illuminations**
>
> Jacob's Well is not mentioned in the Old Testament, but there *is* a mention of Jacob purchasing property near the well thought to be where Jesus spoke to the Samaritan woman. The well has been known since the early Christian era and is currently maintained by the Greek Orthodox Church.

The woman replied that she didn't have a husband. Jesus revealed that he knew that she had, in fact, had *five* husbands, but that the man whom she was with currently was not her husband. This bit of unexplainable knowledge convinced the woman that Jesus was the Messiah, and she ran off to tell everyone about the man at the well who knew her whole life.

Again, there is absolutely nothing to indicate that this woman was Mary Magdalene, but to the early medieval mind, the scandal of having had five husbands and at least one other man to whom she wasn't married made the Samaritan woman yet another who was caught up in the sinfulness of fleshly desire. In short, she *may as well* have been a prostitute, and as such, her identity was added to the list of those applied to Mary Magdalene.

How Mary Magdalene Became a Bad Girl

Now that we know how insult was added to injury through the continual addition of sinful characters to her identity, how did Mary Magdalene come to be thought of as a prostitute in the first place? To understand how this happened, we must come back to the anonymous sinner of Luke and Mary of Bethany. What do these two figures have in common? The anointing scene!

The anointing scene, as we have already seen, was mentioned in all four Gospels. There is some disagreement about whether or not all four Gospels refer to the same anointing scene; it has been argued that there are one, two, or even three different anointing scenes represented, based on the timing of the event. In all cases, a woman anoints Jesus with expensive ointment. She is then criticized either because of who she is or because she has wasted something so precious (ointment was evidently quite expensive). Jesus comes to her defense in all accounts, and in Matthew and Mark, he says that what she has done will always be spoken of "in memory of her."

The following table summarizes who did what in each of the Gospel accounts of this event. (Spikenard was an herb that grew in northern India known for its aromatic qualities. Aside from the anointing scene in the Gospels, the only other mention of spikenard in the Bible is in *Song of Songs*.)

Details of the Anointing Scene by Gospel

Gospel	Location	Anointer	Substance
Matthew 26:6–13	Simon the leper's house in Bethany	Anonymous woman	Ointment of spikenard in an alabaster jar
Mark 14:3–9	Simon the leper's house in Bethany	Anonymous woman	Ointment of spikenard in an alabaster jar
Luke 7:36–50	Simon the Pharisee's house	Anonymous sinner	Ointment in an alabaster jar
John 12:1–8	Martha and Mary's house in Bethany	Mary of Bethany	One pound of ointment of spikenard

As you can see, there are enough similarities and differences between the accounts of the anointing that it would be easy to get confused. There are plenty of details that I haven't included: the day of the anointing relative to the Passover feast, who was present, the reaction of the onlookers, and Jesus' defense of the anointing woman. All of these things affected later writers' ability to distinguish (or *not* distinguish, as the case may be) between the four versions of the story.

Illuminations

The famous alabaster jar that is associated with Mary Magdalene comes from her identification with the woman who anointed Jesus before the crucifixion. In three of the four Gospel accounts, she uses ointment from an alabaster jar for the anointing. There was a connection between alabaster jars and the dead in antiquity; referred to as an *alabastron* (plural, *alabastra*), a jar of scented oil or perfume was often included at a funerary site. The fact that the Gospel narratives mention an *alabastron* of ointment is significant in the foreshadowing of Jesus' death.

Of the four versions, Luke's narrative is the most different, not only because of the alternative description of the host and the anointer, but also because it gives the most drastically different timeframe for the anointing. It takes place quite some time before the Passover during which Jesus is arrested. The three other accounts have the anointing taking place during the week immediately before Passover.

Mary Magdalene is nowhere involved with the anointing of Jesus before the crucifixion. It is almost entirely through the anointing scene that Mary Magdalene, Luke's sinner, and Mary of Bethany intersect. In addition, Mary Magdalene's strong association with Mary of Bethany, who in turn was associated with Luke's anonymous sinner, brought the three into a close relationship.

Some people have accounted for the belief that Mary of Bethany is the same woman as the anonymous sinner of Luke through a reading of the second verse from the Gospel of John given below (my emphasis added):

> Now a certain man was ill, Lazarus of Bethany, the village of Mary and her sister Martha.
>
> *It was Mary who anointed the Lord with ointment and wiped his feet with her hair*, whose brother Lazarus was ill.
>
> —John 11:1, 2

Here, Mary of Bethany is introduced as the woman who anointed Jesus and wiped his feet with her hair. The tricky thing to remember here is that when this verse appears, Mary of Bethany hasn't yet anointed Jesus. It has been suggested that, because the Gospel of John was written later than the other three, the author knew already of Luke's anonymous sinner and tried to harmonize the story by identifying the anointer as Mary of Bethany. Another possibility is that Mary of Bethany did indeed anoint Jesus on two separate occasions, and that she *was* the anonymous sinner of Luke. We'll probably never know for sure.

The fact that Mary Magdalene, as herself, went to Jesus' tomb *after the crucifixion* to anoint his body was further reason to associate her with this memorable act of devotion.

> **It Is Written**
>
> And when the sabbath was past, Mary Magdalene, and Mary the mother of James, and Salome, bought spices, so that they might go and anoint him.
>
> —Mark 16:1

Pope Gregory the Great Speaks Up

Gregory, who came to be Pope Gregory I, was born around 540 C.E. into a prominent political family. He lived as a monk for many years before being appointed as a special ambassador representing papal interests in the court of the Patriarch of Constantinople. In short, without getting bogged down with the details, he was a pretty big deal even before he became pope.

In 590 C.E. he did become pope, whether he wanted to or not. Gregory was a talented administrator with a passion for organization. He spent a great deal of effort straightening out what was often a confused jumble of conflicting theology and doctrine.

Gregory is remembered for the plainchant he helped to develop, which is still referred to as "Gregorian chant," and for developing the Church calendar that was in use for some 13 centuries.

During his reign, Pope Gregory delivered a homily in which he said: "She whom Luke calls the sinful woman, whom John calls Mary, we believe to be the Mary from whom seven devils were ejected according to Mark." This was a fancy way of saying that Luke's anonymous sinner, Mary of Bethany, and Mary Magdalene were the same person.

Since Mary Magdalene scholarship has increased in the last part of the twentieth century, lots of attention has been given to Gregory's homily as the final blow to Mary Magdalene's good name. Although this is true, the more frequently the story is repeated, the more responsibility Gregory bears for making Mary Magdalene into something she was not. In the flurry of excitement about Mary Magdalene in recent years, blame for her reputation has been laid squarely on Gregory's shoulders.

As already mentioned, by the sixth century C.E., there was significant confusion about the various Marys in the Gospels and the women involved in the anointing scene. Depending on where in Christendom you happened to be at the time, you may have been taught that she was the same person as Mary of Bethany but not Luke's sinner, or the same as Luke's sinner but not Mary of Bethany, or any combination of the three. By the time Gregory became pope, no one could agree on who she was.

Gregory made a decision to reduce confusion and to unify Church doctrine. His decision, to conflate Mary Magdalene, Mary of Bethany, and Luke's sinner, may not have been the *best* decision, but it was by no means an innovation. What he *was* responsible for was ending any real discussion of Mary Magdalene's true identity. For about 1,400 years, Gregory's declaration was, officially, the end of the story.

The Least You Need to Know

- Mary was a common name in the New Testament, which led to some confusion about Mary Magdalene's identity.

- Mary Magdalene was not Jesus' mother.

◆ Mary Magdalene has commonly been associated with Mary of Bethany and Luke's anonymous sinner.

◆ The woman caught in adultery and the Samaritan woman at the well were, and still are, thought by many to be Mary Magdalene.

◆ The anointing scene in the Gospels is what led to much of the confusion between Luke's anonymous sinner, Mary of Bethany, and Mary Magdalene.

◆ Although Pope Gregory the Great did not invent the idea that Mary Magdalene was a prostitute, blame for her reputation is often attributed to him.

Chapter 3

How Mary Magdalene Is Remembered Today

In This Chapter

- The power of penance
- She saw it with her own eyes
- Easter, the oldest Christian holiday
- Mary Magdalene gets a day of her own
- She's the patron saint of *what?*

In 1969, the Roman Catholic Church quietly disentangled Mary Magdalene from Mary of Bethany and the anonymous sinner of Luke by changing their official calendar, to demonstrate what had been known for a very long time: There is no Biblical evidence to support the conflation of the three women. It's important to understand, however, that 1,400 years of tradition doesn't just go *poof!* with a reformed calendar. Mary Magdalene is still remembered in her previous roles of prostitute and penitent within Catholicism, and Protestant branches of Christianity that don't answer to Rome have always been free to interpret her identity for themselves.

Regardless of the ongoing controversy about who Mary Magdalene *was*, she still *is* a very important figure in all branches of Christianity. In this chapter, we examine two of her most popular identities, and the two times of the year during which she is officially remembered.

The Penitent

Like it or not, the Mary Magdalene with a checkered past is here to stay. Regardless of official decree, she continues to be recognized as a repentant sinner. Thus we are left with a situation similar to that which existed during the first six centuries of Christianity before Pope Gregory's famous decision: Mary Magdalene's various identities can be mixed and matched however it's convenient. With no central body to determine which teachings are correct or incorrect across all of Christianity, Mary Magdalene is once again subject to the interpretation of individual groups.

There are a couple of different messages sent to believers by recognizing Mary Magdalene as a sinner who changed her life. Most importantly, she serves as an example of what can be accomplished through setting aside past mistakes and establishing a devoted relationship with God. The range of teachings along this line is almost endless, from a simple encouragement to repent of your sins as Mary Magdalene did to lengthy guilt-inducing tracts about how if God could love someone as despicable as Mary Magdalene, surely he could love even *you*.

Many Christians have, regardless of the official teachings of their church, discovered the controversy about Mary Magdalene's identity and have gone to the Gospels themselves to try to decide who she was. Some have decided that it's unfair and dishonest to continue to label her as a penitent whore if the Bible mentions nothing sinful about her pre-Jesus life. Others have suggested that her seven demons, which I discuss in more detail in Chapter 7, were evidence of a sinful life. Still others have taken the fact that the town of Magdala was destroyed for its "moral depravity" to mean that she must have been morally depraved, too, because she lived there.

Sometimes Mary Magdalene is still used as an example of vanity and pride, commonly held medieval ideas about prostitutes, who needed to make themselves beautiful in order to ply their trade and attract customers. Some evangelical Protestant congregations continue to hear sermons about leaving behind the concerns of the flesh, as Mary Magdalene did, to follow Jesus. Sometimes Mary Magdalene is used as an example of why women should refrain from wearing jewelry and cosmetics to enhance their appearance beyond what God gave them.

In some Christian churches, Mary Magdalene is remembered as the sister of Martha and Lazarus as well as the anonymous sinner woman of Luke, and is therefore honored as a penitent. It is often recognized that although there is no Biblical evidence for this stance, the longstanding Christian *unity* tradition can still be honored.

Lingua Magda

Unity refers to the theory or tradition that Mary Magdalene was also Mary of Bethany and the anonymous sinner of Luke.

Before you get the impression that Mary Magdalene's role as penitent is merely a manipulative tool for keeping believers in line, for centuries she has served as an inspiration to people who feel their lives have gotten out of control. Certainly some of the influence has been related to the state of a person's soul, but Mary Magdalene has also served as a symbol of hope. Many people have looked at her as someone who, as a sinner, was able to turn her life around and become a productive member of society.

This hopefulness turned into both a blessing and a curse as, starting in the eighteenth century, special homes and shelters to rescue prostitutes and other debauched women from their sinful lives were set up under Mary Magdalene's name. Many of these institutions were little more than convents, giving the women the opportunity to leave behind their compromised conditions and instead devote their lives to God. *Magdalen houses*, as they were called, continued to spring up and do their work well into the twentieth century, though some gained a bad reputation for using the women they were claiming to help as little more than slave labor.

Magdalen laundries were an offshoot of the traditional Magdalen house, in which unmarried pregnant women were sent to do laundry work until after the birth of their babies. Some of these institutions were, in essence, adoption farms surrounded by scandal; there are women still living today who "served time" at a Magdalen laundry in their youth.

Illuminations

Magdalen laundries have been the subject of recent literary and film projects, including *The Magdalen*, by Marita Conlon-McKenna, and the 2002 film *The Magdalene Sisters*.

For some, Joni Mitchell's 1994 song "The Magdalene Laundries" was the first time they had heard of the practice of sending unwed mothers away. In the song, Mitchell describes what it would have been like for a woman to be unfairly judged and sent away to live a shameful life as a penitent sinner at a Magdalen laundry.

Fortunately, the tide has turned. In America as well as other countries, Mary Magdalene has lent her name once more to rescue organizations offering shelter and other services to homeless women who have often been abused or forced into prostitution. A Seattle, Washington, organization called "Mary's Place" is associated with The Church of Mary Magdalene, an ecumenical, nondenominational ministry. Their mission is to provide a place for women and children struggling to overcome homelessness, poverty, and abusive living situations. Several states have outreach organizations called "The Magdalen House" with similar goals.

The Witness

Regardless of what people have thought of Mary Magdalene's pre-Jesus reputation, she is almost universally recognized as a witness of the resurrection. It is this scene that redeems any darkness that surrounds her, for there must have been a reason why Jesus would have chosen her to be a witness to one of the central events of Christianity. Was it to reward her faithfulness for being one of the brave who stood by him during the crucifixion? Was it her sinfulness, and therefore another statement of his love for humans in spite of their imperfection?

It Is Written

Mary Magdalene went and said to the disciples, "I have seen the Lord"; and she told them that he had said these things to her.

—John 20:18

The answers to these questions depend, again, on the branch of Christianity you belong to, as well as each individual church and clergy member. Mary Magdalene is indeed remembered in her role as witness because of *both* her sinfulness and her faithfulness, as well as the obvious devotion to Jesus that led her to go to the tomb to anoint his body. As one of the myrrhophores, Mary Magdalene was expressing her deep love for Jesus by being willing to fulfill the unpleasant task of preparing his dead body for burial.

It was this determination that led her to be in the right place at the right time, which is usually assumed not to have been a lucky accident for Mary Magdalene, but instead ordained by God. It is therefore up to Christians to interpret why Mary Magdalene was chosen as either the first or one of the first witnesses to the resurrection.

As mentioned previously, Mary Magdalene's earliest identity in Christianity was that of a myrrhophore, which gives us an indication of the importance of this role. St. Augustine pointed out in the fifth century that Mary Magdalene's presence served as "ocular proof" of Jesus' grand feat, which brings another perspective into view. Were it not for the witnesses of the resurrection, how would anyone know it happened? How would Christianity have been founded if it weren't for the "good news" being passed from person to person? It had to start somewhere. By some calculations, there were up to 500 or more witnesses to Jesus' life after death (1 Corinthians 15:6), so it's by virtue of being among the first that sets Mary Magdalene apart.

The Anglican Church honors Mary Magdalene as *first* witness of the resurrection, as noted in this traditional prayer (my emphasis added):

> Almighty God, whose blessed Son restored Mary Magdalene to health of body and mind, and *called her to be a witness of his resurrection:* Mercifully grant that by thy grace we may be healed of all our infirmities and know thee in the power of his endless life; who with thee and the Holy Spirit liveth and reigneth, one God, now and for ever.

Easter Services

Throughout the Christian world, the first Sunday that follows the first full moon after the spring equinox is celebrated as the day that Jesus rose from the tomb, conquering death, transcending his fleshly incarnation, and demonstrating his divinity.

Illuminations

Almost everyone knows that Easter falls on a different Sunday every year, but why the crazy calculation dependent on full moons and the spring equinox? Jesus was said to have been arrested, tried, and executed during the week of Passover. The Jewish calendar is lunar, which means that it is calculated based on the cycles of the moon rather than the cycles of the sun. In order for Easter to be celebrated near Passover, the calculation of Easter was corrected with the Gregorian calendar reform in the sixteenth century. Previously, under the Julian calendar, the date of Easter was determined according to a 19-year table.

Easter has always been the central holiday of Christianity, being surpassed only by Christmas in popularity and secular celebration. It has probably been observed at least since the second century, according to a reference by the historian Eusebius of Caesarea (b. 260 C.E.), in Book 5 of his *Church History*.

The Easter season is often celebrated with a retelling of the Passion cycle, the events leading up to the death and resurrection of Jesus Christ. Depending on the branch of

Christianity, the complexity of the ecclesiastical calendar relies on the date of Easter. Related events are commemorated leading up to the celebration of Easter and afterward, usually referred to as "moveable feasts." Some of these are:

- Ash Wednesday

- Palm Sunday

- Good Friday

- Ascension Day

- Pentecost

- Corpus Christi

It Is Written

Blessed be the God and Father of our Lord Jesus Christ! By his great mercy we have been born anew to a living hope through the resurrection of Jesus Christ from the dead ...

—1 Peter 1:3

Far from just a single holiday, then, the Easter season is a time during which Christians enjoy a renewal of their faith and communities as they commemorate God's love and justice by remembering the resurrection. As Jesus passed through the harrowing experience of death and into new life, so Christians see Easter as a reminder that their religion is a living one; that they can symbolically leave behind their old lives and awaken spiritually through Christ. This has very old connections to the tradition of baptisms occurring only on Easter; in Roman Catholicism, the baptismal font is still blessed on Easter night.

Mary Magdalene figures into the Easter narrative in the customary ways; in some traditions she is remembered as the woman who anointed Jesus during the week before Passover, and she is always mentioned as one of the witnesses of the crucifixion and resurrection. In some churches, she is exalted in her special role as first witness and apostle. Sometimes, Easter dramas are acted out, in which a woman plays the role of Mary Magdalene discovering the empty tomb and the risen Christ.

There is a long history behind Mary Magdalene in Easter plays. In fact, Mary Magdalene was one of the first theatrical characters in Western drama! Although one might suppose that our modern theater productions are descended from the Greek dramas, they are actually descendants of medieval religious plays. In the tenth century, monks started to act out the most basic story of Easter, playing the myrrhophores as they discovered the empty tomb.

This theme grew in popularity and complexity throughout the Middle Ages, and eventually Mary Magdalene came to be the subject of more focused attention. She was often given her own lament in the dramas, and there was a whole genre of plays devoted to the story of her sinful, preconversion life as an allegory for the state of humankind before Christ's ultimate sacrifice. It has been suggested that she grew in theatrical popularity because she had been growing in popularity as a saint otherwise, but maybe this is a chicken-and-egg question. Who came first? The people who liked her and wanted to see her in a play, or the people who liked her *because* she was in a play?

In Eastern Orthodox churches, although it is not an official part of the Easter service, members of a congregation often exchange red eggs with the words "Christ is Risen!" This custom comes from an old traditional story, that although told in many different ways, comes down to this: After Jesus ascended into heaven, Mary Magdalene traveled to Rome and had an audience with Tiberius Caesar. As she dined with him, she complained about the way Pontius Pilate mishandled Jesus' trial. She went on to tell him that Jesus was the Son of God, and that he had risen from the dead. Incredulous, Caesar replied, "A man could no more rise from the dead than that egg in your hand could turn red!" The egg, of course, *did* turn red, and this tale is the source of the celebratory exchange of red eggs on Pascha. Pascha is the Greek word for "Passover," and in Eastern Orthodox Christianity, it refers to the time when Easter occurs. It is used in the way that other Christian traditions use the term "Easter."

A Summer Feast

As early Christians were killed, or "martyred," for their faith, their names were recorded and remembered locally on certain days. Such lists were kept widely and were gradually incorporated into the overall construct of the *liturgical* year. Although feast days started as remembrances of martyrs, during the eleventh century, the designation of "saint" came into more popular use to recognize those who, although not martyrs, had lived holy and otherwise notable lives in service of God and the Church.

Lingua Magda

Liturgy is the public expression of faith, prayer, and worship. The Christian liturgical year and liturgical calendar refer to when the major events of the faith are to be observed.

During the Middle Ages, important feast days required church attendance and sometimes occasioned special community festivals. Feast days were a crucial part of the cultural landscape, and it is from them that we've developed our modern practice of celebrating the holidays. Just look at the words involved and you can see what kind of events the medieval feast days were: the "fest" in "festival" and "festive" comes from "feast," and the "holi" in "holiday" comes from "holy."

The list of feast days was changeable throughout the centuries, and there were sometimes as many as 85 days on which people were obligated to refrain from work. Even though that may sound pleasant to us now, no work meant no livelihood and sometimes no food. The Church worked to reduce the number of these days and the European liturgical calendar remained in flux until well after the French Revolution.

In the Catholic and Eastern Orthodox churches, many saints have been associated with days of the year on which their lives are remembered. Saints are rarely celebrated in Protestant branches of Christianity because it is believed that they were like any other true believers and only God the Father, Jesus, and the Holy Spirit are, well, *holy*. In spite of this, the Anglican Church does have a feast-day calendar that includes saints.

There are some differences between the feast-day calendars of the Eastern Orthodox Church and the Roman Catholic Church. For example, in the Eastern Orthodox Church, several of the people associated with Mary Magdalene are given both separate and common feast days:

- Holy Myrrhbearers Sunday: second Sunday after Pascha
- Mary, Myrrhbearer and Wife of Cleopas: May 23
- Martha and Mary, Sisters of Lazarus: June 4
- Joanna, the Myrrhbearer: June 27
- Salome, the Myrrhbearer: August 3

In all branches of Christianity that recognize saints' days, Mary Magdalene's feast day is observed on July 22. It was first mentioned in the eighth century by the Venerable Bede, an early Anglo-Saxon historian of the Church. Her feast day was mentioned in association with a legend that she traveled to Ephesus, a city in what is now called Turkey, after the resurrection.

When July 22 falls on a day when church services are held, there is usually a special liturgy spoken in her honor. Very often, it includes a reading from the *Song of Songs*. Even so long after Hippolytus's memorable commentary on this poetic work and even though most people don't associate Mary Magdalene with the Shulamite woman, she is on this occasion compared with her as she looks for her beloved. In Mary Magdalene's case, this is similar to her search for Jesus in the garden outside of his tomb.

Besides a reading from *Song of Songs*, a feast-day service usually includes a discussion of her role as witness of the crucifixion and resurrection. Often she is admired for her faithfulness not only during Jesus' ministry, but during the dangerous and torturous time of his public execution. Sometimes prayers are recited that detail her legendary life and request her intercession on behalf of the faithful.

It Is Written

Upon my bed by night I sought him whom my soul loves; I sought him, but found him not; I called him, but he gave no answer. "I will rise now and go about the city, in the streets and in the squares; I will seek him whom my soul loves." I sought him, but found him not. The watchmen found me, as they went about in the city. "Have you seen him whom my soul loves?"
—*Song of Songs* 3:1–3

Mary Magdalene, Patron Saint

Before the eleventh century, people were made into saints in a more or less willy-nilly process. If a person was a martyr or lived an otherwise spectacularly notable life, that person might be called a saint, but it was usually based on local tradition. Around the eleventh century, the Roman Catholic Church defined a process by which people would be canonized, or recognized as saints. There is no specific date on which Mary Magdalene was made into a saint because she had been honored since the beginning of Christianity.

A patron saint is a saint who is chosen to be the protector or guardian of just about anything that is part of the human experience. There are patron saints for occupations, geographical locations, buildings, churches, illnesses, causes, and groups of people. Individuals may take patron saints as their personal guardians. Patron saints are usually chosen based on some similarity between the saint's story and what is to be protected; for example, Saint Nicholas made toys for children in his village, so he became the patron saint of children.

As I mentioned earlier, "Magdalen houses" were opened under Mary Magdalene's patronage, meaning that she was their patron saint and namesake. Because she was such a popular saint, though, there are many different areas of life over which she has been adopted as patron saint.

Perfumers and Apothecaries

How appropriate it seems that Mary Magdalene would be taken as a patron saint by perfumers! Given that she is almost always depicted holding an unguent jar, her association with scented oil and ointment is never far from mind. Modern perfumers and aromatherapy practitioners have also remembered Mary Magdalene; there are a number of aromatherapy tours in southern France to examine not only the flowers of the region but also the sites where Mary Magdalene was venerated during the Middle Ages.

An apothecary was rather like our modern pharmacist; they prepared herbs and medicines for sale. Mary Magdalene's association with apothecaries probably originates with the medieval passion plays, which sometimes featured a humorous apothecary figure. Before the anointing scene, Mary Magdalene would visit the apothecary to purchase her ointment. Often the leering vendor would make cheeky remarks about her previously sinful lifestyle.

Hairdressers

Mary Magdalene's association with hairdressers is just a little more difficult to trace. One possibility is the result of more confusion between Mary Magdalene and another woman, this time, Jesus' mother.

The Talmud has a passage that has been interpreted as a reference to Jesus and his mother, who is called a women's hairdresser. Her name appears as "Miriam megadla nashaia," or "Mary, the women's hairdresser." If you look closely, the word "megadla" sounds very similar to "magdala" and could lead to more mixing of the Marys.

Contemplatives

During the Middle Ages, some very popular legends arose about Mary Magdalene leading a life of solitude and contemplation. Many of these originated in southern France, where she was believed to have retired to a quiet life in a grotto, or small cave, near the town of St. Baume for 30 years. During this time, she fasted and prayed, and was lifted into heaven by angels who would feed her a spiritual food that sustained her body. There are several versions of this legend, but they all agree that Mary Magdalene set herself apart from normal life in order to focus her attention on living the remainder of her days in devotion to God.

Contemplatives, therefore, often took Mary Magdalene as their patron saint. They looked to her example for leading a righteous life, and called upon her to sustain and protect them in their efforts.

Penitents, Reformed Prostitutes

It probably does not need to be said, at this point, why Mary Magdalene would have been a patron saint for penitents and reformed prostitutes. This is the area where Mary Magdalene is most often called upon now, and where her name, as a patron, is most often heard. Her patronage is important and powerful for these groups of people; to take away Mary Magdalene because she wasn't *really* a prostitute would be to ignore centuries upon centuries of tradition and to deny a potent example of devotion to people who desperately want someone who they can identify with. It wouldn't be a bad thing to at least recognize the value in Mary Magdalene's sinful reputation, legendary though it may be, as it relates to people who cling to the hope she offers.

Tanners, Glovemakers, Shoemakers

This is, perhaps, the most mystifying group of occupations to take Mary Magdalene as their patron. There is an obvious association here with leather; tanners are people who work with leather to make it a supple and useful material. Glovemakers use leather, as do shoemakers. But how did Mary Magdalene come to be associated with leather in the first place?

In the twelfth century, King Phillipe Auguste of France passed a charter for perfumers that granted glove makers the right to prepare perfumes, creams, and unguents. By the Renaissance, tanners had developed methods for working delicate scents into fine leather used for gloves and other items of clothing. By the seventeenth century, perfumed gloves were all the rage in Paris.

Illuminations

Marie de Medicis, the woman who ruled France as a regent from 1610 to 1617, reputedly owned more than 300 pairs of perfumed gloves.

So it is by way of Mary Magdalene's association with perfume and scents that she comes in contact with occupations related to leatherworking.

The Least You Need to Know

♦ In spite of official Vatican decisions otherwise, Mary Magdalene is still remembered as a penitent sinner.

♦ Mary Magdalene's oldest identities, those of a myrrhophore and witness of the resurrection, are still her most important.

♦ Easter is celebrated with retellings of the events leading up to and during the crucifixion, culminating with the resurrection, and Mary Magdalene is one of the star characters.

♦ Mary Magdalene is remembered on her feast day of July 22, and has been for at least 1,200 years.

♦ Mary Magdalene is the patron saint for many things, especially anything related to perfume, penitence, or prostitution.

Chapter 4

I'll Bet You Thought Mary Magdalene Was ...

In This Chapter

- ◆ The woman with the long, flowing hair
- ◆ Her association with the color red
- ◆ Mary as *femme fatale*
- ◆ A marriage made in legends
- ◆ A woman of wealth?
- ◆ Leonardo da Vinci's gender-bending John

Whether or not you're a religious person, you've surely come into contact at least once with a secular vision of Mary Magdalene. She has entered into our cultural awareness as the exotic harlot who turned from a life of decadence to one of religious devotion. When the emphasis is removed from her spiritual significance, she has been pictured as everything from a haggard streetwalker to a beautiful and free spirit.

Poets, authors, artists, and playwrights have all contributed to the body of myth surrounding Mary Magdalene, and hundreds of years of creative portrayal has filtered down to us in many ways. Her legendary beauty has been the subject of more than one artistic work, and there are certain things that have come together to create a stereotypical "Mary Magdalene." And although some things can't really be called typical, some modern notions are getting a *lot* of attention.

Her Crowning Glory

Of all of Mary Magdalene's imagined characteristics, it's her hair that is most often remembered. In countless works of art from the Middle Ages onward, one of the easiest ways to identify which figure is supposed to be Mary Magdalene is to look for the woman with long, uncovered hair. Whether pictured as a brunette, blonde, or, most frequently, a redhead (more about that in a moment), Mary Magdalene's crowning glory has been vividly portrayed for millennia.

Hair as a primary attribute is carried to extremes in art where Mary Magdalene is represented as a contemplative. Although most art depicts a very womanly Mary Magdalene with long, flowing hair, she is at times completely covered—from head to toe—with hair. Long hair is one of the things frequently associated with a penitent, who in their prayerfulness and suffering were often thought to neglect everyday concerns such as eating, washing, and keeping their hair trimmed. One second-century author described James, the brother of Jesus, as an ascetic figure who wouldn't permit his hair to be cut, and whose knees were disfigured from kneeling in prayer. Mary Magdalene is depicted very similarly in a sixteenth-century painting called *The Elevation of The Magdalen,* by Peter Strüb the Younger. In this piece, Mary Magdalene is shown as a beautiful hair-covered woman being lifted into the air by angels. The only areas not obscured by hair are her face, hands, feet, and knees, presumably from constant kneeling in penitential prayer.

How in the world did Mary Magdalene become such a well-tressed wonder?

As you learned in Chapter 2, the anonymous woman in Luke who was thought to be Mary Magdalene wept on Jesus' feet. She then dried them with her hair before anointing them. Her hair figures as an important feature in the story, and therefore, it becomes an aspect that was later applied to Mary Magdalene.

Another piece of evidence that leads us to believe that Mary Magdalene's famous hair was the result of her association with Luke's anonymous sinner was that the sinner-woman was believed to have been a prostitute. Prostitutes, apparently unconcerned by a need to maintain their dignity by covering their heads in public, wore their hair loose. On the flip side of the situation was that any woman who wore her hair loose in public was considered to be a prostitute. Either way, prostitutes and hair left to flow in the wind were closely linked in first-century minds.

Seeing Red

Mary Magdalene and the color red have a long and relatively unclear relationship. What we do know for certain is there is nothing Biblical to link her to the color. The figures she is confused with aren't really linked to red either, so this becomes an interesting question. Anything related to Mary Magdalene and the color red is definitely legendary.

Illuminations

More "red" language commonly associated with illicit sexuality: A "scarlet woman" is another word for a prostitute, and a "red light district" is an area where prostitutes are frequently found.

The most likely origins of Mary Magdalene's connection with the color red is as a color associated with harlotry and the wanton pursuit of pleasure. There are a couple of things to consider when thinking about the color red and prostitution:

- In antiquity, prostitution wasn't necessarily thought of as a last resort for women with no income. A prostitute (a term used broadly to describe almost any woman who broke a law of moral behavior) was a woman who was acting on sensual desire.

- Red was a color that came to be associated with blood, life and death, sensuality, and sexuality. Although the color red was used widely in a number of different contexts (even the Virgin Mary was depicted in red for many centuries, for example), it is by far the color most associated with sinfulness, passion, and illicit sexuality.

It Is Written

Come now, let us reason together, says the LORD: though your sins are like scarlet, they shall be as white as snow; though they are red like crimson, they shall become like wool ...
—Isaiah 1:18

There was probably no universal rulebook that said Mary Magdalene *must* be depicted with red hair, and she was certainly portrayed quite often with hair of other colors. But it's the combination of the color red and her loose and flowing locks as they represent a woman with a sinful nature (or the sinful nature of woman, depending on how you look at it) that was a successful combination. Poets and writers picked up on the theme, and there were eventually enough references to Mary Magdalene's fiery tresses scattered throughout literature and art to burn the image into the modern Western folklore from which we continue to draw. So it should come as no surprise that Dan Brown's main character in the book *The Da Vinci Code*, Sophie Nevue, a descendent of Mary Magdalene, herself had red hair.

An Exotic Courtesan

Perhaps the quintessential twentieth-century portrayal of Mary Magdalene is as a *femme fatale*, a sultry and mysterious woman who uses her feminine wiles to entrap men and entice them to sin. The cover of a 1950s pulp novel shows her in a topless belly dance costume, red hair down to her knees, clad in golden jewels as men watch her from the background. She is the very definition of seduction.

> **Illuminations**
>
> The recent film *Moulin Rouge* is a story about a French courtesan (played by Nicole Kidman) who must choose between her love for a poor man and the security offered by her wealthy potential employer.

A courtesan is a high-class prostitute. A king or other noble could hardly hire a common man's prostitute from a common man's brothel, so he would employ the services of a courtesan. It would be her job to keep herself beautiful for her employer and to cater to his every whim. Courtesans have been known since very early recorded history, but were rarely mentioned during the Middle Ages. It wasn't until the Renaissance that courtesans returned to prominence in the West.

Mary Magdalene, of course, as a free-floating symbol for all womankind, received an image makeover as the times changed. She went from being a common prostitute to a pampered seductress given over to the pleasures of wealthy men. It is much more comfortable, after all, to condemn a prostitute who sells herself in order to live in the lap of luxury than it is to condemn a woman who sells herself merely to survive. As a courtesan, she would have actually *liked* her job, which added to her sinfulness.

Renaissance and later art confirmed Mary Magdalene's evolution into a "sensual sinner." Paintings often portrayed her provocatively nude or nearly nude, her long, flowing hair draped around her like silk. It has been suggested that commissioning a painting of Mary Magdalene was sometimes nothing more than a defensible reason for having a naked lady on the wall. And as photography came into popularity as an artistic medium, there was sometimes no better way to get a woman to pose *au naturel* than to ask her to model as Mary Magdalene.

Mrs. Jesus

At the turn of the twenty-first century, whether or not Mary Magdalene was married to Jesus is perhaps the biggest reason why people have become interested in her. This is a pretty complicated subject, and I go into more detail in later chapters, but for now let's take a look at the highlights.

Maybe, Maybe Not

Rumors that Mary Magdalene and Jesus were married aren't exactly uncommon. This is mostly due to the publication of the 1982 book *Holy Blood, Holy Grail*, by Michael Baigent, Richard Leigh, and Henry Lincoln (see Appendix B). *Holy Blood, Holy Grail* is a collection of history, genealogical records, and serendipity assembled to prove that Jesus and Mary Magdalene had children, and that those children went on to start the *Merovingian* bloodline. As the mother of Jesus' children, Mary Magdalene was, literally, the "cup" that carried the blood of Christ: the Holy Grail. The book was controversial from the get-go, and although it has been thoroughly debunked, it still retains a loyal following of conspiracy enthusiasts.

Lingua Magda

Merovingian is the name of the first royal dynasty of Gaul, which would become France. The Merovingian kings ruled from the fifth to eighth centuries C.E. They were replaced by the Carolingians, the dynasty that included Charlemagne.

In spite of what the facts say, *Holy Blood, Holy Grail* has gone on to inspire a whole new genre of books, ranging from the spiritual aspects of such a union to genealogies supporting pretenders to the throne of England and France. Since the popularity of Dan Brown's book, *The Da Vinci Code*, *Holy Blood, Holy Grail* has enjoyed renewed popularity, and a whole new group of readers unacquainted with its history have been captivated by the possibilities. We return to the subject of Mary Magdalene as the Holy Grail in Chapters 19 and 20.

Baigent, Leigh, and Lincoln were not the first to speculate that Jesus may have been married. The Age of Reason, more commonly referred to as "the Enlightenment," which took place roughly between the years 1650 and 1800 C.E., opened many areas of discussion that were previously believed to be sacrosanct, including Christianity and religion in general. Philosophers, artists, and writers started taking a more analytical approach to eternal questions, and were able to contemplate answers with less and less fear of a deadly reprisal for heresy. During the nineteenth century, religious and secular scholars both asked the question "could Jesus have been married?", but there were no clear answers. In 1970, William Phipps, a Presbyterian minister and theologian, published a highly controversial book called *Was Jesus Married?*, in which he examined the evidence for such a possibility.

Illuminations

Who else thinks Jesus and Mary Magdalene were married? In August 2003, *Time* magazine ran an article about Mary Magdalene in which a claim was made that Martin Luther and Brigham Young believed it. This isn't entirely accurate. A contemporary of Martin Luther named Schlaginhaufen claimed that in 1532 Luther made a statement about Jesus committing adultery with Mary Magdalene, but it was very likely said in sarcasm, among friends. Luther's other work demonstrates that he clearly viewed Jesus as celibate. According to his wife, Brigham Young, the early leader of the Mormon church, however, did suggest in a sermon that Jesus had been married to Mary Magdalene.

The main branches of the argument for Jesus being a family man are as follows:

◆ Jewish fathers had five responsibilities to their sons, including finding them a suitable wife. The Gospels mention that four of these responsibilities were fulfilled by Joseph for Jesus (circumcising him, redeeming him in the temple, teaching him the Law, and teaching him a trade), but there is no mention of the last responsibility, finding him a wife, being addressed. The argument goes that if Joseph met the other four responsibilities, then he was likely to have also fulfilled his fifth.

◆ Jewish rabbis needed to be married in order to be viewed as credible teachers of the Law.

◆ The Gospels don't say that Jesus *wasn't* married.

It wouldn't be fair, however, to examine the reasons for without considering some of the reasons against:

◆ Even if Joseph was obligated to find a wife for Jesus doesn't mean that Jesus would have actually married her.

- Jesus wasn't like other rabbis; he acted on the fringes of acceptable behavior for his culture, and bucked tradition in a number of other areas. Why, then, would he have chosen to marry just to satisfy social requirements?

- There are examples of celibate prophets and teachers in Judaism. In addition, some men were allowed to refrain from marrying in order to focus their attention on the study of scripture.

- The Gospels never mention that Jesus *was* married.

Remember that no society follows its own customs perfectly, and Judaism wasn't without its own factions and splinter groups. Some of them held celibacy in high regard, requiring it or encouraging it among members. It's unfair and inaccurate to say that *everyone* in first-century Jewish Palestine held the same beliefs and values.

The truth, of course, is that no one knows for certain, and because the Gospels *are* silent on the issue, there will always be room for argument on both sides. As for whether or not Jesus was married to Mary Magdalene in particular, aside from the theories cited in *Holy Blood, Holy Grail*, one more source deserves mention.

The *Gospel of Philip*

The *Gospel of Philip* was discovered in Egypt in 1945 with a cache of other texts near the town of Nag Hammadi. Collectively, the texts came to be known as the Nag Hammadi Library. The Nag Hammadi Library contained many writings of the early Christian sects known as the Gnostics. Previously, the only things anyone knew about the Gnostics were gleaned from *polemics* written by the people who hated them; not exactly the most balanced reporting. We discuss the Gnostics and the Nag Hammadi Library in more detail in Part 4.

Lingua Magda

A **polemic** is an argument for or against something. In this case, a polemic is a document written to refute Gnosticism, such as Irenaeus of Lyon's *Against All Heresies*, written in the second century C.E.

In the *Gospel of Philip*, two tantalizing passages lead the reader to wonder about the exact nature of the relationship between Jesus and Mary Magdalene:

> There were three who always walked with the Lord: Mary, his mother, and her sister, and Magdalene, the one who was called his companion. His [sic] sister and his mother and his companion were each a Mary.

And the companion of the Lord was Mary Magdalene. He loved her more than all the disciples, and used to kiss her often on her mouth.

There are a few things about these passages to keep in mind. First, let's take a look at the whole kissing on the mouth bit. What's that all about? This might come into more perspective if we look at another passage from the *Gospel of Philip* that comes earlier in the text:

And had the word gone out from that place, it would be nourished from the mouth and it would become perfect. For it is by a kiss that the perfect conceive and give birth. For this reason we also kiss one another.

Based on this verse and others like it, scholars believe that kissing held spiritual significance for the Gnostics who wrote the *Gospel of Philip*. By kissing Mary Magdalene, Jesus was conveying a spiritual truth or teaching, not acting out a public display of affection. The word "mouth" in the verse about Mary Magdalene is misleading as well. In the original version of the *Gospel of Philip*, there is a gap in the text that has been filled in with the word "mouth." Scholars chose that word because it reflects what had been said in this earlier passage.

The New Testament contains several references to a "holy kiss" used in early Christian communities to greet one another. Romans 16:16 says, "Greet one another with a holy kiss. All the churches of Christ greet you." Other verses include 1 Corinthians 16:20, 2 Corinthians 13:12, 1 Timothy 5:26, and 1 Peter 5:14.

Another thing to think about is that in both passages, the word translated as "companion" is *koinonos* in Greek, which could have conjugal overtones. In other words, it's a word that could refer to people who were romantically involved. That doesn't mean that we should immediately jump to the conclusion that Jesus and Mary Magdalene were married, because there are several possible explanations, including a spiritual interpretation.

Lingua Magda

In Gnostic-speak, a **syzygy** is two spiritual ideas, or principles, that are united, and together make a whole. It is highly likely that Jesus and Mary Magdalene were intended to represent a syzygy in the *Gospel of Philip*.

The *Gospel of Philip* in large part revolves around the subject of a rather mysterious practice known as "the bridal chamber," which probably refers to the union of the soul with God. Marital imagery is used heavily throughout the *Gospel of Philip*, so it's entirely possible that setting up Mary Magdalene as Jesus' partner was intended to represent a spiritual pairing, not a literal one. In this *syzygy*, Mary Magdalene modeled our relationship with God.

The last thing you need to know is that the *Gospel of Philip* was written hundreds of years after Jesus and Mary Magdalene lived! It is true that it reflects a tradition of belief held by early Christians, but it definitely wasn't written by anyone who would have had firsthand knowledge of a relationship between Jesus and Mary Magdalene.

All of this may be a little overwhelming, and that's fine; Gnosticism can be very confusing and hard to untangle. You don't need to remember all the details about the *Gospel of Philip;* just keep in mind that there is more than one way to look at the intriguing passages it contains.

Rolling in Dough?

Although this is one of the less-popular ideas, there is often some belief that Mary Magdalene was wealthy, and that it was most likely the result of her success as a courtesan. Although this is entirely possible, it isn't terribly likely.

Mary Magdalene's legendary wealth stems from the New Testament passage that we have already looked at:

> ... and also some women who had been healed of evil spirits and infirmities: Mary, called Magdalene, from whom seven demons had gone out, and Joanna, the wife of Chuza, Herod's steward, and Susanna, and many others, who provided for them out of their means.

> —Luke 8:2,3

The phrase "out of their means" gives us the impression that the women had some kind of material wealth that they used to support Jesus and his followers as they went about their important mission. Much speculation about the source of Mary Magdalene's wealth has been the result, though strangely, very little attention has been given to the fact that she was not the only woman named.

Other than Mary Magdalene's presumed lucrative profession, it has been suggested that she was an older woman who had inherited property from a deceased husband, or that she had been divorced and given a generous "severance package" as specified in her *ketubah.*

Lingua Magda

A *ketubah* is a Jewish marriage contract dating back to the first century. One of the purposes of this legal document was to specify a sum of money and/or property that could revert to a woman in the event of divorce or widowhood.

Even if it really cannot be known how wealthy Mary Magdalene was, and any suggestions about her fiscal position are purely speculative, the short passage about her "means" speaks volumes. It is highly possible that Mary Magdalene was a woman with possessions and/or property. In terms of likelihood, it is much easier to say with certainty that Mary Magdalene was wealthy than to substantiate any of the other claims we've explored so far in this chapter.

Pictured in *The Last Supper*

Next to the *Mona Lisa*, *The Last Supper* is probably Leonardo da Vinci's most famous painting. Although most people have only seen it as a reprint in books, the real painting is a large fifteenth-century mural that covers an entire wall in the dining hall at Convent of Santa Maria delle Grazie in Milan, Italy. Shortly after the painting was finished, *The Last Supper* began to suffer the effects of deterioration, which became more and more serious as time passed. Leonardo da Vinci was known for experimenting with different artistic methods and materials. The method he used for preparing the surface of the wall that would bear *The Last Supper* is one of the reasons it deteriorated so quickly.

The painting has been restored a number of times, though sometimes the "restoration" was more like a "repainting." In 1999, the most total restoration of the mural was completed, and it can now be seen as it might have been intended by the artist.

> **It Is Written**
>
> When Jesus had thus spoken, he was troubled in spirit, and testified, "Truly, truly, I say to you, one of you will betray me." The disciples looked at one another, uncertain of whom he spoke. One of his disciples, whom Jesus loved, was lying close to the breast of Jesus; so Simon Peter beckoned to him and said, "Tell us who it is of whom he speaks."
>
> —John 13:21–24

The painting itself is a picture of Jesus sitting with his 12 disciples at a long table as they partake in their last meal together. During this meal, the Gospels tell us that Jesus revealed that he would be betrayed by one of those present. Leonardo's painting depicts the moment when Peter asks John, long believed to be the Beloved Disciple, who it is that will betray Jesus. John sits directly to Jesus' right, and leans over to the viewer's left, seemingly listening to something being whispered by the man next to him.

The authors of *Holy Blood, Holy Grail* suggested that Leonardo da Vinci was, at one time, the leader of a secret society that protected the truth about Jesus and Mary Magdalene's marriage and children. As the keeper of this secret, Leonardo supposedly encoded symbols in his paintings to give viewers clues to the truth about Jesus and Christianity.

In *The Last Supper*, the figure thought to be John looks very feminine; he has long hair, no beard, hands folded demurely on the table, and is wearing an enigmatic smile. Because of Leonardo's alleged knowledge about Jesus and Mary Magdalene, some have come to wonder whether the figure long thought to be John is actually Mary Magdalene.

This idea has been in circulation since at least 1997 due to the publication of *The Templar Revelation* by Lynn Picknett and Clive Prince, and was picked up again by Dan Brown in *The Da Vinci Code* (see Appendix B for details on both books). Because of *The Da Vinci Code's* popularity, Mary Magdalene's presence in *The Last Supper* is now rumored on a wide scale. In his book, Brown points out that a female symbol, the downward-pointing triangle or "V" shape, can be seen if you trace a line from the top of Jesus' head down to the table and back up to the top of the Beloved Disciple's head. This is a new take on the idea as it had been presented by Picknett and Prince: that if you trace a line over the two figures of Jesus and the Beloved Disciple, you will see an "M" for Mary Magdalene.

Art scholars have responded to the rumor about *The Last Supper* with the traditional wisdom that the figure to Jesus' right in the painting is that of the disciple John. Some of the more convincing arguments against Mary Magdalene as the figure in *The Last Supper* are as follows:

◆ The Beloved Disciple was often portrayed by other artists as a young, slightly feminine man with long hair and no beard.

◆ Many of Leonardo's other paintings and sketches of young men are decidedly feminine in nature.

◆ Leonardo may have been a trickster, but he had to work within the limits of acceptable subject matter for his day. If the figure to Jesus' right really looked like a woman and not a beardless youth, the monks that commissioned the piece would have thrown a royal fit. And if anyone seriously thought he was suggesting that the Beloved Disciple was a woman, he may have faced grave consequences for heresy.

The main thrust of these arguments is that, 500 years later, through the lenses of our modern culture and a good conspiracy theory, we are misinterpreting what we see. Back in Leonardo's day, viewers saw a young man. Now, because young men typically aren't portrayed as feminine, we see a woman.

> **CAUTION**
>
> **Quite Contrary** _____
>
> There is another legend about Leonardo's *The Last Supper*, namely, that he unknowingly used the same model for both Jesus and Judas. The story usually goes that Leonardo found a morally upright man to model for Jesus. Several years later, he searched for a model for Judas, and found a prisoner who would do very well. After modeling for Judas, the man revealed that many years before, it had been he who modeled as Jesus. There are many versions of this story, and they are all false. Leonardo *did* search for a model for Judas among prisoners, but he didn't use the same man for Jesus and Judas.

However you cut it, not many people will deny that the Beloved Disciple figure in *The Last Supper* looks like a woman. Whether or not the feminine figure was intended to actually be a woman, though, or just a young man who isn't yet *manly*, is still up for debate.

Before I leave you to your own consideration, however, I'd like to point out another artist from the same period. Pietro Perugino was a painter who studied with the same teacher as Leonardo da Vinci, possibly at the same time. In Florence, Italy, he was also enrolled with the same group of painters, in the same year, as Leonardo.

In a work of art called *The Galitzin Triptych*, Perugino painted a curious image of the Beloved Disciple John and Mary Magdalene. The work itself depicts the crucifixion.

> **Illuminations** _____
>
> Modern scholar Ramon K. Jusino has written a fascinating thesis examining the possibility that Mary Magdalene really *was* the Beloved Disciple. He argues that the author of the Gospel of John intended the Beloved Disciple to be Mary Magdalene, but that someone else came along later and removed all references to her in that role. You can find more information about Jusino's thesis in Appendix B.

Beneath Jesus' left arm stands John, and up a little hill is Mary Magdalene. John and Mary Magdalene are standing in exactly the same pose, except for the position of their hands. Even their robes fall in exactly the same manner. If you look closely enough, Perugino could have used the same model for both figures.

If we wanted to apply the same conspiratorial methods as with *The Last Supper*, you will notice that the landscape against the backdrop of the sky, as well as the level of each figure's head, contribute to a downward-pointing "V." If you tried hard enough, you could even convince yourself that because the tops of the rocks are angled downward on the outside, that what you see is only the center part of an "M." It isn't highly likely that this is what Perugino intended, but then, it isn't very likely that Leonardo da Vinci intended to paint the Beloved Disciple as a woman, either.

It is entirely possible that there *was* a heretical teaching circulating in fifteenth-century Italy that linked Mary Magdalene with the Beloved Disciple, but even if there was, it doesn't mean that it was a historically accurate belief. Regardless, based on one or two paintings, we can't say for certain that this was the case.

The Least You Need to Know

- ◆ Mary Magdalene has been portrayed for millennia as having long, flowing hair.

- ◆ She was probably associated with the color red because of her legendary sinful nature, and is often depicted as a redhead, although no one knows for sure what color hair she had.

- ◆ A courtesan is a fancy, high-class prostitute, and Mary Magdalene was probably neither.

- ◆ Whether or not Jesus and Mary Magdalene were married is a question that people have pondered for centuries.

- ◆ Mary Magdalene had some financial means of her own, and may well have been wealthy.

- ◆ The Beloved Disciple, John, in Leonardo da Vinci's *The Last Supper*, has recently been suggested to be Mary Magdalene.

Part 2

The Biblical Mary Magdalene

You might be surprised, as I was, to learn that there is nothing in the Gospels that says Mary Magdalene was a prostitute. If there isn't anything in the New Testament to tell us that, then what *does* it say about her?

Mary Magdalene is mentioned more than any other woman in the Gospels except for Jesus' mother. It's pretty sad, then, that she ended up getting such a bum rap for being employed in "the world's oldest profession." In this part, we visit all the references to Mary Magdalene in the Gospels and take a detailed look at the scenes in which she plays a part. With any luck, we'll begin to get an idea of what it must have been like for her to be part of such an extraordinary ministry.

Chapter 5

Jesus and Women

In This Chapter

- The roles of women in first-century Palestine
- The women who influenced Jesus' life
- More parables of Jesus and women
- The place of women in early Christianity

Because this section focuses on how Mary Magdalene was treated in the Gospels and in Christianity, it seems fitting that we should first take a look at what it was like to be a woman at time, and how Jesus treated women. This will help put into context how Mary Magdalene actually appeared to early Christians, and why she may have been one of the more important women in Jesus' life.

Many assumptions have been made about what it must have been like to be a woman in first-century Palestine based on what is said of women in much older Hebrew texts, and based on much later Rabbinical writings. The truth is somewhere in between. When we take a look outside of religious texts at what was written about Jewish women in Palestine and elsewhere in the Roman Empire, a more rounded picture gradually emerges.

Life for a Woman

There seems to be a general attitude among popular writers today that women in first-century Palestine had much less freedom than they really did. Although they certainly didn't enjoy the same kind of independence that women in America do today, it might not have been nearly as bad as it has been made out to be. As I've pointed out already, in every culture there are groups of people who hold different opinions of what should and shouldn't be acceptable behavior; the Jews at that time were no different.

It's also worthwhile to remember that just because there was a law forbidding something, it doesn't mean that the behavior didn't happen. In fact, it's likely that the behavior *did* happen, or there wouldn't be a law to address it. The religious authorities at the time also gave their opinions on many different aspects of society; these opinions might carry weight with people in their local area, but opinions weren't necessarily the same thing as law.

With that in mind, let's take a look at what life might have been like for a woman, perhaps Mary Magdalene, in first-century Palestine.

Family Life

Female children weren't as desirable as male children, but they were provided for nonetheless. Although it was the mother's duty to care for the children, fathers who happened to be priests were known to teach both their sons and their daughters about the *Torah*. Young children spent their time with their mother, who would begin their education in acceptable behavior, but they also had playtime for games and toys just as all children do. As they grew older, daughters would learn how to run a household and observe the responsibilities of a Jewish woman from her mother, whereas her brothers would be further educated in a family trade by their father.

Lingua Magda

When Christians refer to the **Torah,** they are usually referring to the first five books of the Old Testament: Genesis, Exodus, Leviticus, Numbers, and Deuteronomy. For Jews, however, the Torah is a much broader category. It can also apply to the Books of Moses (the five books already mentioned), or to the Written Torah (the whole of Jewish scripture), as well as to the Oral Torah (the interpretation of the scriptures and how to apply the laws), or to all of these combined.

The responsibilities of a Jewish woman encompassed everything associated with keeping a proper Jewish home and family, including the following:

♦ Grinding flour, baking bread, preparing food

♦ Spinning, weaving, sewing, and washing garments

♦ Giving birth, nursing, and caring for children

Naturally, a woman's time would be consumed by her domestic obligations, leaving little time for other activities. In addition to her household responsibilities, Jewish women had three specific religious duties, called *mitzvot*, or "commandments." They were:

♦ *Nerot.* The lighting of candles to mark the beginning of a religious observance in the home, such as the Sabbath

♦ *Challah.* The separating of a portion of bread dough from the rest and setting it aside

♦ *Niddah.* The ritual bath taken by a woman after she is finished menstruating, to restore her cleanliness

The biological reality of menstruation was the source of much concern in Judaism, and women who were bleeding were considered to be unclean. No contact was to take place between a menstruating woman and her husband, or any other man for that matter, lest he be contaminated. In such a case, he would sometimes need to undergo special purification rituals to become clean again. A menstruating woman's uncleanliness rubbed off on anything that she touched as well, making the everyday situation of living with a man especially difficult. After a woman's period had ended, she was to take the ritual cleansing bath, the *niddah*, after which it would be safe to be around her husband again. Likewise, the period after childbirth was one when a woman was considered unclean, but for even longer; if a woman gave birth to a boy, she was unclean for 40 days following the birth, but it was 80 days for giving birth to a girl.

Women were often given in marriages arranged by their parents while they were children, and sent to live with their husband's family while they grew up. Usually the marriage was between a boy and girl of a similar age, because most people knew that marrying a young girl to an older man wouldn't work out for the best. A girl up to the age of 12 was considered a "minor," and she enjoyed certain privileges, namely, she could use birth control. The cruel fact of life was that girls so young were not mature enough to handle the rigors of motherhood, and often died in childbirth. However young some brides were, though, many women were still considered desirable past the age of 20.

As mentioned in the previous chapter, when a marriage took place, a legal document called a *ketubah* was written, in which a sum of money and/or property was set aside for a bride in the event of a divorce or widowhood. Although many people think that women couldn't inherit from her husband or father, in practice, it could be arranged. Even though by law she didn't have many rights to inherit, there were many loopholes through which husbands and fathers who loved the women in their lives were able to leave legacies for them.

> **It Is Written**
>
> Give the water no passage; neither a wicked woman liberty to gad abroad. If she go not as thou wouldest have her, cut her off from thy flesh, and give her a bill of divorce, and let her go.
>
> —*Wisdom of Jesus Son of Sirach* 25:25,26 (a second-century B.C.E. Jewish text)

Divorce was the other way a woman might acquire money and property of her own. Although technically a woman couldn't divorce her husband, it did happen that they were sometimes able to get out of marriages. Regardless of who did the divorcing, though, the *ketubah* was an all-important document for sorting out what the wife would get to keep. Sometimes the sum was so large that the husband would think twice about divorcing his wife for frivolous reasons.

Public Life

Outside of the home, a woman was not obligated to attend synagogue prayer services because it was not one of her religious duties. However, when a woman did voluntarily attend synagogue, she would sit in a women's gallery apart from the men.

How a woman dressed often depended on her station in life. If she was born into a poor family, she would wear clothes she made herself from the wool that her family could afford, usually in plain, undyed colors. If a woman was born into a family that was better off, she might wear clothes dyed in bright colors, made of wool or silk. She might adorn herself with jewelry and wear cosmetics on her face, hands, fingernails, and sometimes her feet and toenails.

The way a woman acted in public was the subject of much controversy. Most religious authorities recommended that the best way to keep a woman out of trouble was to keep her in the house. But the practical demands of life often required a woman to go out to a public marketplace to buy food, wool, and other goods to run her household. While in public, a responsible woman would avoid contact with men as much as possible, and keep her hair covered. A woman who wore her hair loose in public was thought to be immodest, and at a time when prostitution could be defined as broadly as a woman who looked at a man the wrong way, "immodest" wasn't a label most women wanted.

In spite of the fact that women were thought to be best left at home, women were engaged in several occupations outside of the house. Some women might have found a source of extra income by selling bread dough, or items they had woven, sewn, or embroidered. Some women, as the keepers of the house, rented out extra rooms and were thus employed as innkeepers. Women were often employed by other women as hairdressers and mid-wives, and sometimes acting as a midwife led a woman to further study anatomy and healing herbs, and to practice as a physician.

> **CAUTION**
>
> **Quite Contrary**
>
> In Martin Scorsese's movie *The Last Temptation of Christ*, Mary Magdalene was depicted as having elaborate tattoos on her hands, feet, and face. Other more respectable women were depicted with small facial tattoos as well. This is not historically accurate. Although women did sometimes stain their skin with a paste made from the henna herb for cosmetic purposes, it leaves the skin red, not black.

Another fascinating occupation held by women was that of professional mourner. Most funerals had at least one hired mourner to weep and wail, as well as to lead the rest of those present in songs and lamentations.

An Unusual Attitude

As we saw in the first chapter, Jesus' attitude toward women was unusual. Not only was he willing to talk to women, sometimes he was willing to talk to *foreign* women. In the case of the Samaritan woman at the well, she would have been considered per-manently unclean, as if she was menstruating all the time. Jesus not only had a con-versation with her, but he drank water from her jug, showing that the typical rules about ritual cleanliness didn't concern him. This would have had a profound effect on the woman, as well as on Jesus' disciples, who couldn't believe what he had done.

This sets the stage for understanding Jesus' disposition toward women; he just didn't seem to buy into any of the typical attitudes. He treated women as human beings, just as he treated men, while at the same time recognizing that they led different kinds of lives than men. It was his talent to be able to speak to women in a way that would be meaningful to them, and to include them as recipients of his message.

Perhaps most telling, though, isn't what Jesus did say about women, but what he didn't say. He didn't reinforce the rigid rules of behavior that a woman must adhere to. He didn't tell women they should go home and remember their place. Instead, he said, "Follow me," and he said it to *everyone* (Matt. 16:24; Mark 8:34; Luke 9:23; 14:27; John 10:27; 12:26).

The Gospels mention several women who were associated with Jesus during the course of his life. Just like everyone else, he had a mother, but he also had a number of followers and friends who happened to be women.

Lingua Magda

Theotokos means "god-bearer" or "mother of god." This is a title used to refer to the Virgin Mary in Eastern Orthodox churches.

Mary, His Mother

Mary of Nazareth has already been introduced, but we haven't yet taken a look at how she is remembered in the Gospels. It can be difficult to find the humanity in a figure so much larger than life, but in the beginning, the woman now remembered as "the Blessed Virgin" and *Theotokos* was just a girl named Mary.

No one knows how old she was when she became pregnant with Jesus. The Gospels say that she was engaged to be married to a man named Joseph and that she was a virgin; but knowing that women could be given in marriage as young teenagers on into their adult years, it is impossible to say how old she may have been. Regardless, her life was to be forever changed when the angel Gabriel appeared to her to say that she would become pregnant by the Holy Spirit and bear a son who would be the Messiah. The Gospels tell of her quite understandable fear:

> And [the angel Gabriel] came to her and said, "Hail, O favored one, the Lord is with you!" But she was greatly troubled at the saying, and considered in her mind what sort of greeting this might be.

> —Luke 1:28, 29

While Mary was pregnant with Jesus, she and Joseph traveled to Bethlehem to be counted in a census, and it was in Bethlehem that she gave birth. The Gospel of Luke says that she was "great with child," so we can assume that she was in the last stages of her pregnancy, which would have made traveling difficult.

Quite Contrary _____

The Gospel of Luke says that when Jesus was born, he was laid in a manger because there was no room for Joseph and Mary at the inn (which may have simply been rooms rented in someone's home). It doesn't say that Jesus was born in a barn, but because a manger is a contraption for feeding animals, that has become the popular image for his birth. Matthew says that Jesus was in a house when the three magi came bearing gifts, but it doesn't say when they arrived. It could have been years later.

Joseph and Mary fulfilled their obligations to Jesus as any good parents would, but raising the Son of God proved to be challenging at times. Every year, Joseph and Mary took their family to Jerusalem to celebrate the Passover feast. When Jesus was 12, without telling his parents, he stayed behind at the temple when the rest of his family left Jerusalem. When Joseph and Mary realized he was missing, they searched high and low for him, eventually returning to the temple. They found him deep in conversation with religious scholars. Like any mother, Mary asked Jesus something to the effect of, "Do you have _any_ idea what you've put us through!?" Jesus' response was to ask why they had been looking for him because he was going about his father's business, which is to say, God's business (Luke 2:41–52).

An even bigger challenge came when Jesus began his ministry, which was terribly unpopular with the religious authorities and conservative Jews of the time. He got himself thrown out of their local synagogue, and was taunted by people in his hometown. They asked, "Isn't he Mary's son?" This couldn't have been easy for Mary or the rest of his family (Luke 4:16–30; Mark 6:1–6).

Whatever occurred during the course of Jesus' life, any mother would know that nothing could have prepared Mary for what was to occur during his last Passover in Jerusalem. He was arrested, put on trial, beaten, humiliated, and finally crucified. As terrible as it would have been to outlive her own child, it must have been much, much worse to see him killed in such a ruthless manner. The Gospels record his mother as one of the women who remained near the cross during his ordeal:

> But standing by the cross of Jesus [was] his mother …

—John 19:25

While on the cross, the Gospel of John says that his mother and the Beloved Disciple, usually assumed to be John, stood and watched. One of Jesus' last acts was to entrust his mother into John's care:

> When Jesus saw his mother, and the disciple whom he loved standing near, he said to his mother, "Woman, behold, your son!" Then he said to the disciple, "Behold, your mother!" And from that hour the disciple took her to his own home.

—John 19:26–27

The Virgin Mary is also mentioned in the New Testament after Jesus has ascended into heaven. He had told his followers that the Holy Spirit would come to teach them, comfort them, and help them remember his words. The book of Acts says that Jesus' mother was present, along with "the other women," for the event known as the Pentecost: the descent of the Holy Spirit onto his followers (Acts 1:14).

Martha and Mary of Bethany

Two different Gospels, Luke and John, mention women named Martha and Mary, who were sisters. The Gospel of John says they were from Bethany (John 11:1). Some people think that the two Gospels are referring to two different sets of sisters named Martha and Mary, but it does seem likely that it's the same set of women being referred to in both places.

Perhaps the most important thing about Martha and Mary is that Jesus loved them as friends. He and his followers spent time resting and eating at their house when they were in the area, and two of the most important scenes in the Gospels occur during these stopovers: the raising of Lazarus (John 11) and the anointing by Mary of Bethany (John 12:1–8).

Lazarus was Martha and Mary's brother. He became ill while Jesus was in another town, and knowing that he was a healer, the sisters sent for him to come restore their brother to health. Unfortunately, before Jesus could make the journey back to Bethany, Lazarus died and was entombed. Upon returning to Bethany, Jesus was met by Martha, who said that if he had been there, Lazarus wouldn't have died. Jesus responded by telling her that Lazarus would rise from the grave. Martha, not understanding what Jesus meant, said she knew he would be resurrected on "the last day." Jesus corrected her and said that *he* was the resurrection and the life, and that whoever believed in him would have everlasting life. Martha then said that she believed, and went to get Mary.

When Mary came to Jesus, she fell at his feet, weeping. She, too, said that if he had been there, Lazarus wouldn't have died. But this time, Jesus was clearly moved by her grief, and the shortest verse in the New Testament reflects his emotion:

> Jesus wept.
>
> —John 11:35

It Is Written

When Jesus saw her weeping, and the Jews who came with her also weeping, he was deeply moved in spirit and troubled ...
—John 11:33

Then, he ordered the stone to be rolled away from the opening of the tomb, and he called Lazarus out. To everyone's astonishment, Lazarus, in his grave clothes, came forth from his tomb. This was a pivotal event in Jesus' ministry, after which he became a marked man. When everyone who had assembled to mourn Lazarus saw what he did, some of them went and told the religious authorities what had happened. As a result, the decision was made that Jesus had to be arrested and put to death.

We have briefly looked at the anointing by Mary of Bethany already, but not at the details of that particular version of the story. After Jesus resurrected Lazarus, he was in Bethany dining with Martha, Mary, their brother, and his other followers. Mary entered the room and poured a pound of very expensive ointment on Jesus' feet, then wiped them with her hair. So potent was the scent that it filled the entire room. Judas, who we are led to believe was overly concerned about money, complained about wasting something so expensive. Jesus then defended Mary, saying:

> Jesus said, "Let her alone, let her keep it for the day of my burial. The poor you always have with you, but you do not always have me."
>
> —John 12:7

One other story about Martha and Mary in Luke reflects their different personalities and how they show their devotion to Jesus. Jesus was sitting in the house teaching his followers. Martha, the older sister, was overwhelmed by the work of being a hostess while her younger sister, Mary, sat at Jesus' feet listening to him talk. Martha told Jesus that she needed Mary's help serving, and asked him to admonish her for being lazy. Jesus replied:

But the Lord answered her, "Martha, Martha, you are anxious and troubled about many things; one thing is needful. Mary has chosen the good portion, which shall not be taken away from her."

—Luke 10:41

This story has been interpreted as demonstrating two ways of living a Christian life: through service and through contemplation. Martha is an example of active faith, taking charge and getting things done, organizing and serving. Mary, on the other hand, content to sit at her Master's feet, is an example of complete devotion to God and the desire to learn and reflect on his teachings.

Other Followers

For the most part, the Gospels refer to Jesus' female followers collectively as "women," but there are a few who are mentioned either by name or another specific designation:

- Mary the mother of James and Joses: one of the women who watched the crucifixion and one of the myrrhbearers (Matthew 27:56)

- The mother of Zebedee's children: one of the women who watched the crucifixion (Matt. 20:20; 27:56)

- "The other Mary": one of the myrrhbearers (Matthew 27:61; 28:1)

- Salome: one of the women who watched the crucifixion and one of the myrrhbearers (Mark 15:40; 16:1)

- Joanna the wife of Chuza, Herod's steward: one of the women who provided for Jesus' ministry and one of the myrrhbearers (Luke 8:3; 24:10)

- Susanna: one of the women who provided for Jesus' ministry (Luke 8:3)

- "His mother's sister": one of the women who watched the crucifixion (John 19:25)

- Mary the wife of Cleophas: one of the women who watched the crucifixion (John 19:25)

You may be wondering about the references to the woman called "the other Mary." The verses that contain "the other Mary" don't give us any clues as to her identity, only that because she was accompanying Mary Magdalene, it couldn't have been her.

In parallel versions of the same verses, however, we can conclude that "the other Mary" may have been the Virgin Mary. We take another look at how this is possible in the next chapter.

The other woman you may be wondering about is Salome. Perhaps you've heard the story about the daughter of Herodias who danced for her stepfather, Herod, and was offered anything she desired in return. Herodias, who hated John the Baptist, convinced her daughter to ask for his head on a platter. The Gospels never name this dancing girl, but other documents of the time mention that the name of Herodias' daughter was Salome. Was this the same Salome who was a follower of Jesus? It's unlikely. Much is known of the life of Salome, the daughter of Herodias, and it is never mentioned that she became one of Jesus' followers.

Illuminations

The Gnostic texts mention a woman named Salome extensively as one of Jesus' most devoted followers.

Parables and Miracles

It might seem like no big deal now, but it was really quite significant that every aspect of Jesus' ministry involved women to some degree. During the time when he was traveling around Palestine, women weren't usually taught scripture unless they were married to a rabbi, and even then it was at her husband's discretion. Jesus, on the other hand, had women followers, taught lessons that women would be able to identify with, and performed several miracles for women.

We've already gone over the stories of the Samaritan woman at the well and the woman caught in adultery, so let's look at some of the others. This is by no means a complete list, only a few of the most prominent and best-remembered scenes. Rather than including direct quotes from the Gospels, I'm going to paraphrase each story and include the reference for you to go back to later.

The Parable of the Lost Coin (Luke 15:8–10)

Jesus was being criticized by the religious authorities for keeping company with people on the outskirts of society, and in particular, for eating with sinners. Jesus tells a story of how just as a shepherd with 100 sheep would leave 99 to go after 1 that was lost, there is more joy in the repentance of 1 sinner than of 99 who need no repentance.

Then he goes on to further illustrate his point by giving another example. What woman, he asks, who had 10 coins but lost 1, wouldn't light a candle and sweep her house until she found it?

In giving this example to a mixed crowd, that is, to men and women of various financial means, Jesus was including everyone in the lesson. One coin could be a whole day's wages, and if a husband left his wife in charge of the money, she would be responsible for any lost. So the answer is of course a woman with 10 coins would go looking for the lost coin. Not only would she look for it, but she would call her neighbors and share her joy with them when she found it, just as Jesus said that the angels of God rejoice when one lost soul repents.

The Parable of the Woman with a Measure of Leaven (Matthew 13:33)

In this parable, Jesus is explaining the nature of the kingdom of God to an assembled crowd. First he compares the kingdom to a tiny mustard seed. But after planting such a seed, it grows into a large tree in which birds can nest.

He goes on to discuss leaven, which is the yeast that causes bread to rise. He says that the kingdom is like a measure of leaven that a woman hides in three pieces of dough. It started as nothing, but before long, it was all "leavened," or risen. Yeast, or leaven, is an agent of change; it causes bread to rise. Like the mustard seed that grows into a great tree, leaven causes an otherwise unremarkable lump of dough to grow into a loaf of nourishing bread. It is noteworthy that in John 6:35, Jesus said: "I am the bread of life; he who comes to me shall not hunger, and he who believes in me shall never thirst."

> **Quite Contrary**
>
> Many people believe that Jews aren't allowed to eat leavened bread at all, but in fact, it is only during the Passover feast that they are to refrain.

Again, this parable of the leaven is relevant to women, who, as the preparers of food, would be very familiar with how bread is made.

The Healing of the Woman with an Issue of Blood (Matthew 9:20)

Just as the Samaritan woman at the well was considered permanently unclean, the Jewish woman who suffered from a hemorrhage was also considered unclean because of her continual bleeding. You can probably imagine how difficult it would have been for a woman in such a situation; not only must she have felt ill, but she had to obey strict rules that forbade her from coming into contact with men for many, many years.

Perhaps because she thought Jesus would never allow her to touch him, she decided to just secretly touch the hem of his robe in hopes that it would heal her. It did heal her, but Jesus turned around quickly to see who it was that had touched him. He saw her, but instead of condemning her for contaminating him, he told her that her faith had made her whole.

The Poor Widow (Mark 12:41)

Jesus was watching people putting their money into a treasury at the temple. Many rich people came and tossed in lots of money, and then a poor widow woman came and tossed in "two mites," which wasn't very much money at all. Jesus told his disciples that the widow woman had given more than everyone else who had donated to the treasury, because the rich people were putting in only a portion of their wealth, but the widow had given everything that she had.

Everyone Is Equal in Heaven (Matthew 22:30)

How much more democratic can it get than teaching that in heaven, everyone is the same?

Some *Sadducees* came to Jesus and asked him a trick question. What if a man gets married, has no children, and then dies? The wife is then allowed to marry the man's brother in an effort to bring children into the family. (Levirate marriage was a Jewish custom whereby if a man died without any children, his brother would marry the widow in an effort to provide children who could inherit the deceased man's property. This ensured that property was kept within a family.) What if the brother also dies without any children by her? And then what if she remarries the next brother and so on, until finally the seventh brother dies and then the woman dies? Who then, would be her husband in heaven?

Lingua Magda

Like the Pharisees, the **Sadducees** were a powerful sect of Judaism at the time of Christ. They taught strict adherence only to the written Mosaic law.

Jesus answered that no one would be married to anyone else, because everyone will be like an angel of God. The Gospels then record that everyone who was listening was astonished, and we can well assume that any women who were present would have been pretty impressed.

Jesus on Divorce (Matthew 5:32, Matthew 19:9, Mark 10:11, Luke 16:18)

As we've already seen, divorce was mainly the prerogative of the husband. Perhaps it was inevitable that a practice so blatantly unfair to women should be addressed by Jesus at some point. In fact, it is mentioned in a few places.

Jesus' take on the subject was that men and women had an equal right to divorce one another—that is, neither of them should do it. If a man was to divorce a woman, he was making her into an adulterer, and if a woman was to divorce a man, she was making *him* into an adulterer.

Women in Early Christianity

The Gospels of Matthew, Mark, Luke, and John are the only books in the New Testament that record words believed to have been spoken by Jesus. The books that follow the Gospels record the development of Jesus' ministry into a young religion and the efforts of his followers to preach the message of salvation. Some of the most interesting portions of the New Testament are letters sent by Paul, who was considered to be an apostle even though he never met Jesus in the flesh, to the earliest Christian communities throughout the Roman Empire. Although Paul's letters are the best description of early Christian groups and practices in the New Testament, there are records of the activities of Christians mentioned in nonreligious sources as well.

> **CAUTION**
>
> **Quite Contrary**
>
> Many of the letters that are attributed to Paul may not have been written by him. These are called the "Deutero-Pauline" letters, and they include Ephesians, Colossians, 2 Thessalonians, 1 and 2 Timothy, and Titus.

Early Christianity was a fledgling Jewish sect, not the powerful institution that we know today. Husband and wife pairs were often sent as missionaries to spread the message of Christianity into new areas. One of the reasons Christianity appealed to women is because it was from women that they heard of it. Women, as keepers of households, often offered up their houses to be used as meeting places where her friends and neighbors could gather and discuss the new faith. These house-churches were of utmost importance to the young religion, and there is evidence that the women whose homes were used often served as clergy members.

Because Christianity was viewed with suspicion by Roman authorities, believers had to be more equal-opportunity in selecting those who would run things. Slaves and freedmen, men and women could be Christians, and they all shared in performing church functions. There are records of women ministering, preaching, prophesying, baptizing, and even serving the Eucharist to other believers. Women were apostles, deacons, and there is even evidence that there may have been women bishops.

Eventually, however, all forms of Christianity in which women were allowed to fulfill roles of authority were eliminated by the emerging orthodoxy. Second-century church fathers wrote scathing comments about women acting in official capacities, and early Christian texts show a clear indication that there were competing schools of thought as to what the proper roles of women were. In many of these texts, Mary Magdalene figured as an extremely important leader of the Church. It is possible that even though they were written later than the four Gospels of the New Testament, they reflect an earlier tradition that remembered her as an apostle of Jesus.

The Least You Need to Know

- ◆ Although women in first-century Palestine enjoyed many fewer freedoms than we do now, they did have a bit more autonomy than is frequently suggested.

- ◆ Jesus intentionally tailored his message to appeal to people from all walks of life, including women, and he didn't seem to hold the typical attitude about women and uncleanliness.

- ◆ There were many women in Jesus' life mentioned in the New Testament, and there are many stories of how they figured in his ministry.

- ◆ Women fulfilled roles in early Christianity that were later forbidden to them.

6

Mary Magdalene in the Gospels

In This Chapter

- ◆ A bit about the Gospels of Matthew, Mark, Luke, and John
- ◆ A play-by-play look at Mary Magdalene
- ◆ Comparing notes on parallel scenes
- ◆ The silent lady finally speaks

Let's now turn our attention to each of the Gospels in order, to see how Mary Magdalene appears in each one. Some mentions of her show up in all four Gospels, but it is only when they are all taken together that they begin to congeal into a meaningful whole.

The four Gospels themselves—Matthew, Mark, Luke, and John—are separated into the something called the *synoptic* Gospels and John. Synoptic means "to take the same view," which is precisely the case with the first three Gospels: They share much in the way of tone, content, and the order of events. The synoptics—Matthew, Mark, and Luke—were written earlier than John and all share enough similarities to give scholars the idea that they were based on one another. Most scholars today believe that

Mark was written first, and that it influenced the authors of Matthew and Luke. There is evidence that another document, nicknamed "Q," acted as a source for Matthew and Luke as well. To date, no one has discovered a copy of Q, but much has been written about what it might or might not have contained.

The Gospel of John is quite different from the first three Gospels. It contains different stories, different events, and a very different tone. Because it was written last, there is evidence that the author of John was aware of material in one or more of the synoptic Gospels. In one case that we've already seen, the author of John may have tried to explain the anointing in Luke by identifying the anonymous sinner woman as Mary of Bethany.

Matthew

The Gospel of Matthew appears first in the New Testament because from around the second century C.E. onward, people believed it was the first to be written. Scholars now believe that it was not the first, because it contains a lot of material that appears to be based on the Gospel of Mark. Matthew is usually dated at about 80 C.E.

Witness of the Crucifixion and Benefactor

The first mention of Mary Magdalene in any of the Gospels is as one of those women who were present during the crucifixion:

> And many women were there beholding afar off, which followed Jesus from Galilee, ministering unto him: among which was Mary Magdalene, and Mary the mother of James and Joses, and the mother of Zebedee's children. (Matthew 27:55, 56)

Aside from being a witness of Jesus' death, this passage also mentions that the women who were named were some of those who "ministered unto him." "Ministered" has been interpreted to mean that they were the women who provided for his ministry out of their own finances.

Witness of the Entombment

The next mention of Mary Magdalene in Matthew isn't until after the crucifixion has taken place; she appears as one of the women present when Jesus is placed into his tomb.

When the even was come, there came a rich man of Arimathaea, named Joseph, who also himself was Jesus' disciple: he went to Pilate, and begged the body of Jesus. Then Pilate commanded the body to be delivered. And when Joseph had taken the body, he wrapped it in a clean linen cloth, and laid it in his own new tomb, which he had hewn out in the rock, and he rolled a great stone to the door of the sepulchre [a burial chamber or tomb], and departed. And there was Mary Magdalene, and the other Mary, sitting over against the sepulchre.

—Matthew 27:57–61

In this somber scene, Jesus has died on the cross, and Joseph of Arimathaea has been granted the right to take his body to put it in a tomb. He wraps Jesus in a shroud and puts him in the tomb that had been reserved for Joseph himself. Then a large stone is rolled in front of the opening to the chamber. Everyone leaves except Mary Magdalene and "the other Mary."

Being the last to leave gives people the impression that Mary Magdalene was extremely faithful to Jesus. We can imagine that she had probably had a very long day. She watched Jesus die on the cross, something that had to have been extremely difficult, and stayed until the very end. It is for this kind of fortitude that many believe she was rewarded by being the first to witness the resurrection.

Illuminations

Joseph of Arimathaea is mentioned only in connection with getting permission to take Jesus' body from the crucifixion site and providing a tomb for him, but during the Middle Ages several legends sprang up around him as well as the other figures in the Gospels. In some legends, he was a traveling companion to Mary Magdalene. In others, he brought the Holy Grail, and Christianity, to Britain.

Witness of the Resurrection

When reading the Gospels in the order they appear in the New Testament, it is here that we first learn of Mary Magdalene as one of the first people to see the risen Jesus.

In the end of the Sabbath, as it began to dawn toward the first day of the week, came Mary Magdalene and the other Mary to see the sepulchre. And, behold, there was a great earthquake: for the angel of the Lord descended from heaven, and came and rolled back the stone from the door, and sat upon it. His countenance was like lightning, and his raiment white as snow: and for fear of him the keepers did shake, and became as dead men. And the angel answered and said unto the women, Fear not ye: for I know that ye seek Jesus, which was crucified. He is not here: for he is risen, as he said. Come, see the place where the Lord lay. And go quickly, and tell his disciples that he is risen from the dead; and, behold, he goeth before you into Galilee; there shall ye see him: lo, I have told you.

And they departed quickly from the sepulchre with fear and great joy; and did run to bring his disciples word. And as they went to tell his disciples, behold, Jesus met them, saying, All hail. And they came and held him by the feet, and worshipped him. Then said Jesus unto them, Be not afraid: go tell my brethren that they go into Galilee, and there shall they see me.

—Matthew 28:1–10

I've always found the accounts of the resurrection in the synoptic Gospels interesting; there is always a series of events that is a little difficult to unfold in the right order. For example, in the first part of the story, Mary Magdalene and "the other Mary" come to the tomb. Then, it says, there was a big earthquake and the angel came and rolled away the stone. Should we assume that the women also witnessed the earthquake and the coming of the angel? Or did that happen before they arrived? There is nothing that says that the angel had to roll away the stone so Jesus could get out of the tomb, so maybe the angel just came to make everyone aware of the fact that the tomb was empty and to announce the resurrection.

After the angel sends the women to tell the disciples that Jesus is risen, they hurry away. On the road to wherever the disciples were staying, the women are met by Jesus himself. We are given the impression now that the women were thunderstruck by seeing their risen teacher, because it says that they fell down at his feet and worshipped him. Then Jesus gives them instructions again to go tell the disciples the good news.

It Is Written

And when he had considered the thing, he came to the house of Mary the mother of John, whose surname was Mark; where many were gathered together praying.

—Acts 12:12

Mark

The Gospel of Mark is now believed to be the first that was written, probably shortly before or after 70 C.E. Authorship isn't certain, but it's possible that it was written by a man called John Mark who was mentioned several times in the New Testament. John Mark accompanied Barnabas and Paul on a missionary journey, and his mother's home was used as a gathering place. If John Mark *was* the first author of a Gospel, his work proved to have an influence he probably never could have imagined.

Witness of the Crucifixion and Benefactor

After reading the first mention of Mary Magdalene in Matthew, it is easy to see how it could have been based on Mark's passage above—they're almost identical! Here again we see Mary Magdalene standing "afar off" watching the crucifixion.

> There were also women looking on afar off: among whom was Mary Magdalene, and Mary the mother of James the less and of Joses, and Salome; who also, when he was in Galilee, followed him, and ministered unto him; and many other women which came up with him unto Jerusalem.
>
> —Mark 15:40, 41

Just as we saw in Matthew, Mark also contains a reference in the same passage to Mary Magdalene as one of the women who "ministered" to Jesus.

Witness of the Entombment

Although it isn't identical, it is again easy to see the influence that Mark may have had on Matthew by comparing the next passage with its counterpart in Matthew. Mary Magdalene and another woman see Jesus being laid in the tomb.

> And when he knew it of the centurion, he gave the body to Joseph. And he bought fine linen, and took him down, and wrapped him in the linen, and laid him in a sepulchre which was hewn out of a rock, and rolled a stone unto the door of the sepulchre. And Mary Magdalene and Mary the mother of Joses beheld where he was laid.
>
> —Mark 15:45–47

Here, in the *deposition* scene, is our first clue about the identity of "the other Mary." In the parallel passage in Matthew, it was Mary Magdalene and "the other Mary" who watched Jesus being laid in the tomb, but here in Mark, it is Mary Magdalene and Mary, the mother of Joses.

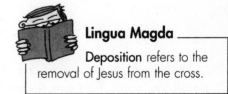

Lingua Magda

Deposition refers to the removal of Jesus from the cross.

Myrrhbearer, Witness of the Resurrection, and Demoniac

In Mark, we see Mary Magdalene for the first time as a myrrhbearer. In Matthew, she went to the tomb only to see Jesus; in Mark, she brought "sweet spices" so she could anoint him. This mention of anointing contributed to the confusion of Mary Magdalene as the woman who anointed Jesus before the crucifixion.

> And when the Sabbath was past, Mary Magdalene, and Mary the mother of James, and Salome, had bought sweet spices, that they might come and anoint him. And very early in the morning the first day of the week, they came unto the sepulchre at the rising of the sun.
>
> And they said among themselves, Who shall roll us away the stone from the door of the sepulchre? And when they looked, they saw that the stone was rolled away: for it was very great. And entering into the sepulchre, they saw a young man sitting on the right side, clothed in a long white garment; and they were affrighted. And he saith unto them, Be not affrighted: Ye seek Jesus of Nazareth, which was crucified: he is risen; he is not here: behold the place where they laid him. But go your way, tell his disciples and Peter that he goeth before you into Galilee: there shall ye see him, as he said unto you.
>
> And they went out quickly, and fled from the sepulchre; for they trembled and were amazed: neither said they any thing to any man; for they were afraid.
>
> Now when Jesus was risen early the first day of the week, he appeared first to Mary Magdalene, out of whom he had cast seven devils. And she went and told them that had been with him, as they mourned and wept. And they, when they had heard that he was alive, and had been seen of her, believed not.
>
> —Mark 16:1–11

> **CAUTION**
>
> **Quite Contrary**
>
> Some people believe Jesus was dead for three days. In fact, if we follow the order of the events, he was dead for two days at the most. If he died on Good Friday, was dead the day after (which would have been observed as the Sabbath) and was risen by Sunday morning, then he couldn't have been dead for more than about 48 hours.

Mark's account of the resurrection doesn't have the thundering intensity of the scene with the angel. This time there is no earthquake; the women just come to the tomb and see the angel inside. Again, the angel instructs the women to go tell the disciples that Jesus is risen and will meet them in Galilee.

In this version of the story, however, Jesus doesn't meet the women on the road. We don't know exactly where it happens, but Jesus singles out Mary Magdalene to be the first to see him alive again. When she told the disciples, they didn't believe her. Most scholars believe that the ending of Mark that includes the resurrection appearance to Mary Magdalene was added at a later date, but no one knows when it was added or by whom.

The identity of "the other Mary" is now becoming clearer. In the parallel version in Matthew, Mary Magdalene and "the other Mary" go to the tomb. But in Mark, it is Mary Magdalene and Mary, the mother of James. It's worth noting that in the first passage we looked at in Mark, in which Mary Magdalene and the other women are watching the crucifixion, she is watching it with Mary, the mother of James and Joses. So Mary, the mother of James, and Mary, the mother of Joses, are probably the same person. Now take a look at this verse, Mark 6:3:

> Is not this the carpenter, the son of Mary, the brother of James, and Joses, and of Juda, and Simon? and are not his sisters here with us? And they were offended at him.

There is another version of this passage in Matthew 13:55. It's therefore possible that "the other Mary" is in fact Jesus' mother, but officially, her identity remains unknown.

Another item of note in this narrative is that Mary Magdalene is described as having had seven "devils" or demons, cast out of her by Jesus. There is no elaboration at all about what the demons might have been, what they did to her, or how she suffered. It's a very plain, matter-of-fact statement.

Illuminations

Like the Gospels, some of the Gnostic Gospels identify the Virgin Mary as "the other Mary."

Luke

The Gospel of Luke is the synoptic Gospel that differs the most from the other two (Matthew and Mark). It is clear that the author used material that appeared in Mark, as well as the mysterious unknown Q, but it also shows evidence of being influenced by additional material not shown in the other Gospels.

Lingua Magda

An **evangelist** is someone who spreads the gospel, as in missionary work. Matthew, Mark, Luke, and John are often referred to as "The Four Evangelists."

It was probably composed around 80 to 90 C.E. by a Syrian man from Antioch named Luke who, in Colossians 4:14, was called a physician. The *evangelist* Luke was likely also the author of the book of Acts, which immediately follows the four Gospels in the New Testament. Because of the different nature of the Gospel of Luke, some scholars believe that it was written outside of Palestine by a non-Palestinian, for non-Jewish Christians.

Demoniac and Benefactor

We have looked at the passage that follows once already, when discussing the women who ministered to Jesus "of their substance" as meaning that they were the ones paying the bills. It is clear by the time this passage appears in Luke that *whatever* "ministering" meant, it was extremely important to Jesus and his ministry, and the women were rendering a very valuable service of some kind.

> And it came to pass afterward, that he went throughout every city and village, preaching and shewing the glad tidings of the kingdom of God: and the twelve were with him, and certain women, which had been healed of evil spirits and infirmities, Mary called Magdalene, out of whom went seven devils, and Joanna the wife of Chuza Herod's steward, and Susanna, and many others, which ministered unto him of their substance.

—Luke 8:1–3

Here again we see Mary Magdalene as a woman from whom seven devils went. This time we aren't told that it was Jesus who sent them out of her, only that she had been healed, so we must draw the conclusion ourselves. Again there is no word on what the "devils" were or how they affected her. We can only assume that she was better off without them because she had been "healed." We will come back to the subject of the seven demons in the next chapter.

Myrrhbearer and Witness of the Empty Tomb

Here we have a very different account of the resurrection. At first it appears similar: The women go to the tomb, find it empty, and speak to angels. They hurry back to the disciples and tell them what they've seen, and the disciples don't believe them.

But this time, that is where the story ends. There is no resurrection appearance to Mary Magdalene or any of the other women.

> And the women also, which came with him from Galilee, followed after, and beheld the sepulchre, and how his body was laid. And they returned, and prepared spices and ointments; and rested the Sabbath day according to the commandment.
>
> Now upon the first day of the week, very early in the morning, they came unto the sepulchre, bringing the spices which they had prepared, and certain others with them. And they found the stone rolled away from the sepulchre. And they entered in, and found not the body of the Lord Jesus. And it came to pass, as they were much perplexed thereabout, behold, two men stood by them in shining garments: and as they were afraid, and bowed down their faces to the earth, they said unto them, Why seek ye the living among the dead? He is not here, but is risen: remember how he spake unto you when he was yet in Galilee, saying, The Son of man must be delivered into the hands of sinful men, and be crucified, and the third day rise again. And they remembered his words, and returned from the sepulchre, and told all these things unto the eleven, and to all the rest. It was Mary Magdalene, and Joanna, and Mary the mother of James, and other women that were with them, which told these things unto the apostles. And their words seemed to them as idle tales, and they believed them not.
>
> —Luke 23:55, 56 and 24:1–11

If you look up this story in Luke in your own New Testament, you will see that it goes on to tell about how Peter goes to the tomb himself to verify that it is empty, and that Jesus appears to two disciples, Cleopas and someone else who is unnamed, while they are on the road to Emmaus. Popular tradition holds that Peter was the other disciple present, and that it was he, not Mary Magdalene, who was the first to see the risen Christ. Thus, the Christian church was founded on the testimony of Peter, and not the "idle tales" of women.

It Is Written

Then he took [unto him] the twelve, and said unto them, Behold, we go up to Jerusalem, and all things that are written by the prophets concerning the Son of man shall be accomplished. For he shall be delivered unto the Gentiles, and shall be mocked, and spitefully entreated, and spitted on: And they shall scourge him, and put him to death: and the third day he shall rise again.

—Luke 18:31–33

John

Because it isn't one of the synoptics, we know right away that the Gospel of John is going to be very different from the others, which, in fact, it is. It was written with a highly evolved theological and literary voice, and it presents a different order of events along with ones that aren't recorded in the other Gospels. Written between 90 and 120 C.E, the authorship of John is unknown. Most scholars agree that it was written by more than one person; there are parts of the Gospel that seem to be the work of a later editor.

Witness of the Crucifixion

John begins his references to Mary Magdalene by placing her at the cross with the other women followers. In John, Mary Magdalene's primary importance is as a witness to the central events of Christianity.

> Now there stood by the cross of Jesus his mother, and his mother's sister, Mary the wife of Cleophas, and Mary Magdalene.

> —John 19:25

Here we have the fourth and final reference to Mary Magdalene as a witness of the crucifixion. We have now seen that as a witness to his death, entombment, and resurrection, Mary Magdalene fulfils an important role: She has seen not only one part or the other, but the entire chain of events. There could have been some question about whether or not Jesus really died, or whether he was really entombed, and most of all, whether or not he really rose from the dead. But with the presence of one person at all three events, the credibility of the story was increased. It wasn't a series of stories spread second- and thirdhand by various people who were in different places at different times, it was all witnessed firsthand by one person: Mary Magdalene.

Witness of the Resurrection

The resurrection account in John is the longest, but it is also the most important scene that Mary Magdalene has in the Gospels, so including the full text is critical.

Rather than commenting at the end of such a long narrative, however, let's break it up into smaller pieces.

> The first day of the week cometh Mary Magdalene early, when it was yet dark, unto the sepulchre, and seeth the stone taken away from the sepulchre. Then she runneth, and cometh to Simon Peter, and to the other disciple, whom Jesus loved, and saith unto them, They have taken away the Lord out of the sepulchre, and we know not where they have laid him. Peter therefore went forth, and that other disciple, and came to the sepulchre. So they ran both together: and the other disciple did outrun Peter, and came first to the sepulchre. And he stooping down, and looking in, saw the linen clothes lying; yet went he not in. Then cometh Simon Peter following him, and went into the sepulchre, and seeth the linen clothes lie, And the napkin, that was about his head, not lying with the linen clothes, but wrapped together in a place by itself. Then went in also that other disciple, which came first to the sepulchre, and he saw, and believed. For as yet they knew not the scripture, that he must rise again from the dead. Then the disciples went away again unto their own home.

—John 20:1–10

In this version of the story, Mary Magdalene goes to the tomb alone, and sees that the stone has been rolled away from the opening. She doesn't wait around to see any angels, she runs straightaway to tell Simon Peter and "the disciple whom Jesus loved," the Beloved Disciple, John. Here is where things get tricky.

Peter and the other disciple ran together to the tomb. The other disciple outran Peter and got to the tomb first, saw the empty grave, and then was joined by Peter. They investigated the tomb and went home.

Illuminations

In the Gospel of Luke, the angel reminds the women that Jesus had said that he would rise from the grave on the third day. In the parallel scene in John, we are told that the disciples didn't yet know that Jesus would be resurrected.

When the story picks up again below, you will see that suddenly, Mary Magdalene is back at the tomb as well. How did she get there? The last time we saw her was back when she ran and told the disciples that the stone had been rolled away. Did she run back with Peter and the other disciple? Did she teleport from one location to the other? The answer is that this is probably an indication of a change made to the text that had been badly matched, leaving some gap in the narrative that is unexplained. Most likely, the section we are about to look at below was added later than the first part. What makes this even more interesting is that it was probably added with the specific purpose of including a detailed resurrection appearance to Mary Magdalene alone.

> But Mary stood without at the sepulchre weeping: and as she wept, she stooped down, and looked into the sepulchre, And seeth two angels in white sitting, the one at the head, and the other at the feet, where the body of Jesus had lain. And they say unto her, Woman, why weepest thou? She saith unto them, Because they have taken away my Lord, and I know not where they have laid him. And when she had thus said, she turned herself back, and saw Jesus standing, and knew not that it was Jesus. Jesus saith unto her, Woman, why weepest thou? whom seekest thou? She, supposing him to be the gardener, saith unto him, Sir, if thou have borne him hence, tell me where thou hast laid him, and I will take him away.
>
> Jesus saith unto her, Mary. She turned herself, and saith unto him, Rabboni; which is to say, Master. Jesus saith unto her, Touch me not; for I am not yet ascended to my Father: but go to my brethren, and say unto them, I ascend unto my Father, and your Father; and to my God, and your God.
>
> Mary Magdalene came and told the disciples that she had seen the Lord, and that he had spoken these things unto her.
>
> —John 20:11–18

Finally, Mary Magdalene has been given a speaking part! The Gospel of John is the only one that actually attributes any words to Mary Magdalene herself.

Lingua Magda

Noli Me Tangere (*no-lee may tahn-gah-ray*) is Latin for "touch me not." This is the name by which this scene has been known for centuries, and there are countless paintings and sculptures depicting that specific moment.

Here we have seen one of the most-often depicted scenes in the Bible, the *Noli Me Tangere*. The reason why Jesus doesn't want her to touch him has been the subject of lively debate since time immemorial, and it is unlikely to be resolved anytime soon. However, in Greek, the verb that is translated as "touch" has many other possible connotations, including "cling." Perhaps Jesus didn't want Mary Magdalene to depend on him as a physical person anymore, because he was now a spiritual presence soon to ascend into heaven.

The *Noli Me Tangere* scene is the one that inspired Hippolytus to compare Mary Magdalene with Eve and the Shulamite woman from *Song of Songs*. Although little is said to give us the impression that she discovered Jesus in a garden outside of the tomb, it is Jesus' description as a gardener that has set imaginations aflame. In many *Noli Me Tangere* paintings, Jesus is dressed as a gardener, sometimes even carrying a shovel or other gardening implement. This scene is closely associated with Easter; from the medieval passion plays to the present day, almost all Easter dramas feature Mary Magdalene discovering Jesus in the garden outside of the tomb.

It's interesting to note that in the sixteenth century, the date of Easter had slipped significantly out of place because of its previous 19-year rotating schedule. So the pope at the time, Gregory XIII, instituted a calendar reform. During his reign, a coin bearing Mary Magdalene's image was minted. It depicts her kneeling before Jesus, who holds a shovel, in a *Noli Me Tangere* scene.

The Least You Need to Know

- The Gospels are divided into two categories: John, and the synoptics, which are Matthew, Mark, and Luke. The synoptics are very similar to one another.

- Mary Magdalene appears in the Gospels as benefactor, demoniac, myrrhbearer, and witness of the crucifixion, entombment, and resurrection.

- Luke is the only Gospel that doesn't have Mary Magdalene seeing the risen Christ before the other disciples.

- John is the only Gospel that has Mary Magdalene encountering Jesus in the garden outside of the tomb, and is the only Gospel to give her any dialogue.

Chapter 7

The Seven Demons

In This Chapter

- ◆ A number in its prime
- ◆ The seven biggest no-no's
- ◆ Some theories on Mary Magdalene's seven demons
- ◆ Demons for all occasions

As we've already seen, the Gospels didn't really have too much to say about Mary Magdalene's seven demons. She had them, she was healed, and they left her. End of story. Still, even those small mentions were enough to ignite imaginations and invite elaboration. What were the demons? Why were there seven? How did they affect her? Where did they go?

To better understand Mary Magdalene's demons, we need to take a look at what the attitude was about such creatures, and what they have been thought to be.

The Number Seven

Of the numbers one through ten, the number that the Greek philosophers and mathematicians thought to be the most beautiful is the number seven.

The number appears with astounding frequency throughout the religious scriptures of the world, including the Bible. Human beings have always been drawn to the number seven, even before the Jewish scriptures that would become the Old Testament were written.

The Epic of Gilgamesh is a work of ancient Mesopotamian mythology, and is the oldest work of literature in the world, dating back to about 2000 B.C.E. In it, the number seven is mentioned as the number of days it took the harlot Shamhat to domesticate the god-man Enkidu. *The Epic of Gilgamesh* also has the oldest written account of a global flood, but in that version, the storm lasts only seven days instead of Noah's forty days and forty nights. In other Mesopotamian myths, the tale of the Sumerian goddess Inanna's descent in the underworld contains references to her seven cities, her seven powers, her seven symbols of queenship, the descent through seven levels of the underworld, the shedding of seven garments, and passage through seven gates.

In Judaism and Christianity, some of the best known stories contain sevens:

♦ God created everything in seven days.

♦ Noah brought "clean" animals onto the ark in sevens, sent a dove out every seven days to check for dry land, and landed on Mt. Ararat in the seventh month.

♦ The dream that Joseph interpreted for the Pharaoh was full of sevens: seven fat cows, seven thin cows, seven good ears of corn, seven withered ears of corn. Joseph revealed that this meant seven years of plenty and seven years of famine.

♦ God commanded the Israelites to observe Passover by not eating leavened bread for seven days.

♦ Joshua circled the city of Jericho every day for seven days, with seven priests blowing seven horns. When they circled the city seven times on the seventh day and then blew the horns again, the walls to the city fell.

♦ Delilah cut off "the seven locks" of Samson's hair, which stole his strength.

♦ In the book of Proverbs, Wisdom's house is built with seven pillars.

♦ Perhaps most significantly, the Sabbath, which itself means "seven," is the seventh day of the week, and is set aside as a day of rest.

Illuminations

The rainbow, symbol of God's promise to Noah that he would never again flood the whole earth, has seven colors: red, orange, yellow, green, blue, indigo, and violet.

All in all, there are more than *400* mentions of the number seven in the Christian Bible.

Since the earliest recorded stories of human history, the number seven has played an important role in almost all of the world's mythology. It is possible that the number became so sacred because it can be observed in a place where the ancients often looked for answers: the stars. Without the benefit of space telescopes, for thousands of years people watched the movement of what they considered to be the seven planets: the sun, Mercury, Venus, the moon, Mars, Jupiter, and Saturn. The movement of the planets was believed to have an effect on the lives of humans; their personalities, how they behaved, and even what their destiny might be.

> **It Is Written**
>
> The number seven, because of its occult virtues, tends to bring all things into being. It is the dispenser of life and the source of all change. For the moon itself changes its phases every seven days. This number influences all sublunar things.
>
> —Hippocrates, fifth century B.C.E. philosopher

The Greek philosophers held the number seven in reverence, and Pythagoras, the father of modern mathematics and philosophy, introduced the seven-note musical scale that is still in use in the West. To Pythagoras and those who followed him, the number seven and the musical scale held mystical properties that linked humans and the divine. The number seven came to be known as the number of perfection, completion, and wholeness.

It isn't known why Mary Magdalene's demons numbered seven and not some other number. It is possible that the number seven was meant to indicate that she was *completely* overcome by whatever her demons represented, but it is equally possible that the number seven was simply inserted into the story of her demonic possession just because it was a popular number. The fact is that we just don't know. This has left an amazing amount of room for interpretation by anyone who has a theory on the subject.

The Seven Deadly Sins

During the Middle Ages, Mary Magdalene's seven demons were often thought to have been the "seven deadly sins," which make a great bridge between our examination of the number seven in the last section and the various interpretations of her demons in the next section.

Knowing what you do now about Pope Gregory the Great, you might find it interesting that he is the source of the seven deadly sins as we have come to know them. Although lists of these cardinal mistakes had circulated previously, it was Gregory the master administrator and organizer who compiled them into an authoritative list. In his commentary *Moralia in Job*, he developed the specific sins that would result in eternal damnation with no hope for heavenly grace.

Although it might seem now that only one or two of the seven sins really seem to fit Mary Magdalene's reputation, to the medieval mind the sins were all linked; the fact that there were seven sins and seven demons brought them into closer association.

Illuminations

Thomas Aquinas, the famous thirteenth-century Christian theologian, wrote about seven virtues that countered the seven vices. The seven virtues he wrote about are faith, hope, charity, prudence, justice, fortitude, and temperance.

The list hasn't always been the same; depending on who was commenting on the sins, or "vices" as they were sometimes known, the specific items sometimes differed. When we compare all of the sins as they have come down to us, though, they all share a common idea: Self-indulgence is bad. Notorious as a sinner, Mary Magdalene was the medieval queen of self-indulgence, and was often cited as an example of what to avoid.

Superbia (Pride)

Previously known as "vainglory," pride is the sense of superiority that leads people to believe they are above the law. An inflated sense of self-importance has long been recognized as the gravest of the deadly sins because it is pride that leads persons to believe they can commit all the others without consequence.

During the Middle Ages, a fairly rigid social structure was in place. It ensured that fields got tilled, seeds got planted, crops got harvested, shoes got cobbled, the land was defended against invasion, and every other necessary role to keep civilization ticking along got fulfilled. Pride led one to believe that he could aspire to greater things than mucking out a horse stall, and at a time when class divisions were viewed as extremely important for maintaining social order, one had to remember his place. Pride was therefore the worst of all sins because it could lead to a breakdown in the status quo.

Biblically speaking, pride is never viewed as a good thing. Perhaps the most famous quotation from the Bible regarding pride is one you've already heard:

> Pride goeth before destruction, and an haughty spirit before a fall.

—Proverbs 16:18

Avaritia (Greed)

Greed also went by various names in the lists of deadly sins, including covetousness and avarice. Although covetousness sounds a lot like "envy," which is another sin on the deadly list, the two are related but different. Covetousness is defined as an inordinate desire for something that leads a person to try, at all costs, to acquire it. Envy, on the other hand, is the dark feeling that you get when you see something that you want but can't have.

By being greedy, a person may gather and hoard the object of his desire to the extent that others may be forced to go without. The greedy person may flaunt his acquisitions in order to get the attention of those around him, or he may be a quiet miser, driven to keep everything to himself and out of public sight.

Not only is a greedy person less likely to be charitable to his neighbor, but he is usually too tied up in an obsessive quest for material possessions and power to devote any time to God. This, of course, is what made greed such a serious offense.

> **Quite Contrary**
>
> We've all heard it: "Money is the root of all evil." But that's only part of the quotation from 1 Timothy 6:10. The whole passage reveals that it isn't money that's the cause of greed: "For the love of money is the root of all evils; it is through this craving that some have wandered away from the faith and pierced their hearts with many pangs."

Luxuria (Luxury)

Luxury is probably an unfamiliar entry on the list for modern readers, so let's discuss it as it has come to be known today: lust. By far, luxury and lust are the sins Mary Magdalene has most been associated with. As a presumed worldly woman, Mary Magdalene would have been too busy indulging the desires of her flesh to lead a life of spiritual piety, and this is precisely the type of behavior tied up in this sin.

Lingua Magda

Hedonism, as it is generally used, is an overwhelming love of and desire for sumptuous comfort and pleasure. Mary Magdalene has often been portrayed as a hedonistic individual, wanton in her craving for carnal delights.

The word "lust" places the focus on sexual craving, but it can also be used to describe the more subtle connotations of "luxury." It is, in addition to the sexuality of the body, the sensuality of living a human existence. It is the act of getting caught up in the *hedonistic* pursuit of things that give pleasure, whether it's sex, soft fabrics, jewels, rich food, or a good cigar.

Luxury and lust call to mind Mary Magdalene in her guise as courtesan, the high-class, "diamonds are a girl's best friend" prostitute. She wasn't selling her body to pay the bills, she was selling her body because she liked it, and because it provided her with the wealth to indulge her senses. In many paintings of the redeemed and penitent Mary Magdalene, she is shown rejecting the symbols of luxury: jewels, fine clothes, and mirrors, which were also symbols of vanity.

Invidia (Envy)

Envy, as already mentioned, is that dark feeling of discontent a person gets when they see that someone else has a thing they can't have. Unlike greed, in which a person wants the object of desire itself, envy leads to a sense of ill will toward the person who possesses that which is desired. Thomas Aquinas, the medieval theologian, said: "Charity rejoices in our neighbor's good, while envy grieves over it."

Illuminations

Jealousy and envy are often associated with the color green. Shakespeare called jealousy "the green-eyed monster," and people are said to be "green with envy."

An envious person may pine away for the thing they want; they may sulk about it, fantasize about possessing it, and even dream about it. But when they actually try to get it, just to have it, then it is greed. The two sins are closely linked in that way.

Spiritually, envy is a problem because it is a twisted kind of love for what other people have. This, in turn, prevents a person from fully loving God and his fellow human beings.

Gula (Gluttony)

Gluttony is usually associated with the concept of overindulgence in food or drink, but it became a sin for the lack of control involved. Like lust, it is a pursuit of comfort and pleasure, in whatever form a person might be inclined. Unlike luxury/ lust, however, it goes beyond the mere pursuit and enjoyment of a thing; it is the enjoyment of something *in excess.*

With regard to food and drink, there are various forms of gluttony that have been condemned, some of them surprising: eating or drinking too much, paying too much for food and drink, being too eager for food and drink, or eating and drinking too delicately. In other words, if you try to extract from something more pleasure than it was meant to give, or you must have something just so, then you are being a glutton. The crux of the issue is giving far more attention to what it is you desire than is necessary or healthful for your body, mind, and spirit.

A person can be a glutton for food and drink, which is the most obvious downfall, but can also be a glutton when it comes to another person's time, or a nonmaterial experience, such as sleeping. Gluttony is a loss of self-control, which has perilous spiritual consequences.

Ira (Anger)

On many deadly sin lists, anger appears as "wrath," and they are, in essence, the same thing: a passionate feeling of hostility, resentment, or displeasure. Anger is an unpleasant emotion often accompanied by an explosive display of aggression, as in fury or rage. In many cases, anger is caused by the perception that one has been or will be wronged by someone else, or when a situation seems confounding.

Everything that leads up to anger could potentially be constructive: identifying a problem or injustice, and even going about a resolution. It is the loss of control and reason that marks anger as sinful, when in the same situation others may respond with patience, humor, and compassion. Like gluttony, anger is a little bit of a healthy thing gone too far.

> **It Is Written**
>
> Let all bitterness, and wrath, and anger, and clamour, and evil speaking, be put away from you, with all malice: and be ye kind one to another, tenderhearted, forgiving one another, even as God for Christ's sake hath forgiven you.
> —Ephesians 4:31, 32

Acedia (Sloth)

Before Pope Gregory the Great's list of deadly sins, sadness (*tristitia*) often appeared instead of sloth. Sadness and sloth intersect at the place where they both represent a weariness that prevents a person from meeting their spiritual obligations. Sloth doesn't mean that a person is necessarily lazy; they might busy themselves with this, that, and the other thing in order to avoid their spiritual responsibilities.

Both sadness and sloth reflect apathy toward things that one should attend to. A person who is slothful is seen as lazy, bored, and self-centered; instead of pulling themselves up by the bootstraps and doing what needs to be done, a slothful person lies about, sighing and making excuses for their negligence. While there are always reasons why a person might be remiss in their spiritual duties, it is the *willful* lack of attention that is represented by the sin.

A Look at Mary Magdalene's Demons

In modern works of scholarship, very little has been written about Mary Magdalene's seven demons because, as we've already seen, the Gospels give us very little to go on. Regardless, there has always been speculation about what her demons may have been.

Real Demons

Perhaps the most obvious place to start is with the belief that Mary Magdalene really was plagued by demonic possession. Since the beginning of recorded history, humans have had some belief in demons as invisible beings that were able to take possession of a human or animal. The concept of demons itself evolved over time, but generally they were thought to be entities that existed somewhere between the gods and humans without corporeal form. When the opportunity arose, a demon might go into a living creature for various purposes, ranging from just a desire to have a physical body to using the person's body to do evil.

Illuminations

During the Middle Ages, goats, cats, and other animals were sometimes killed because they were thought to be possessed by demons.

The Jewish scriptures that make up the Christian Old Testament contain few references to demonic possession. It is in the Gospels that the idea really hits its stride, with Jesus casting out demons left and right. In the next section, we take a look at some of the other demons Jesus encountered.

Whether or not Mary Magdalene was actually plagued by real demons depends a great deal on what you believe about demons. Most Christians today distance themselves from the notion that demons are real entities just waiting in the ether to infect humans for their evil purposes. Some branches of Christianity, however, not only believe it but regularly practice *exorcisms*. The Roman Catholic Church does still employ exorcists, but they have stated that cases of true demonic possession are very rare. Some evangelical branches of Christianity practice exorcisms, either in private or during church services. The demons that people believe can be cast out range from fallen angels with specific names to demons that infect a person with an un-Christian behavior or desire. In one case, at a church I attended once in my youth, a teenage boy underwent an exorcism and was supposedly relieved of "the demon of rock 'n' roll."

Lingua Magda _____

An **exorcism** is a ritual that is performed to remove a demon from a person, place, or thing. Usually an exorcism is performed by a priest, but in some communities any Christian is thought to be capable of casting out demons.

Mental or Physical Illness

Some passages in the Gospels indicate that a demon-possessed person was merely suffering from some illness, which Jesus diagnosed as being caused by a demon. He would then promptly cast out the demon and therefore the illness. Matthew 12:22 says:

> Then a blind and dumb demoniac was brought to him, and he healed him, so that the dumb man spoke and saw.

In this particular case, the man who was possessed was blind and couldn't speak. Although the passage says only that the man was healed, not that Jesus cast out his demon, the passages that follow go on to discuss how the Pharisees heard about it, they wondered how Jesus could cast out demons if he wasn't doing so in the name of the "prince of demons." So we know that this was a case of a man being healed of illness through the removal of his demon. This leads us to wonder whether the other demon-possessed in the Gospels were merely inflicted with various illnesses rather than spewing green pea soup like actress Linda Blair in the movie *The Exorcist.*

Quite Contrary _____

In the Middle Ages, some symptoms of demonic possession were convulsions, foaming at the mouth, protruding tongues, babbling in unknown languages, and the uncontrollable shouting of profanities. Today we know these symptoms could be explained by epilepsy, schizophrenia, and/or Tourette's syndrome.

Demonic possession as an explanation for physical illness is a rather straightforward matter. It is mental illness that is most often cited as the cause for a mistaken diagnosis of demonic possession, because on the outside, it could have looked malevolent and evil to those without medical knowledge. In light of these later realizations about mental illness, it has been suggested that Mary Magdalene suffered from an illness or a set of illnesses that could have been mistaken for demonic possession. Even if she suffered from a physical illness, as we saw from the example of the man who was blind and mute, Mary Magdalene could have had *something* that was explained by the presence of demons as the source of her disease.

Sins

This might seem like an obvious one given Mary Magdalene's reputation. Perhaps, some have suggested, Mary Magdalene's demons were metaphors for the sins in which she was mired in her degenerate lifestyle.

In medieval artwork, Mary Magdalene was sometimes depicted with seven demons fleeing from her body. In the thirteenth century, an illuminated manuscript contained a picture of a woman holding an unguent jar (Mary Magdalene's primary symbol in art) and seven discs that spelled the word "SALIGIA." SALIGIA was an acronym that originated with Pope Gregory's list of seven deadly sins; it is formed from the first letter of each:

> Superbia
>
> Avaritia
>
> Luxuria
>
> Invidia
>
> Gula
>
> Ira
>
> Acedia

The Planets

Perhaps the most recent suggestion about Mary Magdalene's demons is related to a very old notion that there are seven heavens through which one must ascend to return to our original, spiritual home. This idea was present in some Jewish *apocryphal* texts, and appeared again in Gnostic Christianity, in which the process of awakening to humans' true spiritual heritage was imagined as a ladder with seven rungs to represent each of the seven heavens. Each of the seven heavens was overseen by a ruler, or *archon*, and in Gnosticism, one had to know a spiritual secret in order to get past each level and ascend to the next.

The idea wasn't uncommon in the Roman Empire. Some Roman "mystery" religions that were practiced during the first century included seven levels of initiation by which a person gained spiritual knowledge.

Lingua Magda

Something that's **apocryphal** often refers to a writing of questionable origin, but in Christianity, the Apocrypha refers to texts that were included in the Greek version of the Old Testament but not in the Hebrew Bible. The Roman Catholic Bible includes the apocryphal texts but calls them "deuterocanonical," which means "books added to the canon." The Protestant Bible excludes all of the apocryphal texts.

Sometimes the seven planets have been associated with the archons, as the "rulers" of human destiny. The Gnostic mind saw these as forces that conspired to keep humans trapped in a world of matter, to keep them ignorant of their true nature. To break free of the influence of the archons, one had to ascend through each level one by one, until finally reaching a place of transcendence and knowledge: gnosis.

It has been suggested that Mary Magdalene, as someone who was referred to in one Gnostic text as a woman "who understood perfectly," wasn't suffering from demons, but from the planetary and cosmic forces that held everyone captive in the physical world. Jesus, by teaching her spiritual wisdom, helped her transcend the seven heavens, or levels of consciousness, in order to gain what we might now call "enlightenment."

More New Testament Demons

As I mentioned in the preceding section, many demons are mentioned in the Gospels. Let's take a look at some of the demons that Jesus dealt with directly:

◆ The synoptic Gospels (see Chapter 6) tell the story of two men (or one man, as in Mark and Luke) who were possessed by demons. The men had been hiding in tombs and turned back anyone who attempted to pass that way. When Jesus approached, the demons in the men cried out, asking Jesus why he was there.

Then they asked that if Jesus was to cast them out of the men, he allow them to go into a herd of pigs that was nearby. Jesus granted them their request. The demons left the men and went into the pigs, who promptly went crazy and ran off a cliff into the sea. The man who owned the pigs wasn't terribly happy with the solution. (Matthew 8:28–34, Mark 5:1–20; Luke 8:26–39)

♦ In a Galilean town called Capernaum, Jesus and his followers went into a synagogue to observe the Sabbath. A man was there who was possessed by a demon. The demon in the man called out to Jesus, asking why he was there. He went on to say that he knew who Jesus was, and called him the "Holy One of God." Jesus told him to be quiet, and to come out of the man. The demon cried out in a loud voice and left the man. (Mark 1:21–28; Luke 4:31–37)

♦ A Canaanite woman came to Jesus and asked him to cure her daughter, who was possessed by a demon. Jesus answered that God had only sent him to save Israel, not foreigners. The woman showed such great faith in him that he changed his mind and healed her daughter. (Matthew 15:21–28; Mark 7:24–30)

These are only three examples out of several in the Gospels. As you can see, demonic possession was apparently quite a common affliction, and it continued to be seen as so for more than a thousand years. Mary Magdalene was hardly alone in her demon troubles.

The Least You Need to Know

♦ The number seven has been seen as a powerful, mystical number since very early recorded history.

♦ Although Mary Magdalene has been associated with the seven deadly sins as a group, it is *luxuria* or lust that she has most often been accused of.

♦ Several possible explanations have been offered to explain Mary Magdalene's demons, including illness, spiritual transcendence, and possession by real demons.

♦ The Gospels contain many stories of Jesus casting demons out of people, and often the demons are used as explanations for physical illnesses.

Chapter 8

The Crucifixion

In This Chapter

- Early images of crucifixion
- Skulls, suffering, and death
- Who was present at the crucifixion
- The end of the story?

If you approach just about anyone on the street and show them a picture of Jesus on the cross, and then ask them what religion it's associated with, they will answer correctly: Christianity. The scene is so much a part of our culture that you don't need to be a Christian to understand what's going on in the picture. There's Jesus, dying on the cross. There are the two thieves on crosses next to him. And almost inevitably, there are the women standing nearby, weeping and mourning for their lost teacher.

Jesus did many things during his ministry. He taught people that the kingdom of God was already here. He preached in synagogues that scripture had been fulfilled by his coming. He healed the sick and the demon-possessed, and sometimes raised the dead. But honestly, would we expect anything less from the Son of God? It is the two-part culmination of his life here on earth that really sets him apart: the crucifixion and the resurrection. These two things, more than any others, were the foundational events on which Christianity was based. In this chapter, we look more closely at the crucifixion and Mary Magdalene's role in it, and in Chapter 9 we look at the resurrection.

Christianity Starts Here

Early Christians weren't particularly fond of the crucifixion or the cross as a symbol of hope. It's understandable when you think about it. The man they worshipped as the Son of God was put to death in one of the most gruesome manners possible, and many may have even lost friends or relatives to such an execution. It therefore wasn't the victorious image that it has come to be for some Christians today, and early believers avoided it for centuries. Rather, they adopted some common symbols to their new Christian meaning. "The Good Shepherd" was a popular pre-Christian theme that was cast in a new light. The catacombs beneath Rome where many Christians were buried contain several Good Shepherd paintings as well as other optimistic scenes, including the Virgin and child, and the raising of Lazarus. There are also images of the older story of Jonah and the whale, which represents the resurrection.

One of the earliest depictions of the crucifixion dates back as far as the fifth century C.E., in a panel on the door of the Santa Sabina basilica in Rome. It features an open-eyed crucified Jesus who is so large that you can't really see the cross behind him. The two thieves are on crosses on either side of him. This image shows how early artists minimized the traumatic effect of seeing their savior on the cross; he was alive, awake, whole, and didn't really look like he was in pain.

Illuminations

Before the eighth century, Jesus was depicted with his eyes open on the cross. Technically, this is known as *christus triumphans*, "triumphant Christ." After the eighth century, crucifixion images changed to depict Jesus with his eyes closed, which came to be known as *christus patiens*, "dead Christ."

We know that the earliest Christians did remember the crucifixion, because Paul and others wrote about it. Even though it may not have been an image used to gain converts, everyone knew that Jesus' sacrifice was an integral part of the story leading up to the glory of the resurrection.

The Scene on Golgotha

Undoubtedly, you're familiar with the scenario. Three crosses stand atop a hill on a dark day. Mourners wail and passersby point and jeer. Centurions stand at various posts, controlling the crowd, monitoring those who are being executed, and gambling at the foot of Jesus' cross. Three men hang in agony, waiting to die, and Jesus, beneath a placard, with a crown of thorns on his head, still manages to look compassionate in his suffering. Through centuries of art, from paintings to movies, this is the image that has come to represent the crucifixion.

"The Place of the Skull"

It is unknown, exactly, why Golgotha has come be known as a hill or mountain; the Gospels never say anything to give that impression. Nonetheless, the belief that it was on a slope of some kind stretches back to the early centuries of Christianity. After the Gospel accounts, nothing more is said of the place where Jesus was crucified until the fourth century, when the place was called *monticulus*, or "little mount." The only thing we really know about the location is from the New Testament book of Hebrews, which says that it was a place outside of the city. Still, pictures of three crosses standing on a hill are common.

A few different words have been used to describe the location where the crucifixion took place:

- Golgotha—*Aramaic*
- Calvary—Latin (from *calvaria*)
- Kranion—Greek

Lingua Magda

The language that was spoken by Jews in first-century Palestine was **Aramaic**. This is the language that Mary Magdalene would have spoken.

All of these words mean pretty much the same thing: "the place of the skull." The Gospels don't clue us in on why skull imagery was connected to the location, but there are four running theories:

- It was a place of frequent executions, and there were bones and skulls littering the site.
- It was near a cemetery.
- It was a hill that physically resembled a skull.
- It was the legendary location of Adam's remains.

The last notion is probably surprising to most people. It isn't commonly known that there was a legend that the remains of Adam (of Garden of Eden fame) had been passed from person to person until finally being buried at Golgotha. This was

It Is Written

And that same place is the centre of the earth, and the grave of Adam, and the altar of Melchisedek, and Golgotha ...

—*The Book of the Cave of Treasures*, a sixth-century Christian text

suggested very early on in Christianity, and was to later have an effect on the way the crucifixion was depicted. If you look closely at many paintings of the crucifixion, you will see at the foot of the cross a skull and bones. This is the legendary grave of Adam.

Theologically, Adam's grave became valuable as a symbol of redemption. Adam, the first man, along with Eve, the original sinner, represented the fallen condition of humankind. Jesus, through his sacrifice and bloodshed, rescued everyone from Adam's deathly error. In the Middle Ages, the imagery behind this concept was sometimes gruesome; Jesus' blood flowed down the cross, into Adam's grave, symbolically restoring him to life. In some paintings, instead of a skull and bones at the foot of the cross, you see a tiny man rising from a tiny sarcophagus, very much like the later depictions of Jesus' own resurrection.

The Passion

The Passion refers to the events in Jesus' final days culminating with the crucifixion. But it also refers to Jesus' own suffering; the idea is that if it weren't for Jesus' passion for humankind, he wouldn't have submitted himself to such pain. In other words, he must have loved everyone a *lot*.

The term "passion" probably originates with a passage in the book of Acts, 1:3: "To them he presented himself alive after his passion by many proofs, appearing to them during forty days, and speaking of the kingdom of God."

The word was retained in many of the earliest versions of the New Testament, and was also in use in other texts as early as the third century. There are examples of martyrs who identified their own suffering with the suffering of Jesus, and several commentaries were written about the Passion, but it wasn't until the Middle Ages that it became a subject of popular devotion and contemplation.

The Crusades were military campaigns undertaken by Christians beginning in the eleventh century C.E. to recover "the Holy Land" from the growing forces of Islam. It was a political movement driven by religious rhetoric, and it was the faithful, promised a guaranteed ticket into heaven, who went as soldiers to wage holy war. As a side effect of the intense preaching during this time to convince Christians to take up arms and make the long journey, the notion of the Passion was raised in popular awareness, and it became more and more common as a devotional subject. By the thirteenth century, it was prevalent, and art of the time showed the new focus on Jesus' suffering on the cross.

> **Quite Contrary** _____
>
> One of the saints often recognized for her role in the Passion is St. Veronica, who was said to have wiped Jesus' face with a cloth as he carried his cross to Golgotha. Upon inspecting the cloth, she found a perfect image of his face. There is no mention of Veronica in the Gospels. Her name comes from the Latin words *vera icon*, which mean "true image," which were gradually adopted into common language as "veronica" and then attributed to a person as a name.

Typically, the Passion includes the following events from the Gospels:

- Judas' betrayal of Jesus to the authorities

- The preparation for the Passover feast

- The last supper

- Jesus' prayers in the Garden of Gethsemane

- Jesus' arrest and trial

- Peter's denials of Jesus

- Jesus' appearance before Pilate

- Pilate's attempts to find a way to free Jesus

- The freeing of Barabbas

- Jesus' scourging

- The crucifixion

In the seventeenth century, pictures of the Stations of the Cross became common. The Stations are images of specific events that occurred during the Passion, and are usually hung in a certain order in a church. The faithful can then move from Station to Station, praying and meditating on each individual incident.

For centuries, Christians have found inspiration in meditating on the sufferings of Jesus, some even displaying physical manifestations of his wounds called *stigmata*.

Mary Magdalene's only real contribution to the Gospel account of the Passion is as a witness to the crucifixion, although, as we've already seen, she took on an increasingly important role in the medieval Passion plays as she grew in popularity.

About Crucifixion

In Jesus' case, crucifixion was a Roman method of execution, not a Jewish one. The Romans weren't the first to come up with such a torturous way to put someone to death; there are records of the Persians and the Greeks in particular using this form of capital punishment. The Romans probably learned about crucifixion from the Greeks, and they put it to great use. Although Roman citizens were exempt from crucifixion, that still left it as an option for all the noncitizens in the empire, especially military enemies (especially rebels and insurrectionists), thieves, foreigners, and slaves.

Typically, persons sentenced to crucifixion were first scourged, or whipped, which was thought to hasten death later. Afterward, they were made to carry the crossbeam, not the entire cross, to the execution site. Their hands were then tied or nailed to the crossbeam, and they were hoisted onto the upright portion of the cross that already stood in the ground. Then their feet were tied or nailed as well; the block beneath the feet was a later innovation.

It Is Written

[Crucifixion is] the most miserable and most painful punishment appropriate to slaves alone.

—Cicero, *Against Verres* 5:169 (first century B.C.E.)

Because breathing in such a position is so difficult, the cause of death in crucifixion was usually asphyxiation, though heart failure, exposure, blood loss, and shock have also been mentioned as possibilities. Occasionally, a victim's legs would be broken to help the process along; without the ability to push up with his feet, the person being crucified wouldn't be able to draw a proper breath. This is what happened to the two thieves who were crucified next to Jesus. Jesus was spared such a "mercy" because by the time the bone-breakers got to him, he was already dead.

All of this is terribly depressing to think about, and it is with gladness that Christians saw Emperor Constantine, who legalized Christianity in the Roman Empire, abolish it as a method of punishment. It is with these agonizing details in mind that Christians have considered Mary Magdalene's faithfulness during the crucifixion. Certainly anyone who was willing not only to witness a loved one experiencing such a death, but to also risk it herself as a follower of the condemned, must have been as devoted as it is humanly possible to be.

Who Exactly Was There?

Like so many other things, the Gospels don't entirely agree on who was present during the crucifixion, so we'll just gather the names together here in one place. Let's take a look now at who stuck around for the final act.

The Two Thieves

Granted, the two thieves who were on the crosses next to Jesus weren't there by choice, but they were there nonetheless. The synoptic Gospels agree that the two men were criminals; one names them as thieves. It is likely that they were political rebels of some kind, but the Gospels aren't specific. In Matthew, we're told that everyone who passed by mocked Jesus, telling him that if he was the Son of God he should save himself and come down from the cross. The thieves—ridiculously, given their questionable position—joined in the jeering.

The Gospel of Luke, however, tells a different story. One of the thieves mocked Jesus, daring him, if he was the true Messiah, to save himself and them, too, while he was at it. The second thief showed some good sense and asked his fellow, "Don't you have any fear of God, considering that you're suffering the same fate?" The second thief then pointed out that he and the first thief were getting what they deserved (being criminals and all), but Jesus had done nothing to warrant such a punishment.

> **Illuminations**
>
> In the late fourth or early fifth century, there arose a legend that Emperor Constantine's mother, Helena, discovered "the true cross" in Jerusalem. With it were the two crosses on which the thieves had been crucified.

And here is where it gets really interesting. The "good" thief then went on to recognize Jesus as the savior, and asked that Jesus remember him in his kingdom. Jesus answered that before the day was through, the thief would join him in paradise.

In early Christianity, there was a great desire to know more about the life of Jesus, and several "infancy gospels" were written to meet this need. These texts were written to embellish the early life of Jesus and his mother, but none of them were included in the compilation of texts that became the Christian Bible. In one such infancy text, Joseph, Mary, and the baby Jesus were traveling through a desert they knew to be inhabited by thieves, so they tried to slip through unnoticed at night. Two thieves, named Titus and Dumachus, stopped them. Titus, who recognized the holiness of the family, urged his cohort not to do them any harm, going so far as to offer him money to leave them alone. Mary thanked Titus for his kindness and told him that God would protect and forgive him. Then, the baby Jesus spoke and told his mother that in 30 years, he would be crucified next to the two thieves, and that Titus would enter paradise before him. Mary, apparently unfazed by her talking infant, asked that Jesus be preserved from such a fate.

The Centurions

The Gospels say that there were members of the Roman military present at the crucifixion, which seems reasonable considering it was the Romans who were carrying out the sentence. There are a few specific mentions of soldiers who were on the scene:

♦ Soldiers gambled at the foot of the cross for Jesus' seamless robe.

♦ A soldier held up a sponge filled with vinegar and *gall* to Jesus' lips, presumably to ease his suffering.

♦ Soldiers broke the legs of the crucified thieves.

♦ A soldier pierced Jesus' side to see whether he was really dead.

♦ A soldier, seeing the events that surrounded Jesus' death, exclaimed that he must have been the Son of God.

> **Lingua Magda**
>
> In this context, **gall** was probably a bitter herb that was mixed with wine vinegar and offered to Jesus to ease his pain.

The Gospels never mention any of the guards by name, but two of them came to be known as Stephaton and Longinus. Stephaton was the soldier who held the sponge of vinegar up for Jesus to drink, and very little has been said of him. His name first appeared in the tenth century in a text called *Codex Egberti*.

The soldier who thrust the spear into Jesus' side first appeared with the name Longinus around the fourth century, in a text called *The Acts of Pilate*. Later, an entire post-crucifixion story was invented for him. Apparently, Longinus suffered from an eye disorder that was miraculously cured after he thrust the spear in Jesus' side and some blood splashed in his eyes. He then cried out, "Truly, this was the Son of God!" Afterward, he became a Christian, following the apostles and eventually becoming a monk. Unfortunately, he was persecuted because of his faith, and was tortured by having his teeth and tongue removed. Even so, he continued to be able to speak clearly, and set about smashing all of the idols in the room, whereupon evil spirits flew out of them. The evil spirits attacked the governor, who was present for Longinus's torture, and caused him to go blind. Eventually, the governor ordered Longinus to be beheaded, and when he was thus executed, blood that splashed onto the governor's eyes restored his sight.

Illuminations

In some of the earliest crucifixion images, instead of the Virgin Mary and John standing beneath the cross, we see Longinus with his spear and Stephaton with his sponge-on-a-stick.

Joseph of Arimathea

Joseph of Arimathea was the man who convinced Pilate to release Jesus' body into his possession and then laid him in a tomb. We don't know much about Joseph; we can assume he was a man of some influence because he was able to get a request to Pilate for Jesus' body, and his request was granted. The Gospel of Luke refers to Joseph as a member of the Jewish high council who disagreed with the decisions and deeds of the other council members; this has led some to speculate that he was a member of the political party that lobbied for Jesus' execution.

There are a great many medieval legends about Joseph of Arimathea. Some say that he accompanied Mary Magdalene, Martha, and some other people on a boat from Jerusalem that landed on the shores of Southern France. Still others say that he traveled to Britain with the Holy Grail, alternately thought to be the cup that caught Jesus' blood at the crucifixion and the cup Jesus used at the last supper. Among other things, Joseph was said to have …

- ◆ Brought a vial of Jesus' blood to Britain.
- ◆ Brought Longinus' spear to Britain.
- ◆ Founded Glastonbury Abbey.
- ◆ Struck his staff in the ground at Glastonbury, which flowered and grew into a thorn, the descendant of which is still thought to grow today.
- ◆ Been Jesus' uncle.

Illuminations

The modern address for Glastonbury Abbey is on Magdalene Street.

Clearly, Joseph of Arimathea was a fascinating figure in the Middle Ages, as the wide variety of legends indicate. We revisit his importance in grail stories in Chapters 20 and 21.

The Beloved Disciple

The Gospel of John is the only one that mentions a mysterious, anonymous disciple who is referred to only as the one who Jesus loved. Since the second century C.E., John has been supposed to be the author of the Gospel as well as the Beloved Disciple himself. There have been, however, arguments with that theory, and most recently it has been suggested that Mary Magdalene herself was the Beloved Disciple. This theory suggests that the text was written to conceal the fact by not naming her, and by changing pronouns from "her" to "him."

Regardless who the Beloved Disciple was, "he" is mentioned as being one of the witnesses of the crucifixion, and the one who was entrusted with the care of Jesus' mother. In no other Gospel account does Jesus speak from the cross directly to a person. Later traditions say that after Jesus ascended into heaven, John, the Beloved Disciple, took Jesus' mother to Ephesus. It was in Ephesus, then, that both John and the Virgin Mary were said to have been buried.

The Women

The women who were present at the crucifixion, of course, have already been discussed in Chapter 6 when we looked at the New Testament passages about Mary Magdalene. In two cases, Mary Magdalene was named first in the list of women at the cross. To recap, the following women were there:

- Mary Magdalene
- Jesus' mother
- Mary, the mother of James and Joses
- The mother of Zebedee's children
- Salome
- Jesus' aunt (his mother's sister)
- Mary, the wife of Cleophas
- "Many other women"

> **Quite Contrary**
>
> Mary Magdalene's name doesn't appear first in *every* list of Jesus' women followers in the Gospels, but it's pretty close. Of the eight lists that mention her name, seven of them mention her first.

Matthew, Mark, and Luke say that the women watched from "afar off," but John says that they stood by the cross. Early pictures of the crucifixion place the Virgin Mary and John immediately beneath Jesus as he hangs on the cross. When the other women were depicted at all, it was as a group standing and watching from a distance.

The Crucifixion. *Relief in bronze by Antonio Pollaiuolo (1432–1498).*

(EclectiCollections)

In the late Middle Ages and Renaissance, the women became more central figures in crucifixion scenes, with Mary Magdalene often at the foot of the cross. In the illustration, there are two women at the foot of the cross, both in typical poses for Mary Magdalene. The one who is grasping the cross, dressed in finer clothing and has longer hair, however, displays more common Mary Magdalene symbolism, so it is probably that figure who is intended to be her. In Chapter 22, we go over some of the best ways to identify Mary Magdalene in art.

The Entombment

So now we know all about crucifixion and who was there, but what happens next in the story? Compared to the drama of the crucifixion and the resurrection, very little attention is paid to the activities that took place in between. Because that space of time was often depicted in medieval art, let's devote some space to taking a look at what happened.

The Final Moments

Just before Jesus died, the sun went dark, and he uttered some last words:

> My God, my God, why hast thou forsaken me? (Matthew 27:46, Mark 15:34)

> Father, into your hands I commend my spirit. (Luke 23:46)

> It is finished. (John 19:30)

Illuminations

The sanctuary of the temple in Jerusalem contained the Holy Place, where only priests were allowed, and the Holy of Holies, where only the high priest was allowed to go once a year. A curtain, or veil, separated the two spaces.

After speaking his last words, whatever they were, some pretty amazing things happened. There was an earthquake that shook open graves, and dead people were resurrected, appearing to many throughout the city. The veil in the temple was split in half, presumably revealing the most sacred space, the Holy of Holies, where God was thought to reside.

It was the end of the day before the Sabbath, and because Jewish law prohibited the bodies to remain on the crosses overnight, the centurions went and broke the thieves' legs so they would die faster. When they got to Jesus, he was already dead. Just to make sure, the centurion later named Longinus thrust a spear into his side, whereupon blood and water flowed from the wound.

Joseph of Arimathea then came on the scene, and begged Pilate for Jesus' body. Pilate granted his wish, and Jesus' body was taken down from the cross and put into Joseph's custody. He saw that the body was wrapped in fine linen and placed in his own empty tomb. Nicodemus came with a hundred pounds of aloe and myrrh, which were wrapped up with the linen around Jesus' body. The spices wouldn't have been for embalming; in Judaism, bodies must return to the earth, and anything inhibiting the decomposition process is avoided. Rather, the spices were used to offset the scent of death that would have been a quite a problem in such a warm climate.

Mary Magdalene and the other women were present when the stone was rolled in front of the opening to the tomb. The scene was now set for the next great event.

First-Century Burial Practices

Jesus was buried in accordance with Jewish custom of the time. Before sunset, he was removed from the cross. Although the Gospels don't mention it, he probably would have been washed in observance of the ritual cleansing of the dead called *taharah*, which means "purification." Someone would also close the eyes of the deceased person, and a chin band would be wrapped around his head to prevent his mouth from opening.

Before being laid in the tomb, Jesus was wrapped in clean linen that contained the hundred pounds of spices brought by Nicodemus. Another cloth, usually referred to as a "napkin," would have been placed on his face.

After being duly washed and wrapped, Jesus' body was laid on a stone platform inside a tomb that was hewn out of rock. During the first century, it was customary to leave a body in such a place for about a year, after which time the family of the deceased would return and place the bones in a stone box called an *ossuary*. But according to Christians everywhere, because of the resurrection, Jesus' family was to never have a need for performing such a reburial.

The Least You Need to Know

- Early Christian art didn't focus on the crucifixion as much as it did later in the Middle Ages.

- Mary Magdalene's role in the Passion is as a witness of the crucifixion.

- Mary Magdalene was only one of many people who witnessed the crucifixion.

- Mary Magdalene was present at Jesus' entombment, which took place according to the Jewish customs of the time.

Chapter **9**

The Resurrection

In This Chapter

- ◆ An earthquake, angels, and an empty tomb
- ◆ *Noli Me Tangere:* Touch me not
- ◆ Disbelief among the disciples
- ◆ A psychological evaluation

The resurrection is the second half of the two-part climax to Jesus' appearance here on Earth. The preceding chapter revolved around the subject of death; here we shift gears and focus instead on life after death, and how Jesus' resurrection, as the central event of Christianity, was witnessed first by one woman: Mary Magdalene. Although she wasn't alone in some instances, it is Mary Magdalene who is most remembered as the woman who discovered the risen Jesus.

It is as a witness of the resurrection, of course, that Mary Magdalene enters the Christian story in a really big way. Contrary to her invented reputation as the harlot who anointed Jesus' feet, the resurrection narrative is the very source of her biblically *legitimate* fame.

What Did Magdalene See?

Of the four Gospels, only three of them say that Mary Magdalene was either *the* first person or one of the first to see the resurrected Jesus. Because we've already taken a detailed look at the accounts in the Gospels, let's instead focus on the major elements of the narrative that she would have encountered that morning.

The Earthquake

Jerusalem, the location of the crucifixion and resurrection, is about 25 miles from a major fault line called the Jordan Valley Fault. The Jordan Valley Fault is known to have high-magnitude earthquakes every 1,000 years or so, with the last event being in 1033. It isn't known how big the earthquakes were that occurred during the crucifixion and resurrection (they didn't have Richter scales back then, after all), but it wouldn't have been unusual for one to have occurred. If a large earthquake occurred during the crucifixion, it's entirely possible that an aftershock could have occurred up to a week later. That's the scientific explanation.

By way of a spiritual explanation, the Gospel of Matthew attributes the earthquake to the descent of an angel of God to tell the women about the resurrection. It happened on the morning that Mary Magdalene and the other women went to anoint Jesus' body in the tomb, and is described as a "great" earthquake.

Anyone who has been in an earthquake can testify that it is a disconcerting experience. It feels rather like being on a ship at sea even though you're standing on dry land; even in a small earthquake this is enough to cause imbalance, confusion, dizziness, and anxiety.

It Is Written

And Joseph took the body, and wrapped it in a clean linen shroud, and laid it in his own new tomb, which he had hewn in the rock; and he rolled a great stone to the door of the tomb, and departed.

—Matthew 27:59, 60

The Rolled-Away Stone

Although we don't know how big the round stone was that was placed in front of the opening to the tomb, we know that it was big enough for Mary Magdalene and the other women to worry about who might be there to move it for them. Estimates are often in the 1,000+ pound range, so we can safely assume that it would have been a job for at least one strong man using a pole for leverage.

Whether or not an angel moved aside the stone, for the women to see such a large object in a place where it shouldn't be, they would immediately know, as Mary Magdalene did in John, that something unusual was afoot. They probably would have suspected that such a thing couldn't have been done in secret, and because guards were posted outside the tomb, it would have been done with their knowledge and approval. Understandably, this could have made the women extremely nervous.

The Angels

Throughout the Bible, angels serve as messengers of God. They come to earth with a message, deliver it, and then usually go on their way. In the resurrection scenes, angels come to announce that Jesus had risen.

In Matthew, an angel descends amid an earthquake and rolls the stone away from the opening of the tomb. Not only that, but the guards who were posted at the tomb were so terrified that they fainted. The women, however, somehow managed to keep their composure long enough for the angel to tell them to not be afraid.

CAUTION Quite Contrary

Far from being the cute little winged babies that we've all seen in pictures, angels, we can assume, are actually fearsome creatures. Passages in the Bible that include angels are often accompanied by instructions to have no fear, which leads us to believe that there *must* be some reason to say that. (Of course, this could be because of their appearance or simply because they are otherworldly, but fear is almost always mentioned as a side effect of an angelic appearance.)

In Mark, an angel was already at the tomb when the women arrived. He is described as a young man in a shining white garment who sits inside the tomb. Again the women were afraid, and again he reassures them.

Luke's angels are a little different. The women go to the tomb and find the stone rolled away. But this time, *two* angels appear in shiny clothes. The women are so afraid that they bow down in front of the angels, but there are no kind words to calm them. The angels get right down to the business of announcing the resurrection.

John, being a very different Gospel, has a very different perspective on what occurred with the angels. After Mary saw that the stone had been rolled away, she didn't waste any time in going to tell the disciples. Peter and the other disciple ran to the tomb, checked it out, and left. Mary stayed, and went back inside the tomb where she found two angels dressed in white. This time, they were sitting on the platform where Jesus had been laid, one at the head and one at the foot. They asked her, "Woman, why are you weeping?" She answered, "Because they have taken away my Lord, and I don't know where they put him."

Presumably, she thought that his body has been stolen, not resurrected. She said "they," but didn't indicate whom she was referring to. The guards? The gardeners? We pick up the scene at this point in the next section of this chapter, "*Noli Me Tangere.*"

The Empty Tomb

Imagine this: Your loved one has recently died, and you go to the tomb to see him or her one last time. But when you get there, everything is in a state of disarray. As you enter the tomb and your eyes gradually adjust to the darkness, you notice that it's empty.

> **Illuminations**
>
> Tombs like the one Jesus would have been put into were often carved out of a rock face, and were often very low with small openings. Far from being a giant room with a full-size doorway, people who went into Jesus' tomb probably would have had to crawl inside, or at least crouch low. Luke 24:12 says that when Peter went to examine the tomb, he "stooped down" to see inside.

First thought? Grave robbers! I don't know about you, but the very act of walking into a place of the dead and seeing no dead body would be enough to give me a serious case of the heebie-jeebies. Imagining that someone had absconded with the body of my loved one would be enough to make me faint.

After thinking of grave robbers, if my loved one had predicted that he would rise from the dead, I would still be very upset. After all, human beings are conditioned to believe there's no coming back after you make your "final exit." If I was in a dark tomb looking for someone I knew to be dead, well, I'm sure the hairs on the back of my neck would be standing at full attention.

Graves are inherently creepy places, and even though people today have much less contact with their dead than would have been the case in the first century, it's still likely that the sight of an empty tomb would have been shocking, to say the least. Mary Magdalene must have felt all of these emotions and probably more in the moments of confusion leading up to the angels announcing the resurrection.

After going through the ordeal that we covered in the last chapter, Mary Magdalene must have been at least a *little* relieved that it was all over. But then an earthquake, angels, and an empty tomb. How much could one woman bear?

Noli Me Tangere

Mary Magdalene would eventually be repaid for her fortitude under such trying circumstances. Although Matthew, Mark, and John all remember her as the first witness of the resurrection, it is the Gospel of John that gives her the prominence due such an honor.

Magdalene's Time to Shine

Here we pick up the resurrection narrative in John where we left off in the last section.

After having the conversation with the angels in the tomb, Mary turned back toward the garden. She saw a man there, but she didn't know it was Jesus. Like the angel, he asked her why she was crying, and then asked who she was looking for. Mary thought he was the gardener, so she said, "Sir, if you've taken him, tell me where you've laid him and I will take him away."

Before we rush into the next, most famous portion of this scene, let's stop for a moment. Mary Magdalene says *she* will take Jesus' body away. She doesn't say, "I'll go get the disciples and *we'll* take his body away." She's ready to go pick up Jesus' body herself and carry it back to the tomb or to some other location. She is ready to take Jesus' corpse into her own possession. Now *that's* devotion.

After Mary said this, Jesus responded by speaking her name. She instantly recognized him for who he was and exclaimed, *"Rabboni!"* Jesus then told her not to touch him, words that are recorded in older Latin texts as *Noli Me Tangere:* "Touch me not."

Artistic depictions of this scene are imagined very dramatically: Mary falls to her knees before the triumphant Jesus and reaches for him, prompting his instruction to not touch him. The Gospel of John doesn't actually say that Mary fell to her knees or that she reached for him; this is just assumed because Jesus was obviously concerned about it.

Lingua Magda

Rabboni is an honorific title that means "my teacher" or "my master."

Stop, in the Name of Love

In addition to her presence in images of the crucifixion, the *Noli Me Tangere* is the scene in which Mary Magdalene most often appears. If you are interested in art, you can always recognize a *Noli Me Tangere* painting or sculpture because it will feature Jesus, sometimes dressed like a laborer and holding some sort of gardening implement, holding up his hand as if gesturing "stop," toward a kneeling woman who is reaching for him.

> **It Is Written**
>
> The watchmen found me, as they went about in the city. 'Have you seen him whom my soul loves?' Scarcely had I passed them, when I found him whom my soul loves ....
>
> —*Song of Songs*, 3:3, 4

That, perhaps more than anything else that has been written or painted during the last two thousand years, is the very essence of Mary Magdalene. Passionate, unrestrained, uninhibited, always searching and reaching for Jesus. In this, Hippolytus was very astute in comparing her to the Shulamite woman in *Song of Songs*.

The Skeptical Disciples

Before riding too high on the knowledge that Mary Magdalene received a lot of recognition in the New Testament, remember that the disciples didn't even believe her when she announced the resurrection to them.

In Mark, Jesus appeared to Mary Magdalene at some unknown place. She went and found the disciples, who were mourning and weeping for Jesus' death. She announced the resurrection as she had been instructed, but they didn't believe her. The text doesn't lead us to believe that it is something personal. Some have suggested that she wasn't believed simply because she was a woman, but that doesn't seem to be the case here. Jesus appeared to a second set of disciples who also went to tell the rest about the resurrection, but *they* weren't believed either. It wasn't until Jesus appeared among all of them at once that they realized what Mary Magdalene had said was true.

The Gospel of Luke, however, does leave questions about why the women weren't believed. They spoke with the angels at the tomb about the resurrection, then ran to tell the others. But this time they were dismissed by the disciples, who characterized the women's testimony as "idle tales." Peter jumped up and ran to check it out for himself, saw the empty tomb, and then wondered to himself about what really happened. There is no happy ending for Mary Magdalene in the Gospel of Luke; she and the other women are never acknowledged as the first witnesses of the resurrection.

> ![CAUTION] **Quite Contrary**
>
>   Some modern writers have suggested that the disciples didn't believe Mary Magdalene because Jewish law prohibited women from being legal witnesses. This isn't quite true; women *were* allowed to be witnesses in certain types of legal cases, including testifying about a man's death so that his wife could receive the amount specified in her *ketubah*. On the types of cases which women were allowed to act as witnesses, their testimony carried as much weight as a man's.

A similar scene occurs in the Gospel of John, of course, with Peter and the Beloved Disciple running to the tomb to see for themselves. Except in John, that isn't the end of the story for Mary Magdalene. She goes on to meet Jesus in the garden.

"A Half-Frantic Woman"

Celsus was a second-century *pagan* writer whose work comes to us mainly through the Christian theologian Origen, who quoted Celsus extensively in his book *Against Celsus*. According to Origen, this is what Celsus had to say about Jesus and the notion of the resurrection:

> ... while alive he was of no assistance to himself, but that when dead he rose again, and showed the marks of his punishment, and how his hands were pierced with nails: who beheld this? A half-frantic woman, as you state, and some other one, perhaps, of those who were engaged in the same system of delusion ....

> **Lingua Magda**
>
>   Pagans were those who followed the Roman religion; those who sacrificed to the Roman gods and belonged to mystery cults. It was later applied more widely to refer to non-Christians in other areas of the world who followed their local religions.

Let's take a closer look at what has been said of the resurrection, and therefore at what the earliest opponents of Christianity believed about the quality of Mary Magdalene's testimony.

Pagans and the Resurrection

Christianity started in the hotbed of religious thought that was the Roman Empire. There were a great many cults—groups of people or a community that honored a particular deity or saint with religious observances—available for the choosing, and pagans often selected several as it suited them. Because Paul was a very effective Christian evangelist and missionary, the young religion spread from among Jews to among non-Jews throughout the empire, as far and wide as Paul himself, or his letters, could travel.

Strangely enough, the notion of a resurrected Son of God wasn't terribly unique among pagans. They had long been accustomed to stories of Dionysus, Attis, Adonis, and Osiris, all pagan gods believed to have died and been resurrected afterward. The resurrection itself wasn't offensive to pagans; there were plenty of other things about Christianity that annoyed them. One of the largest areas of disagreement was the Christians' bold refusal to make sacrifices to the gods, and oddly enough, another common claim was that Christians were atheists. During the Roman period, atheism wasn't defined in the same way we define it now. Today an atheist is someone who doesn't believe in god at all. Then, an atheist was someone who didn't believe in the providence of the gods, or who rejected all of the Roman gods, as was the case with Jews and Christians.

Unfortunately for our study of Mary Magdalene, very little anti-Christian material exists from the earliest centuries C.E. After Constantine legalized Christianity, and it later became the state religion, material that was contrary to Christian beliefs was burned. This prevents us from knowing, other than Celsus's harsh indictment, exactly what pagans thought of her.

Mental Magdalene

Among those who disbelieve the resurrection account, there are several "naturalistic" suggestions to account for what really happened. Four of them stand out:

- **Hallucination.** Witnesses of the resurrected Jesus imagined that they saw him.

- **Conspiracy.** The disciples stole the body and told everyone that Jesus rose from the dead.

- **Swoon.** Jesus didn't really die; he just passed out or went into a coma.

- **Myth.** The resurrection was a later innovation by Christians.

It is beyond the scope of this book to detail each one of these ideas and provide arguments for and against. What concerns us here is how Mary Magdalene figures into these scenarios.

Obviously, with his characterization of Mary Magdalene as a "half-frantic woman," Celsus seems to have been the father of the hallucination theory. This idea came back into view during the nineteenth century, when all of the naturalistic explanations for the resurrection came into vogue. A scholar named Ernest Renan suggested that a delirious Mary Magdalene, who had been possessed by seven demons and was therefore not the most reliable eyewitness anyway, had only imagined the risen Jesus.

It Is Written

Had his body been taken away, or did enthusiasm, always credulous, create afterwards the group of narratives by which it was sought to establish faith in the resurrection? In the absence of opposing documents, this can never be ascertained. Let us say, however, that the strong imagination of Mary Magdalene played an important part in this circumstance. Divine power of love! Sacred moments in which the passion of one possessed gave to the world a resuscitated God!

—Ernest Renan, *Life of Jesus*

More recent critics of the resurrection follow this with suggestions that Mary Magdalene's excitement then infected the other disciples, who began to see Jesus, too. And so it went, eventually resulting in the mass hallucination of a group of 500 people. I leave it to you to make your own judgment on the reality of resurrection, but suggest that Mary Magdalene has once again managed to become the subject of controversy. Only this time it is because of something that she, by all accounts, *did* do.

The Least You Need to Know

♦ All the elements in the resurrection accounts were things that would have been upsetting to any human being under any circumstances.

♦ Mary Magdalene's best-known episode in the Gospels is what is often called the *Noli Me Tangere* scene.

♦ When announcing the resurrection, the disciples didn't believe Mary Magdalene, probably simply because it is natural to assume that people don't really rise from the dead.

♦ From the earliest pagan writings against Christianity to skeptical arguments of today, Mary Magdalene's sanity has been questioned as a result of her resurrection testimony.

Part 3

The Legendary
Mary Magdalene

If it weren't for some stray bones in the Middle Ages, we might not be talking about Mary Magdalene today. The medieval preoccupation with holy relics was the fuel behind the most extraordinary legends about Mary Magdalene. We're still feeling the effects of the legends today as they are interpreted and reinterpreted to support new theories about who Mary Magdalene may have been.

In this part, we visit medieval France and find out how Mary Magdalene's relics became such a hot topic in the eleventh century, and how two churches competed for tourism dollars by claiming to have them. We also take a look at the effect that Mary Magdalene had on some of the most influential Christian thinkers of the Middle Ages, and how she is connected to the monastic movement. Finally, we take a tour of some different places around the world and see how they remember Mary Magdalene today.

Chapter 10

Legends and Dedications

In This Chapter

- ◆ The life and times of Mary Magdalene
- ◆ *The Golden Legend:* a thirteenth-century page turner
- ◆ Holy molar! The relics trade
- ◆ Who has the real Mary Magdalene?

Beginning with Hippolytus's commentary on *Song of Songs* that introduced his readers to Mary Magdalene as the New Eve, the Apostle of Apostles, and the Bride of Christ, legends have sprung up around her like wildflowers, in about just as many varieties and colors.

The thirst for more knowledge about the life of Jesus led to a parallel desire to know more about the other figures in the Gospels, including Mary Magdalene. Where was she from? Who were her parents? What happened to her after Jesus was gone? Writers began to set down details of her life either as it suited them or as they circulated in popular legend, and it is these kinds of stories that we take a look at next.

Magdalene's Many Biographies

Several accounts of Mary Magdalene's life still exist, and although it's tempting to attribute the stories they contain to the writers, it might not be the case. Some authors were simply recording the legends that they were hearing from the faithful, who heard it from someone else, and so on. This is the nature of legends; a piece of information gets passed along from person to person, until finally a whole framework of myth is constructed around the original tidbit (which might or might not still resemble the original story). We're lucky that certain individuals had the time, patience, and devotion to record some of the tales that were circulating.

Earliest Tales

Not much was said of Mary Magdalene's history in the earliest days of Christianity, but in the sixth century, Gregory of Tours, a historian, mentioned the legend that Mary Magdalene had gone to Ephesus. At that time, a tomb believed to be hers was revered as a very holy place. Modestus, the ruler of Jerusalem in the seventh century, described Mary Magdalene's death in Ephesus as one of a martyr.

Modestus also describes a scene in which Mary Magdalene appears as a "pure crystal" to her executioners. This is very much like a scene in the *Acts of Philip*, a fourth-century text. In it, Mary Magdalene accompanied Philip and Bartholomew on missionary journeys. Eventually they ran afoul of the authorities because Mary Magdalene (who is called Mariamne in the text) healed a woman named Nicanora, the proconsul's wife. Philip and Bartholomew were stripped, searched for magic charms, and then tortured. But when Mary Magdalene was assaulted, something unusual happened (my emphasis added):

> But Mariamne on being stripped became like an *ark of glass full of light and fire* and every one ran away.

Lingua Magda

A **martyrology** is a text that records details about the lives and deaths of people who died for their faith, which in our case is Christianity. Martyrs usually went on to become saints.

An Anglo-Saxon *martyrology* that appeared in the ninth century offered a new take on Mary Magdalene's post-ascension life. So sorrowful was she, it suggested, that she retired to a life of contemplation in the desert. The legend contained in this particular document bears a striking resemblance to later medieval stories; she lived in a cave for 30 years, fasting and praying, her only nourishment in the form of spiritual food given to her by angels as they lifted her up into heaven every day. This particular tale also appears to be influenced by the legend of St. Mary of the Desert, whose history appeared in an earlier text.

The *Vitas*

Vita is the Latin word for "life," and it is used to describe the different legends that were created during the Middle Ages to account for Mary Magdalene's life. Beginning in the ninth century, certain stories arose to describe details about what she did after Jesus ascended into heaven; where she went, who she went with, miracles she performed, and so on.

The first *vita* to appear was in the ninth century; a text known as the *Vita eremitica beatae Mariae Magdalenae*, or "the hermitic life of blessed Mary Magdalene," originated in southern Italy. In the *Vita eremitica*, Mary Magdalene appeared much as she did in the Anglo-Saxon martyrology, although this time her reason for retiring to the desert wasn't sorrow over Jesus' death, but penitence for her sinful life. She lived in the desert naked and without food.

A text called *gesta episcoporum Cameracensum* ("the chronicles of the bishops of Cambrai") showed up in the eleventh century, and it seems to have been the first to suggest that Mary Magdalene's remains were somewhere in France. The *gesta* said that her body had been buried in Jerusalem, but it was transferred in the eighth century to Vézelay, in the Burgundy region of Gaul, by a monk named Badilon. As discussed in the next section, Mary Magdalene's remains were a hot topic in medieval French religious politics.

> **Illuminations**
>
> *Vitas* aren't reserved for Mary Magdalene, and the word is used in a number of different ways. *Vita* could refer to a text, as in "the *Vita eremitica beatae Mariae Magdalenae*"; it can refer to a particular version of Mary Magdalene's life; it can refer to the lives of other saints, and it can refer to a specific kind of life, such as a contemplative life, *vita contemplativa*.

Although there were a few more developments to Mary Magdalene's legendary life in between, the next crucial step in her imagined career came in the eleventh century *vita apostolica*. In this legend, Mary Magdalene and many others were put in a boat and set to sea from Palestine. Through providence, the boat was guided to the shores of Marseilles. The Christians immediately set about evangelizing, and Mary Magdalene was able to convert the town of Aix-en-Provence.

To keep track of all the legends, you need to know the *vitas*, and to keep track of her *vitas*, you really need a scorecard.

Mary Magdalene's Medieval *Vitas*

Name	Legend
Vita eremitica	Lived as a hermit in penitence for her sins
Vita apostolica	Arrived on a boat, Christianized southern Gaul
Vita apostolico-eremitica	Arrived on a boat, Christianized southern Gaul, and then became a hermit
Vita evangelica	Combination of all Gospel passages about her life into a coherent whole
Vita evangelico-apostolica	Combination of all Gospel passages about her life into a coherent whole, plus an account of her voyage to Gaul
Vita active	Led a life of active devotion through penitence, works of mercy, and preaching
Vita contemplative	Led a life of contemplation through solitude, asceticism, and mystical experiences
Vita mixta	Led a life of both active and contemplative devotion

Medieval preachers could draw on all of these different types of legends of Mary Magdalene, and they did so with great frequency. Often several of the different types of legends were combined to create very flexible composite images of Mary Magdalene as she could best serve as an example for certain communities.

The Golden Legend

In the thirteenth century, a Dominican friar named Jacobus de Voragine wrote a book called *The Golden Legend*. Jacobus de Voragine was one of those who combined the various *vitas* in his account of Mary Magdalene; he composed a narrative of her life based on the gospels, then went on to describe her journey to Gaul, her preaching, and her eventual retirement to a life of solitude. To this he added a mix of miracles that she was said to have performed.

" " **It Is Written**

(A) man was holden in prison for debt of money, in irons. And he called unto his help ofttimes Mary Magdalene. And on a night a fair woman appeared to him and brake all his irons, and opened the door, and commanded him to go his way; and when he saw himself loose he fled away anon.

—Jacobus de Voragine, *The Golden Legend,* 1275 (translated by William Caxton, 1483)

Mary Magdalene, according to *The Golden Legend,* was placed in a rudderless boat with several others, including Martha, Lazarus, Salome, a man named Maximin who had been a disciple of Jesus, and Joseph of Arimathea. God took control of their destiny and they landed on the banks of Marseilles, where they immediately started preaching the good news.

After performing many miracles, Mary Magdalene retired to a contemplative life in a *grotto,* where she lived for 30 years. During that time, she fasted, prayed, and was lifted into heaven by angels for spiritual nourishment. The legend continued to account for her last days: From a distance, a priest saw angels lifting her into the air one day, so he went to find her. When he arrived, she told him that she would be leaving this world, and gave him a task. He was to go to Maximin, who was the bishop of nearby Aix, and tell him to watch for her in his oratory the next day. Faithfully, Maximin watched for her, and she appeared in the air in his oratory, held aloft by angels. He administered the Eucharist to her, during which she cried an abundance of tears and then died. Afterward, he anointed her body with various perfumes and buried her sweet-smelling remains.

Lingua Magda

A **grotto** is a small cave or carved-out impression from stone. Mary Magdalene is often depicted in a cavelike setting in art; these are references to her life in the grotto.

In addition to writing an account of her life unprecedented in detail, Jacobus de Voragine answered a question that had been, and still is, the subject of debate: why Jesus appeared to Mary Magdalene first after he rose from the dead. Jacobus gave five reasons:

 ◆ Because she loved him so much

 ◆ To show that he died for sinners

- Because he had said that prostitutes would enter the kingdom of heaven before Pharisees (Matthew 21:31)

- Because women are messengers of life (as they are of death)

- To show that she had received a measure of grace greater than that proportionate to her sin (Romans 5:20)

By far the greatest story of Mary Magdalene in *The Golden Legend* is that of how she helped a prince and his wife conceive a child, and how she restored them to life. A prince and his wife were trying to bear a child and were sacrificing to idols to help achieve their goal. Mary Magdalene appeared to the wife three times in dreams, the last time to the prince also, telling them that they needed to give some of their riches to support the people of God. After the last dream, during which Mary Magdalene chastised the prince and his wife for not heeding the first two dreams, they decided to see her. They invited Mary Magdalene and others into their home and provided for their needs, while Mary preached to them. The prince said he would believe what she said if her god was to grant them a child. Mary Magdalene prayed on their behalf, and finally they were able to conceive. The prince then said he was going to travel to visit Peter, who was in Jerusalem, to confirm what Mary Magdalene had preached of Jesus. The wife begged and begged, and although she was in her final stages of pregnancy, the husband allowed her to come along on the trip.

Illuminations

The Golden Legend contains more than one story about how Mary Magdalene aids in fertility and protects children. Other related legends say that couples who wanted children would visit her tomb to ask for her help in conceiving.

During the voyage, a storm arose and tossed the ship to and fro, causing the woman to go into labor. She delivered a son, but died in childbirth. The husband was beside himself with grief, having lost his wife, and he knew that his son, too, would die without any way to feed him. The sailors took the ship to a small island, where they put the mother and the child on the shore under a cloak and left them there.

The husband went to Jerusalem and found Peter, who saw immediately how consumed by sorrow the prince was. Peter told the prince that God gives and God takes away, and then when he sees fit, he *gives back* and turns sadness into joy. The prince then spent two years learning about everything Jesus had done and said.

Finally, the prince left Jerusalem to sail back to Marseilles. On the voyage back, the ship somehow ended up back at the island where he had left his wife's body and his baby son. To his great surprise, a little boy was on the shore, throwing stones into the sea. Having never seen other humans before, when the men from the ship approached him, he ran back to his dead mother on the shore, climbed under the cloak with her and began to nurse. He had thus been miraculously sustained for two years while the prince was gone.

The prince took his son in his arms and spoke aloud to Mary Magdalene, saying that he would be happy if only his wife were alive. Suddenly, the dead woman took a breath and was restored to life, and the three of them returned to Marseilles together, where they found Mary Magdalene preaching with "her disciples." After telling her everything that had happened, they were baptized by Maximin, and set about smashing icons and building churches. The prince made Lazarus the bishop of Marseilles and Maximin the bishop of the nearby town of Aix.

Quite Contrary

Depending on whom you ask, Mary Magdalene and the others landed at different places on the southern shores of Gaul. This is because there are so many similar legends, each of them tailored to the locale. The oldest reference to Mary Magdalene coming to France says that she landed at Marseilles.

The Golden Legend went on to become the medieval equivalent of a bestseller, with translations into every common European language and more than a hundred different editions. It had an enormous effect on how Mary Magdalene was viewed from that time forward.

Everyone Wanted a Piece: The Relics Trade

In the summer of 2002, I had the good fortune to travel to New York, where my husband and I roamed the halls of the Metropolitan Museum of Art. Among the many works of art related to Mary Magdalene displayed in the Met, I came across an oddly shaped object that appeared to be made of gold, with what looked like a large crystal egg in the center. As I peered into the crystal, I realized that it contained something rather macabre: a tooth. I was looking at a medieval *reliquary*, built for the sole purpose of displaying one of Mary Magdalene's teeth.

Believe it or not, a majority of the medieval French legends of Mary Magdalene appear to be closely tied with the fascination with her *relics*. What may seem a little morbid to us today was serious business in the Middle Ages. The faithful believed that saints blessed the regions that possessed their relics, aiding in everything from harvests to military campaigns, with an emphasis on the miraculous. In addition, believers who felt a devotion to certain saints would travel to view their relics, and this burgeoning tourism industry was an enormous incentive for churches to get popular relics of their own.

Lingua Magda

A **relic** is usually the corpse (or a piece of the corpse) of a holy person, but it could also refer to something associated with them. For example, Mary Magdalene's alabaster jar was considered a relic, as was the cross and Jesus' crown of thorns. A **reliquary** is a container built to contain a relic; it may be as small as a pillbox or as large and elaborate as a sarcophagus. It may be meant for personal use only or for public display. Some were very simple, made of wood, and others were encrusted with precious metals and jewels.

The history of Mary Magdalene's relics is a thoroughly complicated one. It all revolves around something called *furtum sacrum*, or "holy theft": the practice of thieving relics from one church to bring them back to your own. Far from carrying the stigma usually associated with stealing, *furtum sacrum* was a blessed occupation, often celebrated by the townsfolk on the receiving end.

From the time that it was founded in the ninth century until the eleventh century, the abbey at Vézelay was under the patronage of the Virgin Mary. It gradually fell into disrepair until 1055, when an abbot named Geoffrey took over. Abbot Geoffrey was a man with a plan. To bring the faithful back into church and restore appropriate devotions, he would need to give them a reason to come. Mary Magdalene, it turned out, was that reason.

Although nobody knows exactly how he did it, Geoffrey knew the right people who had enough influence to generate a holy buzz. Soon, popes were issuing statements that Mary Magdalene's genuine relics were located at Vézelay. Texts began to appear detailing the miracles (courtesy of Mary Magdalene) that were being performed there. Believers far and wide started to make pilgrimages to Vézelay, and it became the center of the Magdalene cult in France.

Soon, however, the monks at Vézelay were under pressure to actually *show* the relics, which no one had ever seen, and to explain how they got there. Various stalling tactics ensued, until finally a flurry of legends erupted to account for their origins, including the *gesta episcoporum Cameracensum*, which I've already discussed earlier in this chapter. The monk Badilon, it seemed, had performed a *furtum sacrum*, and transferred her relics to Vézelay from Provence. That was the story that stuck.

In the thirteenth century, a prince in southern Gaul named Charles of Salerno discovered that, lo and behold, Mary Magdalene's remains weren't at Vézelay at all, but in the Provence church of Saint-Maximin. The body he discovered smelled of sweet apothecary spices and had a small green plant growing out of its tongue, evidence that it was the corpse of the Apostle of the Apostles. From the tongue of Mary Magdalene was professed the good news of the resurrection, and the tender plant symbolized the living word. Soon, a similar flurry of documents and miracles started to pour out of Saint-Maximin to prove that theirs, not Vézelay's, was the *real* body of Mary Magdalene.

> **Illuminations**
>
> When the bodies of holy people have been exhumed for various purposes, they are sometimes said to exude a sweet smell, described as flowery or, in the case of Mary Magdalene, like apothecary spices. Often the sweet smell is accounted as one of several miracles that leads the holy person to be considered a saint.

Vézelay and Saint-Maximin weren't the only places to claim relics of Mary Magdalene, however. If we were to tally all of the pieces and parts that turned up during the Middle Ages, the poor woman would have left behind at least …

◆ Five full corpses.

◆ Eight arms.

◆ A jawbone.

◆ A breastbone.

◆ Several fingers.

◆ Several teeth.

◆ An untold amount of hair.

In addition to the body parts listed, one of her skulls bore a piece of perfectly preserved skin on her forehead. This was believed to be the spot where Jesus touched *her* as he was telling her not to touch *him* in the *Noli Me Tangere* scene.

As you might have guessed, based on Mary Magdalene's many corpses, the medieval relic trade was often based on spurious claims. One church, for example, claimed to have the brain of Saint Peter, but when it was moved, it was discovered to be nothing more than a piece of pumice stone.

Magdalene in Ephesus

Very little record of Mary Magdalene's life in Ephesus remains. Her sepulcher in Ephesus was known as a holy place from around the sixth century, and was near the Cave of the Seven Sleepers.

The Seven Sleepers of Ephesus is a legend that was told at least since the sixth century. The story goes that in the third century, during the reign of Decius, Christians were being persecuted for not following the laws of the state religion. Seven Christian men in Ephesus were found guilty, so they went into a cave to pray and prepare for the worst. As they said their final prayers, they fell asleep, and stayed asleep for 200 years. When they woke up and went out to buy food, they found a Christian empire where there had been a pagan one before. The new emperor, Theodosius, declared their long slumber a miracle that proved the resurrection.

After the men died, they were buried in the cave in which they had slept for so long. It isn't known whether Mary Magdalene's grave was there before or after the legend of the seven sleepers came into circulation. One might find it interesting, however, that the earliest record of Mary Magdalene's remains are found in strong association with the number seven, this time of a miraculous, rather than demonic, variety.

In the ninth century, Mary Magdalene's remains were transferred to Constantinople, the capital of the Byzantine Empire. There she was laid to rest next to the man assumed to have been her brother: Lazarus.

Magdalene in Gaul

Gaul was the name of the region that contained territories that would later become France. Although Gaul stretched northward to include much of modern-day Germany, Belgium, and Luxembourg, it is primarily the area that would become southern France that we're concerned with here. Within Gaul, the Burgundy (modern-day Borgogne) and Provence regions were most important to the rise of Mary Magdalene in medieval thought.

The real beginnings of Mary Magdalene's presence in Gaul began, as we've seen, with the eleventh-century *vitas*. Of primary importance, it seemed, were the details surrounding the location of her relics, and in fact, some of the *vitas* may have been written to support Vézelay's claims to her body.

Vézelay

As we've already seen, it is highly possible that Mary Magdalene's initial association with the church at Vézelay was the result of some elaborate planning on the part of Abbot Geoffrey. Nonetheless, it became one of the holiest shrines in Christendom and the place where Mary Magdalene was most venerated for 200 years.

Vézelay certainly wasn't the earliest church dedicated to Mary Magdalene in France, nor the first to claim her relics. It was, however, the first to widely publicize its dedication to her and become a major pilgrimage site for believers all over Europe. As such, it enjoyed attention and visits from members of the uppermost levels of society, including:

- Thomas Beckett, the former archbishop of Canterbury, who went there to publicly excommunicate Henry II

- Bernard of Clairvaux, who preached as the Second Crusade was launched from Vézelay

- Philip Augustus of France and Richard the Lion-Hearted of England, who went there to announce the Third Crusade

During the thirteenth century, plagued by power struggles, jealous neighbors, and scandal, Vézelay's fame and revenues began to decline. Even the "miraculous" rediscovery of Mary Magdalene's body, which the monks at Vézelay had been so hesitant to display all along, wasn't enough to rescue the ailing abbey. The eleventh-century legends that were circulated by Vézelay to establish the legitimacy of their claim to Mary Magdalene's relics came around, as it were, to bite them in the backside.

Saint-Maximin

Charles of Salerno, as we've already seen, oversaw the miraculous discovery of Mary Magdalene's body at Saint-Maximin in the late thirteenth century. The monks at Saint-Maximin probably wouldn't have been able to stake a legitimate claim to her relics if it hadn't been for the documents generated by Vézelay in the eleventh century. The legends placed Mary Magdalene's body in Provence to begin with before being stolen and transferred to Vézelay. It was therefore easy for Provençals to claim that poor Badilon's *furtum sacrum* had never really taken place, or that he had transferred someone else's body, leaving the *real* Mary Magdalene at Saint-Maximin.

Not long after the discovery of her remains, the necessary supporting documents appeared, and miracles began to take place. The pilgrims that had once gone to Vézelay now steered south to Saint-Maximin. Not only did Saint-Maximin have her relics, but two other significant sites were nearby: the grotto in which she was said to have lived for years; and Marseilles, where she was said to have landed with the others in a rudderless boat. Saint-Maximin just had too much of a good thing for Vézelay to ever recover its previous prestige.

It Is Written

In the year 1283
The Prince of Salerno,
From kindness and out of love for the Lord
Displayed her in gold,
Decorated with a sacred crown.
Therefore, Mary, be our pious patron
Protecting him while living and in death.

—Inscription on the reliquary at Saint-Maximin that contains Mary Magdalene's skull

Where Is She Now?

During the French Revolution, most of Mary Magdalene's relics at Saint-Maximin were lost, but her skull is still displayed there. It is encased in crystal and embedded in a gold reliquary, and on her feast day, July 22, the whole reliquary is carried about the village in a procession. After marching her skull around town, the procession wraps up in the basilica, where the faithful sometimes dress in period costumes and retell the medieval legends.

Down in the darkness of the crypt at Vézelay, a gold reliquary box holds another portion of Mary Magdalene's remains. Although Saint-Maximin is by far the site that receives the most attention as her final resting place, Vézelay still receives many pilgrims wishing to honor their beloved Mary Magdalene.

The Least You Need to Know

- Many, many people wrote about what Mary Magdalene may have done after the ascension of Jesus.

- Several very specific categories of Mary Magdalene legends arose during the Middle Ages.

- Some of the legends of Mary Magdalene may have been written to justify claims to her relics.

- Vézelay was the first place in Gaul to have a very popular Mary Magdalene cult, based largely on the presence of her relics.

- Saint-Maximin's claim to Mary Magdalene's relics overshadowed Vézelay, and it is there that she is most commonly known to have been laid to rest.

Mary Magdalene's Influence

In This Chapter

- ◆ Preachers just like Mary Magdalene
- ◆ Francis meets Mary Magdalene at the foot of the cross
- ◆ Why Mary Magdalene's apostleship was rejected
- ◆ The weeper has awakened

It has been said that because Jesus and his mother were examples of absolute purity, Mary Magdalene was provided by God as an example of penitence. In the Middle Ages this was vital as monastic orders were founded to reach the people in a way that the institutional Church no longer could. Salvation, they taught, would only follow repentance. Mary Magdalene emerged as an extremely important influence during this time then, not only because of the race for her relics in France, but as a legendary penitent. This, in turn, led to even more ways to view her.

Many people in the Middle Ages have emerged as extremely important Church personalities, and many have mentioned Mary Magdalene. Here we take a look at some of the best-known medieval Christian figures, including the two men at the heart of the monastic movement, and how their ideas may have been influenced by Mary Magdalene.

Dominic of Guzman (1170–1221)

Dominic of Guzman is best remembered as the founder of the Order of Preachers, better known as the Dominicans. Born as Domingo in the Castile region of Spain in 1170, Dominic was the child of well-to-do, perhaps even noble, parents.

Little is known of his father, Felix Guzman, but his mother, Joan of Aza, was a devout Christian, eventually being recognized by the Church for her sanctity. His brothers, Antonio and Manes, were also known for their faithfulness. Dominic was well educated, and early on he displayed a rare piety and concern for the poor.

Dominic entered the service of God while still a student, assisting the reform of a local cathedral. His real mark on history begins, however, when his bishop brought him on an assignment in the Languedoc region of modern-day France, to minister to the heretics there known as the Albigensians, also called the Cathars.

> **Illuminations**
>
> Dominic's mother had a vision while she was pregnant with him that he was a dog carrying a torch in his mouth, setting the world on fire. The symbol of the Dominicans became a dog bearing a torch, and they were known as "the Dogs of the Lord."

The Cathars, who we return to in Chapter 20, appointed clergy that led lives of impeccable sanctity. In contrast to this, the Cistercians, an older monastic order that represented the Roman Catholic Church in Languedoc at the time, lived the lives of pampered nobility. The heretics, Dominic noticed, would never come around to the Church's doctrines if those sent to preach to them couldn't begin to match their own leaders in piety and holiness.

Dominic and his bishop therefore appealed to the clergy in Languedoc to adopt a more spare way of life, and to preach to the people more as Christ's apostles had. The result was measurable in increasing numbers of converts.

> **It Is Written**
>
> As princes of the Church and envoys of the pope, the Cistercians traveled in great state, a suite of retainers, bodyguards, servants, and sycophants always at their beck and call. To the spiritual seekers of Languedoc, the legates appeared as pampered hypocrites, unable to speak to the soul. The times called not for feudal swank but for genuine material destitution.
>
> —Stephen O'Shea, *The Perfect Heresy: The Revolutionary Life and Death of the Medieval Cathars*

Foundation of the Dominicans

It was on his journeys through Albigensian territories that Dominic conceived of the idea of his Order of Preachers, to combat heresy and promote the word of God through preaching. In 1215, his Order was finally realized, and before long, the pope was bestowing churches on the brotherhood in which it was to grow into an organization uniquely suited to ministering to the laity.

Two other orders were founded by Dominic. While in Languedoc, he established a convent for young women who had been protected previously by the clergy of the Cathars. This was later called the Second Order of St. Dominic.

The "third order" is the Militia of Jesus Christ, formed of everyday men and women who are tasked with safeguarding the interests of the Church, both doctrinal and material, wherever they may be. Shortly after starting this particular organization, Dominic fell sick and died in 1221.

Mary Magdalene and the Dominicans

It is here that we begin our look at Mary Magdalene in her very important role as the figure symbolic of the movement toward penitence in the twelfth and thirteenth centuries. Dominic's Order of Preachers was one the first orders of *mendicant* preachers that was to arise during the Middle Ages, and we can see Mary Magdalene's influence on their approach.

Toward the end of the thirteenth century, some interesting changes were in store for the Dominicans. After Mary Magdalene's remains were discovered at St. Maximin, the Dominicans were established at her tomb. In the next two years, her feast day was instituted as a mandatory observance in the Order, and she became their patron saint.

Lingua Magda

A **mendicant** order is one that depends on the alms and charity of others, with its members often begging for their sustenance rather than owning property and earning money.

The most important thing to consider when thinking about Mary Magdalene's influence on the Dominicans is her role as apostle. The Order was founded as, as the name says, an order of preachers. Mary Magdalene's later legends in France revolve a great deal around her activities in preaching and evangelizing the pagans who met her on the shores of Marseilles. It was primarily in this apostolic role, then, that Mary Magdalene was lauded by the Dominicans.

Francis of Assisi (1181–1226)

It might not come as a surprise to know that one of the other most popular saints is one who modeled himself, to some extent, after Mary Magdalene. Francis of Assisi was born in 1181 in the Umbrian region of Italy to a wealthy cloth merchant father. Little is known of his mother.

He didn't receive the fine education that Dominic did, being educated by priests and troubadours, but it's likely that an expensive education would have been lost on Francis anyway. He wasn't the serious student that Dominic was, and by many accounts he, in essence, partied his youth away.

> **CAUTION**
>
> **Quite Contrary**
>
> Francis of Assisi wasn't always "Francis." He was baptized as Giovanni de Bernardone. His nickname was Francesco, out of his father's admiration for France, where he often did business.

After living a lavish life for his first 20 years, Francis turned to military service, which was interrupted by illness and strange dreams that turned his attention toward things of a more spiritual nature. Finally, in 1205 he returned to Assisi, after which he seemed to be a changed man. It was during this time that he set aside his interest in worldly things and began to live a life of devotion to God.

In 1208 he took the final step toward his fate and realized his calling after hearing a sermon one morning. In it, the priest talked about Jesus' exhortation to his disciples to go forth and preach, but to do so in poverty.

From then on, Francis and his little band of followers gave up all of their remaining worldly possessions and went forth to preach and perform work in exchange for all they needed to survive.

Foundation of the Franciscans

In 1209, having 11 or 12 followers, Francis went to Rome and sought the pope's approval for his new order. Pope Innocent III gave verbal approval to Francis's new "rule," the guiding document for how members of his order should live.

The Friars Minor, as the order was called, grew quickly, and as a result, the rule was tweaked by some of the members of the order while Francis did missionary work abroad. Francis tried to resist softening his original rule, but he did finally rework it, and it was approved in 1223. The three main vows of the order were obedience, chastity, and poverty, and it is the rule still in use by the Franciscans today. Francis died in 1226.

Mary Magdalene and the Franciscans

Where the value of Mary Magdalene to the Dominicans was in her role as preacher, to the Franciscans it was her role as penitent. The Franciscans placed a great deal of emphasis on the Passion, with meditation and devotion focused on the suffering of Jesus. Mary Magdalene, then, in her role at the foot of the cross, was a representative of humanity; a complex figure who could sum up several important concepts.

She was a penitent, first and foremost, and her repentance was exemplary. Mary Magdalene was also a symbol of the errors of humanity that led to Jesus' necessary sacrifice, so her previous life of vanity and indulgence was cited as an indication of the worldliness that should be left behind. Additionally, she was both a symbol of the active life, as a preacher, and the contemplative life, as a hermit. The Franciscans followed the *vita mixta*, modeling their behavior on Mary Magdalene's balance between the interior relationship with God and the exterior service to humankind.

It Is Written

And he called to him the twelve, and began to send them out two by two, and gave them authority over the unclean spirits. He charged them to take nothing for their journey except a staff; no bread, no bag, no money in their belts; but to wear sandals and not put on two tunics.

—Mark 6:7–9

The Franciscan devotion to Mary Magdalene was to change the way that the crucifixion was depicted. Prior to the thirteenth century, Mary Magdalene was rarely pictured at the foot of the cross. As the mendicant orders grew, however, she was frequently pictured there either alone or with Francis or another monk. Often the monks were pictured at the foot of the cross alone, in what they saw as her place.

Thomas Aquinas (1225–1274)

Thomas was born near the end of 1225 in Italy to noble parents; his father was the count of Aquino. As a child, he excelled in his education and as a young man joined the Dominican order. So enraged was his family that his mother bade Thomas's brothers to capture him, which they did, and kept him locked up in the house for two years. During that time his family seemed to soften somewhat to his resolve to live in service to God, and they finally released him to his brothers in the Dominican Order of Preachers.

After being freed to pursue his life of devotion, he continued his education in association with the order. He was ordained as a priest in 1250, and led an extremely busy life. He fulfilled the duties of his offices as well as studying for his Doctor of Theology appointment, which finally came through in 1256.

Thomas of Aquinas is known for his book the *Summa Theologica*, in which he presented everything that one would need to know about the Christian religion. It is formatted as lists of questions and answers, much in the way that modern catechisms are organized.

> **It Is Written**
>
> Therefore, it does not seem becoming for Christ's Resurrection to be manifested first of all to the women and afterwards to mankind in general.
>
> —Thomas Aquinas, *Summa Theologica*, Question 55, "The Manifestation of the Resurrection"

Aquinas didn't have much to say about Mary Magdalene, but it was significant that he referred to her as "holy intercessor and advocate of sinners." Here again the faithful are being urged to access her as a symbol for their penitence, and to seek redemption as she had.

On a less-positive note, Aquinas commented on the role that Mary Magdalene and the other women played on the morning of the resurrection. In a blow to any potential for women's leadership in the Church, he wrote that although the women were privileged to see the risen Jesus first, what they did subsequently did not qualify as apostleship.

They had acted as witnesses of the resurrection to the other disciples, but because they were women, they couldn't act as public witnesses. This is why Jesus forbade Mary Magdalene to touch him in the garden while later allowing Thomas to put his hand in the wound in his side in order to believe. The women announced the resurrection, Aquinas taught, but they didn't preach the good news.

Catherine of Siena (1347–1380)

Born in 1347 as the twenty-third child of Jacomo Benincasa in Siena, in the Tuscany region of Italy, Catherine was a lovely child whose parents had hopes that she would someday marry. Early on, Catherine had visions, among them visions of St. Dominic, who urged her to join his order, probably a result of living near a Dominican monastery. At the age of 12, she cut off her long, blonde hair to repulse potential suitors, but it wasn't until she turned 15, when smallpox marred her forever, that her wish to never be married became a reality. At 16, she entered the Dominican order of penitents.

Catherine's life is marked by her mystical marriage to Jesus, which occurred in her visions. She gave Jesus her heart, and in return, he gave her his sacred heart. In another vision, she was betrothed to Jesus when he placed a ring on her finger; it was invisible to everyone but her. She also received the *stigmata*, but the marks, too, were invisible until after her death.

Like many people of her time, Mary Magdalene's importance to Catherine was primarily as a penitent; though to Catherine, Mary Magdalene's humility in renouncing her former life of luxury was also to be imitated. When she spoke of Mary Magdalene, it was usually to extol her ability to ward off pride through humility.

Lingua Magda

Stigmata is the name for the phenomenon wherein a person manifests the wounds of Christ on their body. Francis of Assisi was the first stigmatist, developing the wounds after a period of prolonged isolation in the wilderness while following Mary Magdalene's example of a contemplative, hermitic existence.

What made Catherine of Siena's view of Mary Magdalene different, though, was that she saw her as a maternal figure. The Virgin Mary appeared to Catherine in a vision and gave Mary Magdalene to her as a second mother. Catherine's biographer, Raymond of Capua, wrote "… for it was proper for penitent to be united with penitent, lover with lover, contemplative with contemplative."

Although this maternal identity for Mary Magdalene wasn't as incredibly popular as her roles, there is evidence of others during the Middle Ages looking to Mary Magdalene as a spiritual mother. In this identity she took on a nurturing aspect as she taught others how to worship, repent, and devote themselves to Christ.

Margery Kempe (1373–1438)

Margery Kempe is at once a fascinating and puzzling figure. Born in 1373 to the mayor of her hometown of Lynne, in Norfolk, England, the most significant thing that can be said of Margery's childhood is that she wasn't taught to read. At this time, literacy could well be expected of middle-class girls, so it's an unusual feature that appears to have had some impact on her later. Toward the end of her life, she dictated her memoirs, *The Book of Margery Kempe*, and it survives as the first medieval autobiography.

After the birth of her first child, Margery suffered from a fever and went mad, to the point where her husband had to confine her. After some time in isolation, in her state of raving, she had a vision of Jesus that returned her to health. She recovered instantly and went about a re-entry into her community as a new woman.

After undertaking a couple of commercial ventures that eventually failed, she set on a new course of religious devotion. She became a religious *mystic* of a sort quite annoying to those around her, weeping, wailing, and carrying on whenever she took communion. Accused more than once of being a charlatan and hypocrite, she persevered through the abuse of others by the encouragement given her by Jesus and the Virgin Mary in her mind.

Lingua Magda

A **mystic** is someone who engages in contemplation or other religious and spiritual activities with the goal of developing a personal knowledge of, or some kind of spiritual union with, God. Medieval mysticism rose in practice as a result of what many felt was an impersonal approach to Christianity by the Church.

Quite Contrary

Think that women couldn't inherit property in the Middle Ages? Think again. Margery Kempe inherited a handsome sum upon her father's death, and it was hers to keep. In fact, it was from her inheritance that she agreed to pay her husband's debts in return for his agreement to allow her to live chastely.

Margery's antics weren't entirely unique at the time; weeping and extreme penitence were characteristic of medieval women's mystic practices. Catherine of Siena also had "the gift of tears," and undertook the abuse of her own body in order to despise herself and quell pride. Mary Magdalene was a key figure in these kinds of severe devotions as the one with whom the penitents identified.

During the course of her life, Margery gave birth to 14 children. This was the cause of great consternation for her, because virginity was the ideal. It was through Jesus' love for Mary Magdalene that she found solace. There was a common view that Mary Magdalene's post-conversion life was one of unimpeachable chastity. As a result, she was almost as pure as a true virgin, and some estimated that she was even awarded a virgin's crown in heaven. Mary Magdalene was a virgin in mind, rather than in body, because she had turned her attention toward Jesus.

With this in mind, Margery cut a deal with her husband of 20 years by which they would sign a chastity agreement and he would no longer pursue her for sexual favors. From then on, she lived life as a penitent, modeling her sometimes strange behavior on the life of penitence exemplified by Mary Magdalene.

The Least You Need to Know

- ◆ The Dominicans held Mary Magdalene in high esteem as a preacher.

- ◆ The Franciscans revered Mary Magdalene as a perfect penitent.

- ◆ Catherine of Siena was one of the few in the Middle Ages who viewed Mary Magdalene as a mother figure.

- ◆ Margery Kempe, an example of women's devotions during the Middle Ages, also viewed Mary Magdalene as a role model for penitence.

Chapter 12

Mary Magdalene Around the World

In This Chapter

◆ Basilicas built on bones

◆ Brotherhoods of Mary Magdalene

◆ Visiting the Holy Land

◆ Adopting Mary Magdalene's legends

All around the world, in countries where Christianity is part of the cultural landscape, Mary Magdalene is remembered in direct, and sometimes not-so-direct, ways. She has left an indelible mark on the face of the Christian world, and is unlikely to be forgotten anytime soon.

Although most of the areas we cover in this chapter are in European countries, there are small towns and villages all over the globe that count Mary Magdalene as a patron. There are far too many to include all of them here, so we only visit some of the most historic, colorful, and unusual.

France: Root of the Legends

So popular was Mary Magdalene in France that to this day, many places bear her French name: *Sainte Marie-Madeleine.* Although you could probably go just about anywhere in France and find some amount of devotion to her, there are two places that reflect much more dedication to her than others.

St. Maximin la Sainte Baume

St. Maximin la Ste. Baume is the town where you will find one of the two French *Basilicas* of St. Mary Magdalene. The one in St. Maximin la Ste. Baume was begun at the end of the thirteenth century to house her relics. The town itself has a population of about 12,500, and is located about 31 miles from Marseilles in the Provence region of France. It is situated near the Ste. Baume mountain range, from which it takes its name.

The two most important locations in the St. Maximin la Ste. Baume area are the basilica and the nearby grotto where Mary Magdalene was said to have lived for 30 years.

The Basilica of St. Mary Magdalene at St. Maximin la Ste. Baume is well known not only as the resting place for Mary Magdalene's skull, but because it is the largest Gothic structure in Provence, and because it contains an *enormous* pipe organ. Every July and August, a large music festival takes place in the basilica, and visitors can attend free organ concerts every first Sunday of the month from April until October.

The basilica was begun in the late part of the thirteenth century after the body of Mary Magdalene was discovered in the old church on the same site, and it took more than 200 years for it to be completed. Before the construction, Benedictine monks had been the caretakers of the site, but afterward,

> **Illuminations**
>
> In the French language, words can be masculine or feminine. When it comes to saints, there are two spellings: "saint" and "sainte." In general, "saint" refers to men, and "sainte" refers to women. The words are abbreviated "St." for "saint" and "Ste." for "sainte."

> **Lingua Magda**
>
> Originally, a **basilica** wasn't a church but a Roman public building where business was conducted. It is the architecture that defines a basilica: a tall, long hall lined by a row of columns on either side which separates the main aisle from aisles on either side. In the fourth century, after Christianity was legalized, basilicas started to be constructed as places of worship.

the Dominicans took over. Although there were a few shifts in authority over the years, the Dominicans remained until 1957.

Just outside the town of St. Maximin la Ste. Baume is a steep rock face called a *massif*. About halfway up there is a small cave in which Mary Magdalene was believed to have lived for 30 years, being fed only by angels. Visitors can undertake the steep journey up the footpath to the grotto, where they will find it has been turned into a small chapel. A lovely sculpture of a kneeling penitent Mary Magdalene commemorates her long and solitary life in the cave.

Vézelay

Tourists say that the best way to visit the Basilica of St. Mary Magdalene in Vézelay is to park at the entrance of the town at the bottom of the hill and walk all the way up. The main street curves as it ascends, and nearby streets are lined with houses from all periods of history. At the top is the church, still a major stop on pilgrimages, and a park that has a stunning view of the surrounding valley.

Vézelay is a small village in the Borgogne (Burgundy) region of France, roughly 155 miles southeast of Paris, with a population of about 500. During the Middle Ages, at the height of its popularity as *the* place to honor Mary Magdalene, it had a population of about 15,000 and was visited by some 100,000 pilgrims a year. The day before Mary Magdalene's feast day in 1120, a fire destroyed part of the church, which was then rebuilt amid great controversy between the local villagers, the monastery, and the abbot.

Quite Contrary

Vézelay never had an easy existence. Even after the church was rebuilt after the twelfth-century fire, much of the basilica was destroyed yet again during the French Revolution. It was rebuilt again in the mid-nineteenth century.

Exceptionally well lit for a structure of its size and age, the Basilica of St. Mary Magdalene at Vézelay is known for the sculpted art it contains. Pillar capitals depict different scenes from the Bible, and a very large Romanesque relief portrays a majestic Jesus among his disciples as they receive the Holy Spirit on the Day of Pentecost. In addition to her relics housed in the crypt, the church also contains a sculpture of Mary Magdalene, smiling faintly and cradling her ever-present ointment jar.

The Basilica of St. Mary Magdalene, Vézelay, France.

(Photo by Martin Gray)

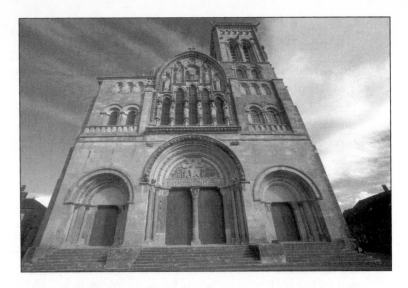

Spain: The Spirit of Brotherhood

To medieval Christians, Spain was a very important place. It was, and still is, the home of one of the best-known pilgrimage destinations, following only Jerusalem and Rome in popularity: *Santiago de Compostela*, or "Saint James of the Field of the Star." Santiago de Compostela itself is a church built on a site where, in the ninth century, a hermit had visions of Saint James. Spanish legend has it that James brought Christianity to the shores of Spain much the way French legends say that Mary Magdalene and her companions brought Christianity to France. After the hermit's vision, James' tomb was miraculously discovered. Although a small chapel was erected initially, as the site grew in popularity, the large cathedral eventually replaced it.

> **Illuminations**
>
> Seashells were very common medieval badges of a pilgrim traveling to Santiago de Compostela. Pilgrims wore them on their clothing, and on the main pilgrimage routes to the cathedral, shells were used to designate places where pilgrims could stop for food or lodging.

It was while on the *Camino de Santiago* ("Way of Saint James") that pilgrims defined many other important stops along the most popular routes, including Vézelay. As an overwhelmingly Roman Catholic country, Spain maintains several traditions that reflect devotions to the saints, including Mary Magdalene.

Holy Week

All over Spain, the week before Easter is a time for remembering the Passion. Known as Holy Week in English-speaking countries, *Semana Santa* in Spain reflects the devotion of the Roman Catholic population. In many locations, particularly in northern Spain, Passion plays take place. Perhaps the most fascinating Spanish observation of Holy Week, though, is the practice of bearing large wooden images of Jesus, the Virgin Mary, and the saints through the streets in solemn processions.

The images themselves are life-size, and look rather like wooden mannequins. They can be dressed in different garments and adorned with jewels, flowers, and other finery. They are then placed on elaborate and sometimes extremely heavy platforms that are usually carried by the faithful along the procession route.

Such elaborate images of Christianity's holiest figures aren't treated carelessly, and their maintenance requires organized efforts. Religious brotherhoods therefore have sprung up as the guardians of the images in an example of spiritual and civic responsibility. The brotherhoods, or *cofradías*, are often active within their communities, assist in organizing the Passion processions, and provide for the upkeep of their particular image, and do so in a spirit of fraternity.

> **It Is Written**
>
> The stars in the sky sleep and in the Earth not a slight murmur sounds.
> Alone under the cross, the Magdalena
> Hears his moan in the silence!
>
> —Hermandad de Santa Maria Magdalena ("Brotherhood of Saint Mary Magdalene"), Hellin

There are many brotherhoods of *Santa Maria Magdalena* in Spain with the sole purpose of caring for her images that are carried in procession during Holy Week. Some of the towns in which *cofradías* have formed around Mary Magdalene images are:

- Cieza
- Hellin-Albacete
- Baena-Cordoba
- Castellón de la Plana
- Liria

One town, Zaragoza, has a brotherhood named after the images that it maintains: *Slavery of Jesus the Nazarene and Conversion of Saint Mary Magdalene.* These two elaborate floats depict Jesus in captivity before the crucifixion, and Jesus forgiving a penitent Mary Magdalene. Zaragoza is also known for a shrine to Mary Magdalene that rests in relative obscurity due to the much more popular nearby basilica, *Catedral Nuestra Senora del Pilar,* which is dedicated to the Virgin Mary.

Anguiano

Anguiano is a small rural town in the Spanish state of La Rioja, in a mountainous region about 12 miles south of Nájera. Every year, the villagers commemorate the feast day of their patron saint, *la Magdalena,* by moving a small icon from the main church to a small shrine dedicated to her for the three-day feast. By itself, such a practice isn't anything terribly special. It is the way that they move the icon that's significant: while dancing on stilts to the music of bagpipes and drums. The ritual is called *Danza de los Zancos.* The name of this Spanish tradition literally reflects the nature of the event: "dance of the stilts," or "stilt dance."

Eight young men wearing colorful skirted costumes perch about three feet off the ground on their wooden stilts, whirling in circles and dancing from one end of the town to the other as onlookers line the cobblestone streets. They do this every year on July 21 to begin the three-day celebration of Mary Magdalene's feast. On the last day, they do the same ritual in reverse, dancing her icon back up to the main church.

The first written reference to *la Danza de los Zancos* was in 1603, and Anguiano celebrated 400 years of the stilt dance in 2003. The dance is a tradition that has been carried out by the oldest families of the area, passed from father to son for many generations. Spinning in tight circles as they descend and ascend stairs and go down curving, roughly paved roads is a skill that requires great dexterity and courage. The dancers insist that theirs is an act of devotion to their patron saint, who will protect them from harm.

Mary Magdalene is referred to by those in Anguiano as "the one with ways about her a little freer than modesty allows," a reference to her reputation as a harlot before meeting Jesus.

Israel: Following in Mary Magdalene's Footsteps

Much of first-century Palestine is today known as modern Israel. The places where Mary Magdalene would have lived, therefore, are within Israel's borders. Thousands of Christians from all over the world travel to Israel every year to walk in the places that Jesus would have walked, to see the place where he was crucified, buried, and where Mary Magdalene first encountered him after the resurrection.

Jerusalem

Jerusalem, of course, is the place where Jesus was tried and executed, and since the early Middle Ages many of the sites that are honored today have been the destinations of pilgrimages. The most central place of worship is the Church of the Holy Sepulcher. This church is a structure built on the site believed to have been Golgotha, and it encompasses not only the crucifixion site but the tomb where Jesus is believed to have been buried. As such, it also contains the place where Mary Magdalene would have met the risen Jesus outside the tomb.

The Chapel of St. Mary Magdalene is also known as the Chapel of the Appearance of the Risen Christ to St. Mary Magdalene. It is maintained by the Franciscans, one of the many Christian groups that have claimed ownership of the various parts of the building. Because such an ornate structure has been erected on the site, it is a bit difficult to imagine what it would have looked like in the first century, but it still represents one of the holiest places in all of Christendom.

> **Quite Contrary**
>
> Dan Brown, author of *The Da Vinci Code* (see Appendix B), wrote in his novel that many of the churches built by the Knights Templar during the Middle Ages were round in order to acknowledge the "sacred feminine." Actually, most scholars believe they were round to honor the Church of the Holy Sepulcher in Jerusalem, which was also a circular structure.

Another important site in Jerusalem is the Russian Orthodox Church of St. Mary Magdalene, consecrated in 1888. A stunning example of Russian architecture with enormous gold onion domes, the church sits on the slope of the Mount of Olives—the place where Jesus is believed to have ascended into heaven after the resurrection—in the Garden of Gethsemane, where he prayed before being arrested. Inside the church are large murals depicting the life of Mary Magdalene painted by well-known Russian artist Sergei Ivanov. The murals include a magnificent image of her holding an egg in reference to the Orthodox legend that she visited Tiberius Caesar. Today the church is a place of daily worship for the nuns of the nearby Convent of St. Mary Magdalene, but visitors are also welcome.

Migdal

In spite of historical uncertainties, Migdal is known as the birthplace of Mary Magdalene. Today, a small agricultural settlement stands in place of the once-prosperous fishing village. Rusting signs, fenced-off unfinished archaeological digs, and graffiti are all that greet visitors looking for first-century Magdala; hardly a shining endorsement for a saint of such renown.

What *does* remain of ancient Magdala is a structure whose exact nature hasn't quite been agreed upon: a villa, a synagogue, or a kind of a well-house for a natural spring. Migdal isn't a tourist center or major pilgrimage destination by any stretch of the imagination; Christians wanting to see remnants of first-century Galilee often go to nearby Capernaum instead.

Illuminations

In the fourth century, Emperor Constantine's mother, Queen Helena, was evidently a very busy lady. Not only did she discover the cross from the crucifixion, leading to the construction of the Church of the Holy Sepulcher, she also was said to have discovered Mary Magdalene's house in Magdala. A church was built there to enclose the house, and pilgrims from the ninth to the thirteenth centuries wrote about it. Today nothing is known to remain of the church or Mary Magdalene's house.

Greece: Memories of Maries

There is a an island in the Ionian Sea off the coast of Greece called Zakynthos that holds another secret about Mary Magdalene. A local village called the Maries commemorates the local legend that in 34 C.E. (approximately one year after the crucifixion), Mary Clopas and Mary Magdalene landed there while traveling from Jerusalem to Rome. They came ashore and were the first to spread Christianity to the island.

Strangely enough, this legend bears up to the Eastern Orthodox traditions that Mary Magdalene traveled to Rome after the crucifixion. It is as if she just had a brief stopover during the journey, and Zakynthos bears the ancient memory.

Zakynthos isn't the only place in Greece important to Mary Magdalene legend. Mt. Athos, a southeastern peninsula of Greece, is home to 20 monasteries and magnificent collections of religious texts and art. In 1974, a fourteenth-century copy of a fourth-century text was discovered there. It was the *Acts of Philip;* the text in which Mary Magdalene turns into a box of glass and shining light.

Italy: Celebrating in Style

Like Spain, Italy is a predominantly Roman Catholic country, and as such it celebrates holy days with festivals. During the month of July, many towns in Italy observe the feast day of Mary Magdalene with festivities ranging from one day to a full week. Related events include musical programs, outdoor street fairs with food for all tastes, and, after the sun goes down, fireworks displays. It appears that when it comes to honoring a saint, Italy really knows how to make merry!

Some of the towns that observe *Festa di Santa Maria Maddalena* (Feast of Saint Mary Magdalene) include the following:

- Casamicciola
- Atrani
- Torre San Giovanni
- Busana
- Umbria

In the small town of Paulilatino in the Sardinian region of Italy, the feast of Mary Magdalene is celebrated with displays of horsemanship; first a procession, then exhibitions, folk dancing, shows, and plays, in addition to a local crafts fair.

Serbia and Kosovo: An Unusual Acknowledgment

Kosovo might not be the place that comes immediately to mind when thinking about Mary Magdalene. There is a fascinating epic poem called *The Maiden of Kosovo* that begs closer examination as a work related to Mary Magdalene. Although the main character of the poem, the Maiden, is never named as Mary Magdalene, the figure is quite definitely influenced by her legends. The poem, along with others in the cycle, has become a symbol of Serb national identity.

To truly understand the importance of *The Maiden of Kosovo*, it's necessary to discuss a little bit of its history. The current circumstances in the Balkan region are highly charged

It Is Written

On a Sunday early in the morning
The Maid of Kosovo awoke to brilliant sun ...

—from *The Maiden of Kosovo*, translated by John Matthias and Vladeta Vuckovic with political, ethnic, and religious controversy, and it is far beyond the scope of this book to go into too much detail. It is only how Mary Magdalene's legends became imprinted on a nationalist poem that concerns us here.

Six hundred years ago, in the late fourteenth century, the Ottoman Empire, which was Muslim, was rapidly expanding due to military conquests. The Balkan areas that hadn't yet fallen to the Turks were part of the Byzantine Empire, the birthplace of Eastern Orthodox Christianity. In 1389, a sultan named Murad led the Turkish army against Serbia, the region in which Kosovo resides. A Serb prince named Lazar brought together an allied military force to defend against the Turkish onslaught, and they met at a place called *Kosovo Polje* ("field of the blackbirds").

Both sides fought fiercely, and much blood was shed. At some point during the battle, a Serb noble named Milos Obilic, posing as a deserter, was able to infiltrate the Turkish ranks and kill Sultan Murad. Unfortunately, Murad's son took command of his father's army and led them to victory. Prince Lazar was killed on the field of battle and Serbia was lost to the Ottoman Empire.

This is where *The Maiden of Kosovo* enters the picture. For centuries, a number of "heroic ballads" have been passed through oral tradition commemorating the loss Serbia suffered in 1389. In the poems, Prince Lazar is cast as a Jesus figure, with 12 disciples and even a betrayer. One of the poems in the cycle is *The Maiden of Kosovo*.

In the poem, a woman wanders amid the bodies of soldiers fallen on the battlefield. She is carrying bread and two golden cups, one of which contains wine, and the other water. When she finds a soldier still living, she cools him with the water, and gives him wine and bread "as if in sacrament." Finally she ministers thus to a man who asks her why she wanders through such a place of death. Was she looking for a brother? A father? So she tells her story.

Illuminations

The Maiden also makes an appearance in one of the other poems in the cycle, called *Musich Stefan*. In this poem, a man leaving for the battle sees her carrying a golden goblet in each hand and a helmet from a fallen soldier under her arm.

Before marching off to battle, Prince Lazar had all of his soldiers go to church to receive communion. She happened to be standing in the doorway when three great warriors came in. As they passed, each warrior gave her an object to remember him by. Milos, the first, gave her a colorful cloak. The second warrior, Ivan Kosancic, gave her a golden ring. Each of the first two men said that when they returned, they would be groomsmen in her wedding to their friend, the third warrior, Toplica Milan. When Toplica

Milan passed her, he called her his beloved, and gave her a golden bracelet. And so it was that the Maiden of Kosovo was on the field of battle searching for her bridegroom.

The soldier to whom she tells her story then reveals that all three warriors were killed in battle, and points out where their bodies lie. He advises her to return home lest her clothing become covered with blood. She does as he says, and then wails:

> O pity, pity! I am cursed so utterly
> That if I touched a greenly leafing tree
> it would dry and wither, blighted and defiled.

The similarities that the Maiden of Kosovo bears to Mary Magdalene are subtle, but still recognizable.

Parallels Between the Maiden of Kosovo and Mary Magdalene

Maiden of Kosovo	Mary Magdalene
Golden cups	Ointment jar
Searching for her beloved on the battlefield	Searching for her beloved in the garden
Tears, lamentations	Famous for her weeping and laments in the Middle Ages
Is cast as a bride	Bride of Christ/Shulamite woman
Symbol for Serbia	Symbol for the Church
Went to the battlefield early on a Sunday	Went to the tomb early the day after the Sabbath
Associated with the "Serbian Golgotha"	Witnessed the crucifixion on the original Golgotha

The Maiden of Kosovo, as I've mentioned, has become a Serbian national symbol. Each year Serbia observes Vidovdan, the feast day commemorating the 1389 Battle of Kosovo, and the Maiden is never far from thought. Perhaps one of the most postmodern manifestations of this nationalist pride is in popular culture. Serbia, like many countries all over the world, has beauty pageants to select the loveliest woman to represent the nation. Unlike other countries, though, Miss Serbia receives the weighty title "Maiden of Kosovo" for a year.

Philippines: The Meeting of Cultures

Although the primary celebration of Kawit, a small Filipino town, is an observation of the Nativity of Jesus on December 24, their patron saint is Mary Magdalene. A beautiful wooden image of her stands in the parish church, but although influenced by the Spanish images marched in procession during Holy Week, it has a slightly different look. Kawit's St. Mary Magdalene has very light skin and long black hair, with deep, dark eyes. Contrasting against her fair complexion are scarlet robes embroidered with gold. She holds an ornate golden ointment jar.

The Least You Need to Know

◆ Mary Magdalene's feast day is observed in many places all around the world.

◆ Celebrations in which Mary Magdalene is honored reflect local cultures and traditions.

◆ Several places claim to have had visits from Mary Magdalene in the years after the crucifixion.

◆ Mary Magdalene is sometimes honored indirectly through her inspiration of other legends.

Part 4

The Gnostic Mary Magdalene

For more than a thousand years, the only way anyone had heard of Gnosticism, a branch of early Christianity, was through the writings of people who didn't like it. So it wasn't until the 1800s, when a few important Gnostic texts were first discovered, that anyone suspected how important Mary Magdalene had been to this early competitor of mainstream Christian thought. Not only had she been important, but a whole gospel had been named after her.

For about 500 years, until finally being eradicated, the Gnostics gave the Christian "church fathers" a run for their money. Mary Magdalene was there in the beginning of the movement and in the end. At some points in between, she was held up as a symbol of Gnosticism's struggle to survive in opposition to the new orthodox Christianity. In this, too, then, she was at the root of controversy, which never seems to be too far away where Mary Magdalene is concerned.

What Is Gnosticism?

In This Chapter

- ◆ A different kind of Christianity
- ◆ Sophia and other figures in Gnostic mythology
- ◆ Schools of Gnostic thought that are no more
- ◆ Arguments that preserved history
- ◆ Gnosticism today

Before we can develop any real understanding of Mary Magdalene's importance in Gnosticism, we first have to understand what Gnosticism is. With the exception of a brief definition in Chapter 1, this might be the first time you've ever run into the term. Or it's possible that you've heard of Gnosticism but don't really know what it's all about. Here we take a look at what it is, some of the most basic Gnostic ideas, and how we've come to know about them.

Many people have the impression that Gnosticism is something separate from Christianity, which is not entirely true. It's different from Christianity as we know it today, but back in the early days, Gnosticism was only one of many branches of Christian thought. And as we will learn in this chapter, the variation between the different groups classified as "gnostic" was extreme. Some, but not all, Gnostic groups held Mary Magdalene in very high regard as a woman who understood Jesus' message better than anyone else.

Gnosticism in a Nutshell

In the early centuries of Christianity, many different interpretations of Jesus' teachings sprang up. Remember that there was no central authority that rubber-stamped ideas as official doctrine; there were only people passing stories along to one another. If they were lucky, they had access to some of the people who may have known Jesus, but most Christians were far away from what had happened, and therefore needed to depend on missionaries to tell them what it all meant. Some of the interpretations of Jesus' teachings didn't gain much support, and therefore dwindled away quietly. Others grew rapidly in popularity and became fully fledged branches of Christianity.

Gnosticism was one of those different interpretations of Jesus' teachings. Actually, it was a whole set of different interpretations that just get classified together because they share a certain central idea: the pursuit of *gnosis* (pronounced KNOW-sis), which means "knowledge." Gnosis isn't some everyday kind of knowledge, though, like knowing where you parked your car outside the supermarket or knowing your spouse's favorite color. Gnosis is a special spiritual knowledge that's something like what we might call "revelation." It is a deeply understood spiritual insight into the true meaning and nature of things.

Illuminations

Some scholars have dated the Gnostic *Gospel of Thomas* as early as 50 C.E. That would place it in the same time frame *or before* Mark, the earliest of the four canonical Gospels. The majority opinion, though, is that it was written in the mid-second century.

By most accounts, the seeds of Gnostic thought existed even before Christianity came along. Influences included Asian, Greek, Babylonian, and Syrian religions, astrology, and Judaism. Christianity combined with Greek philosophy—such as Platonism and Stoicism—and this highly syncretic mix of influences sparked a religious movement that rivaled the more orthodox branch of Christianity. As early as the late first century, Gnostic Christian teachings started to be written down.

It didn't take the legalization of Christianity in the Roman Empire for disagreements to begin about what the *true* teachings of Jesus had been, and several early Christian theologians argued harshly against Gnosticism. In fact, until the twentieth century, most of what we knew about Gnosticism was based on texts written against it.

What was it that these men found so disagreeable about Gnosticism?

For the most part, it was the fact that Gnostics believed that humans contained within themselves part of the Divine (God), and that they had it within their own power to achieve salvation. This was a radical departure from the emerging orthodoxy, which taught that salvation was only obtainable by the grace of God through the sacrifice of his son, Jesus. Gnosticism was also extremely tolerant of other religious views, and was known to be more accepting of women's involvement. Orthodox Christianity and Gnostic Christianity were set for a major clash of ideologies.

As orthodox Christianity gained a solid foothold in the empire, Gnosticism was labeled a heresy and efforts were undertaken to root it out. By the fifth century C.E., Gnosticism was almost completely destroyed. Since the recent discovery and publication of Gnostic texts, however, Gnostic Christianity is once again being explored as an alternative to mainstream Christianity.

> **It Is Written** _____
>
> Gnosticism wasn't *completely* destroyed. Mandaeism, often classified as a form of Gnosticism, survived through to the modern era. Worldwide, there are fewer than 100,000 Mandaeans practicing today, and they are concentrated mostly in Iraq and Iran.

Gnostic Mythology

Because Gnosticism was based at least in part on individual revelations, there were a great many sects and a great many texts describing a great many ideas. As a result, several different versions of the central Gnostic myth were recorded. It would take a much longer book to introduce all of them, so let's just take a look at some of the most basic ideas.

The Creation of the World

The Gnostic creation myth is a fascinating, and to many people foreign, set of concepts. It begins with the idea of God, not God as we have come to understand him through the past 2,000 years of Christianity, but God as a completely transcendent entity, unknowable through our limited human senses. This God—sometimes called the One, the Divine, the Source, the Unknowable, or the Good—created a series of lesser beings called Aeons.

Aeons were principles, or basic spiritual elements, such as Truth, Faith, Love, and Intelligence. They were created in pairs that would complement one another, and they all lived together harmoniously in a place called the *Pleroma*, which means "fullness." The Pleroma is a little like the Gnostic version of heaven.

But according to Gnostic creation myth, one of the Aeons in the Pleroma wasn't quite content. Her name was Sophia, a Greek word that means "wisdom," and she wanted to know where she had come from. So earnestly did she strive to know her origin that she created another being from within herself. Although he sometimes received names such as Ialdaboth, her child was often just referred to as the *Demiurge*, which means "craftsman" or "creator."

It Is Written

And when [Sophia] saw the consequences of her desire, it changed into a form of a lion-faced serpent. And its eyes were like lightning fires which flash. She cast it away from her, outside that place, that no one of the immortal ones might see it, for she had created it in ignorance. And she surrounded it with a luminous cloud, and she placed a throne in the middle of the cloud that no one might see it except the holy Spirit who is called the mother of the living. And she called his name [Ialdaboth].

—*The Apocryphon of John*, second century C.E. Gnostic text

Because the Demiurge was created accidentally, he was flawed. He was also completely unaware of how he had come into existence, and not knowing about his mother, Sophia, the Aeons, the Pleroma, or the transcendent God who had created them all, he mistakenly thought that *he* was everything there was to be. He thought *he* was God. And so, as God, he decided to create the universe, which he did in seven days.

Does this sound familiar? To the Gnostics, the God of the Jewish scriptures was the flawed being known as the Demiurge. Depending on the Gnostic group, the Demiurge was a tragic but benign figure or an evil alien deity. Jealous, fitful, and prone to genocidal rages, the Demiurge was more like a petulant child in need of discipline than a benevolent fatherlike creator.

Sophia, seeing the mess that the Demiurge was making, knew she was responsible for his actions, and she wasn't very well regarded by her fellow Aeons. She was shamed as a result, so she set about trying to make things right. She sent a small spark of herself into each human so that they might awaken to their divine heritage, shake off the fetters of the physical world in which the Demiurge had trapped them, and ascend to their true home, the Pleroma.

The Garden of Eden

One of the ways that Sophia was able to accomplish her mission of imbuing humanity with her spark of wisdom was through the familiar scene in the Garden of Eden. The Gnostics also viewed this as a pivotal event in the history of humankind, but not in the same way as their Jewish and orthodox Christian counterparts.

The tree that God (as the Demiurge) told Adam and Eve to avoid was the tree of the knowledge of good and evil. In other words, the Gnostics reasoned, the creator God wanted humans to remain in ignorance, which was a bad, oppressive thing. Sophia went into the Garden of Eden, made an appearance as a serpent, and convinced Eve to eat the fruit from the tree. This Sophia did to free humans from the bondage of ignorance forced on them by the Demiurge. Each human who came afterward therefore *benefited* from Eve's disobedience by having the ability to discern between good and evil.

In some Gnostic texts, Sophia doesn't make the trip to Earth in order to give humans wisdom. In these versions, humans as created by the Demiurge are rather robotic and dull creatures until Sophia sends part of herself into them. This part of herself is called *Zöe*, which means "life."

Jesus' Role

At this point, I'm sure you can see why Gnosticism was considered a heresy, but it gets even better. There are a number of opinions about exactly what Jesus' role was in Gnostic theology, and how he may have functioned as a redeemer. In general, though, Gnostics seem to have believed that Jesus' role wasn't as a sacrificial lamb, but as a revealer come to kindle the spark of divinity that lay smoldering within every person. He was crucified and resurrected to demonstrate that everyone was able to achieve eternal life.

Some Gnostics thought that Jesus wasn't human at all, but only *seemed* to be human, and therefore didn't suffer the pain of death during the crucifixion. Some Gnostics believed that Jesus and Christ were separate beings; Jesus was the human and Christ was the spiritual principle that enabled him to do great things. Others describe Jesus

Lingua Magda

In its most simple definition, **logos** is Greek for "word." It has more complex connotations associated with "reason," both as humans experience it as a drive to know the Divine and as a universal principle that could describe "the mind of God."

as becoming the Christ when Sophia or another Aeon called *Logos* descended on him at his baptism.

Although there were many different interpretations of Jesus' exact nature and what the crucifixion and resurrection really meant, it usually was seen as a spiritual allegory more than literal, historical fact. By following Jesus' (or the Christ's, depending on how you looked at it) example, some Gnostics believed that humans could symbolically die to the physical world and "resurrect" through knowledge of the Christ within.

Matter: The World We Live In

Much has been written recently about how Gnostics believed the world was evil. Indeed, some of them did, but it's not quite as simple as that. The universe and everything in it, as a flawed creation of the Demiurge, was made up of *matter:* the physical stuff of existence. Humans, containing the spark of wisdom that connected them to the Divine, were ignorant to the fact that they weren't really the walking, talking bags of flesh that they identified as Self, and this was the primary problem.

Some Gnostics wanted nothing whatsoever to do with the material world, and did whatever possible to break their ties to it, including refusing to have sex or procreate.

Illuminations

The 1999 movie *The Matrix* (and its sequels) is built around very Gnostic themes, particularly that the world humans move around in from day to day is an illusion, and that there is a deeper truth to which they must awaken. In the film, a character named Trinity plays a Mary Magdalene-like role as the woman who loves the savior figure, Neo.

They were therefore not introducing any more people into a flawed world and doing as little as possible to link themselves to it. Still other Gnostics took a slightly less-strident view and felt that the only real problem with matter was that people tended to be caught up in the concerns of this world rather than awakening to spiritual truth. Regardless, matter was, in one way or another, a trap to be escaped.

Some Gnostic texts give the impression that a person could only truly be free after they achieved gnosis and subsequently died, thereby breaking free from the world of matter completely. However, still other Gnostics took Jesus' words "the kingdom of heaven is here" as a message that spiritual transcendence was achievable in this life, in this body, right here and now; that *freedom* is *within*.

Archons

I've already mentioned the archons in Chapter 7, in the discussion about Mary Magdalene's seven demons. The archons were the rulers of the levels of heaven, which were often viewed in very abstract ways; they weren't necessarily literal places, but modes of consciousness and subtle levels of existence. The archons, in general, were viewed as principles that conspired to prevent humans from escaping their earthly prison, and the task of the Gnostic was to overcome their influence.

Schools of Gnostic Thought

There were many, many different Gnostic teachers, many groups of varying sizes, and almost just as many texts. Here we take a look at only a few of the biggest Gnostic Christian systems to become popular in the early centuries C.E.

Basilidians: One Unknowable God

Very little is known about Basilides (pronounced "bah-SILL-ih-dees"), for whom this Gnostic sect is named. He was alive during the second century, but we don't know when he was born or when he died. Basilides was from Alexandria, in Egypt, and was therefore familiar with Egyptian and classical Greek, or *Hellenistic*, thought. He was a scholar who was also well acquainted with Jewish thought and Christian teachings. Almost none of Basilides's writings survive today, so it is from other writers of his era that we learn about his teachings.

To Basilides, there was one unknowable God who was distant from human experience and who created many different orders of beings and angels. He created five different Aeons: *Nous* ("mind") or Christ, *Logos* ("word"), *Phronesis* ("prudence"), *Sophia* ("wisdom"), and *Dynamis* ("power"). Sophia and Dynamis had a kind of illicit love affair, which resulted in the creation of 365 angelic beings. These angels governed 365 heavens (which correspond to the days of the year), and it was they who were responsible for the creation of the material universe. And so humankind was born. The ruler of this lower class of angels was Abraxas, who was the equivalent of the Jewish God.

The unknowable God at the beginning of the story (otherwise known as "God the Father") sent Christ-Nous ("mind") to earth to illuminate humans to their plight and to assist them in breaking free from their bondage under Abraxas. This was done through Jesus. Basilides's teachings had a decidedly *docetic* angle; Jesus was never crucified, he only appeared to be crucified. In reality, Basilides taught, the Romans crucified Simon of Cyrene, the man who had carried Jesus' cross for him. Meanwhile, the Christ-Nous returned to God the Father.

Marcionites: Two Antithetical Forces

The theologies developed by the man Marcion in the second century turned into one of the longest-lasting and most widely spread of the Gnostic schools. It was robust enough to withstand several centuries of persecution and had taken root not only in urban environments but also in rural communities; in places, entire villages were Marcionite.

Marcion's ideas are not entirely Gnostic in the strictest sense, but he is usually included in discussions of Gnosticism because of the many similarities in his theology.

The primary motivation behind Marcion's philosophy is an absolute division between the God of the law as presented in the Jewish scriptures and the God of salvation as revealed through the Gospels and the apostle Paul's teachings. Marcion saw these two beings as diametrically opposed to one another, with no reconciliation between the two. Jesus' mission on earth took place pretty much as written in the Gospels, but the reason was to free humankind from the despotic rule of the creator God.

Of all the early Gnostic groups, Marcion was the first to establish a real church. He even put together a canon of texts that included an edited Gospel of Luke and several Pauline letters. His compilation had an influence on the orthodox Church's later selection of the texts that would make up the Christian New Testament. Marcion's teachings were softened somewhat by his later students, but the main idea of two antithetical forces remained.

Valentinians: A Mystical Approach

Also in the second century, a Christian teacher named Valentinus started to dissemi-
nate Gnostic concepts. He was a functional part of the mainstream Christianity of
his time, and was even considered for the post of bishop of Rome (an office which
was later to be called "pope"). Valentinus was born and educated in Alexandria around
the same time that Basilides would have been teaching there; it's not known exactly
how Valentinus developed his ideas, but they do appear to be influenced by Basilidian
thinking.

At the root of Valentinus's teaching was the
thought that one could practice the orthodox
Christianity but also take a more mystical
approach to uncover truths that lay hidden
within the words. He believed the teachings
of Christianity could be interpreted through a
knowledge of other non-Christian philosophies
to gain insight and reveal obscured truths. By
doing so, Valentinus developed much of the
mythology that has come to define classical
Gnosticism, some of which was described earlier in this chapter.

It Is Written

Mysticism today often con-
jures up images of fortune tellers,
crystal balls, and psychic detec-
tives. In its original meaning,
however, mysticism describes an
immediate, personal experience
of transcendence or an insight
into the nature of God.

Valentinus also developed in his theology the notion of salvation through gnosis of
the savior, the self, and God. It was a very mystical approach to the question of
redemption, and it was to have a long-lasting influence on non-Christian and Christian thinking alike. The medieval Christian mystics and monastic orders owe at least
a small debt to Valentinian thought.

How the Early Church Fathers Viewed Gnosticism

The men who have come to be known as the "Church fathers," those who developed
much of the earliest Christian theology, lived during the time when Gnosticism was
an active branch of their own religion. Here we take a brief look at some of the men
who wrote about Gnosticism and what their own experiences were with the belief system they called a "heresy."

Irenaeus

As a young man living in Smyrna (near Ephesus) in the early second century, Irenaeus had the opportunity to hear a fellow named Polycarp speak, who in turn as a young man had heard the apostle John speak. Irenaeus was thus only two generations from a witness to Jesus' life, and he was an extremely important early influence on Christianity. He became the bishop of Lyon in southern Gaul in 178 C.E., and committed a great deal of effort to writing against Gnosticism.

His most important work was written around 185 C.E., called *Against Heresies.* In it, Irenaeus detailed the Gnostic ideas circulating at the time, and contrasted them against the true teachings of the Church. He discussed the unity of God as opposed to the duality of the creator God and the unknowable God of the Gnostics. He also referred to the four Gospels, those that we know now, as complete and divinely inspired, contrary to Marcion's heavily edited Gospel of Luke. Until the discovery of more Gnostic texts in the twentieth century, most of what we knew of Gnosticism was from Irenaeus' writings.

> **Illuminations** _____
>
> Who you knew was very important in early Christianity, because the validity of your teaching depended on whether or not you received it from a source close to Jesus. Therefore, something called *apostolic succession* developed; an apostle taught somebody, who taught somebody else, who in turn taught somebody else, and so on. Authority was granted based on the perceived legitimacy of a person's line back to Jesus. The modern Roman Catholic Church claims an apostolic succession back to Peter.

Tertullian

The other writer from whom we were able to learn about the Gnostics was Tertullian, another extremely important early Christian theologian. Born around 160 C.E., he lived in Carthage in North Africa and was educated as a lawyer. He converted to Christianity in 195, and began writing texts to defend his religion at a time when Christians were being persecuted. Tertullian was the first person to use the term "trinity" to describe the nature of God: Father, Son, and Holy Spirit. His writings on the doctrine of original sin and Jesus' nature as both human and divine would be highly influential in later years.

To give you some idea of the volume of work Tertullian produced against Gnosticism, here are some of his titles:

♦ *Against All Heresies*

♦ *Against the Valentinians*

♦ *Prescription Against Heretics*

♦ *Five Books Against Marcion*

It Is Written

What indeed has Athens to do with Jerusalem? What concord is there between the Academy and the Church? what between heretics and Christians?
—Tertullian, *Prescription Against Heretics*, Chapter VII

Tertullian also, then, was a valuable source of knowledge about Gnosticism when few Gnostic texts were available to speak for themselves.

Clement of Alexandria

Born in 150 C.E., Clement was probably from Athens originally, and then settled in Alexandria after making many travels and explorations for spiritual and philosophical truth. Where Tertullian was profoundly practical and puritanical, Clement was speculative and intellectual. In 190 C.E., Clement succeeded as the head of a school teaching Christian principles that would eventually be passed on to the famous theologian Origen, his student.

Clement of Alexandria never produced the volumes of anti-Gnostic writings that Tertullian did, but he did argue against their teachings. At the same time, his writings are thought to resemble Gnostic teachings in certain ways; his works described a "true gnosis" to which Christians should aspire. In spite of using similar language as some of the Gnostics, he argued that creation wasn't the product of a flawed Demiurge, defended the Jewish scriptures, and rejected the duality inherent in Gnostic teaching.

Hippolytus

The same Hippolytus that brought us the influential commentary on *Song of Songs* in which Mary Magdalene was given some of her legendary identities also wrote against Gnosticism. Although we don't know when Hippolytus was born, we do know that he lived during the last part of the second century C.E. He has been identified as an anti-pope, that is, a man who claimed that the papal chair was legitimately his even though someone else was elected to the office. He was sent into exile on the island of

Illuminations

The name *Hippolytus* means "loosed horse." There is a legend that he died by being torn to pieces by horses, but it is thought that this is a confusion between him and a Greek legend about Hippolytus, son of Theseus, who was killed in the same manner. Perhaps not surprisingly, Hippolytus the Church father became the patron saint of horses and riders.

Sardinia, where he died in 236. Because his remains were returned to Rome and he was commemorated as a martyr, we can suppose that he was eventually reconciled with the Church sometime before his death.

Toward the end of his life he wrote an important work titled *A Refutation of All Heresies,* in which he detailed some of the Gnostic ideas prevalent at the time. In the second part of the book, he gives a description of 33 different Gnostic systems. He suggests that the Gnostics developed their philosophies not based on Christianity but on the "wisdom of the heathen."

Modern Gnosticism

Since the discovery of a cache of Gnostic documents near Nag Hammadi, Egypt in 1945, interest has been steadily growing in the early ideas that rivaled orthodox Christianity in popularity. The term "gnostic" itself has come to describe wildly differing belief systems, ranging from what could be considered New Age spirituality to alternative Christianity. Right or wrong, many people are eager to describe their religion as a "gnostic" one, meaning that it is based on revealed knowledge rather than on literalism and dogma.

One group in southern California, called Ecclesia Gnostica, has developed a fully functional Gnostic church reconstructed from the many classical Gnostic texts and set into a "high-church" framework based on Anglican rituals. Overseen by Bishop Stephan Hoeller, the Ecclesia Gnostica is the sacramental-liturgical arm of an organization called the Gnostic Society, which aims to further the understanding and study of Gnosticism. There are four branches of the Gnostic Society in the United States and one in Norway.

Gnosticism is a growing religious trend in the United States and new religious groups are springing up all of the time that base their teachings in whole or in part on the ancient Gnostic texts.

The Least You Need to Know

- Gnosticism's most fundamental ideas are dualism between matter and spirit, and salvation based on spiritual knowledge.

- Sophia, or wisdom, was a central figure in Gnostic myth, and was personified as female.

- The Gnostic Jesus came to save humankind by imparting wisdom, not by shedding his blood.

- There were many different schools of Gnostic thought, some of which were more similar than others.

- Until the twentieth century, most of what we knew of Gnosticism came from the early Church fathers who wrote against it as heresy.

- Since the rediscovery of some Gnostic texts in 1945, Gnostic ideas have begun to appear more frequently in modern religious expressions.

Chapter 14

Paper Treasures

In This Chapter

- ◆ Good things come in dusty packages
- ◆ The sayings of Jesus
- ◆ Some questions are better than others
- ◆ More variations on Mary's name
- ◆ Honorable mentions

The discovery of Gnostic texts in 1945 could read like a scene in a movie. An ordinary man who is otherwise going about his business stumbles across a buried jar. He hesitates before breaking it for fear it may contain evil spirits, the *jinn*, but eventually his curiosity and the lure of golden treasure within leads him to raise his digging tool and let it fall onto the clay vessel. Now we see the man's eyes open wide as he waits for the dust to clear and we hold our breath. Is it an evil spirit? Is it a treasure?

Although we usually think of "treasure" as something gold and sparkling, the dusty pages discovered in Egypt in the mid-twentieth century are as priceless as treasures come. In this chapter we take a look not only at the legendary discovery of the Nag Hammadi Library, the cache of books found in 1945, but other Gnostic texts whose discoveries were less sensational.

The Nag Hammadi Library

The cache of Gnostic documents that has gotten by far the most publicity is the Nag Hammadi Library. In December 1945, an Arab man named Mohammed Ali Samman was digging in a mountainous area near his village, looking for mineral-rich soil to use as fertilizer. To his surprise, he uncovered a large, red earthenware jar, which he broke open. What lay inside didn't look like treasure as we would normally imagine it, but it was valuable almost beyond estimation.

> **Lingua Magda**
>
> **Coptic** is a late Egyptian language written mostly in Greek characters. Today, the Coptic language survives as a liturgical language in the Coptic Orthodox Church.

The jar contained papyrus texts that were arranged in codices, books bound in leather, not scrolls. They were written in *Coptic*, and weren't the original documents; all of them had been copied from older Greek texts. Some of the books in the cache were already known to us, such as the *Gospel of Thomas* and Plato's *Republic*, but most were new discoveries.

The Nag Hammadi Library, as it became known, is composed of 52 different texts contained in 13 codices. They had been gathered together and buried in the jar around the year 390, probably by a monk from a nearby monastery. Earlier in the fourth century, a group of Christian bishops gathered for a landmark event called the Council of Nicaea, during which some of the most basic doctrines of the Christian faith were established.

This unification of Christianity led to a more organized destruction of alternative Christian ideas, and many texts were burned. It's likely that whoever buried the Nag Hammadi Library did so to preserve the wisdom contained in the texts, although I'm sure he didn't think that it would take almost 1,600 years for them to be discovered again!

> **Lingua Magda**
>
> Around the first century, a new school of religious and philosophical thought called **Hermetism** grew up around the mythical figure of Hermes Trismegistus. Hermetism and its modern descendent, **Hermeticism,** have much in common with Gnostic thought.

The kinds of documents included in the Nag Hammadi Library are varied. Among the texts are Gnostic, *Hermetic*, and apocryphal texts, and a rewriting of Plato's *Republic*. One of the most fascinating things about the discovery is that it gave us some insight not only into Gnostic thought itself, but also into the kinds of writings that were influencing Gnostic thought. The discovery was also important to scholars who study the origins of books; the Nag Hammadi Library contained some of the oldest bound books known to exist.

After discovering the texts in the jar, Mohammed Ali Samman took them back home. Without realizing their worth, he put them on a stack of kindling used by his mother for the cooking fire. We don't know how many pages were lost, burned, or thrown away, but there are several gaps in the texts that could have been caused in this way.

At some point unknown to us, Mohammed Ali Samman must have begun to think the texts had some value. His family was involved in a blood feud at the time, and he eventually entrusted his find to a local priest. The priest then sent a sample of the texts to an Egyptian historian.

After passing through a few hands, all the books except one ended up at the Coptic Museum in Cairo, where they received the care due such historical treasures. The last book was sold on the black market and ended up being purchased as a birthday gift for the late psychologist Carl Gustav Jung. That particular book is still known today as the Jung Codex.

In 1977, the Nag Hammadi texts were published together for the first time in English, after being translated by a group of scholars organized by a biblical scholar named James M. Robinson. The texts of the Nag Hammadi find were included together with texts that had been discovered in the late nineteenth century, including the *Gospel of Mary*. (We'll take a closer look at the *Gospel of Mary* in the next chapter.)

Mary Magdalene is an important figure in many of the Nag Hammadi texts. Not only is she mentioned in the roles given to her in the canonical Gospels, the Gnostics place much more importance on her as a companion of Jesus. Some of the Nag Hammadi texts that included references to Mary Magdalene are as follows:

- The *Gospel of Philip*
- The *Gospel of Thomas*
- The *Gospel of Mary*
- The *Sophia of Jesus Christ* (as Mariamne)
- The *Dialogue of the Savior* (as Mariam)

We take a more detailed look at how Mary Magdalene appears in the Gnostic texts in Chapter 16.

Quite Contrary

The "Sophia" of Jesus Christ? Although Sophia is a women's name, it is also the Greek word for "wisdom." So the text is also known as *The Wisdom of Jesus Christ*.

The *Gospel of Thomas*

In the late nineteenth century, some papyrus fragments were found on a garbage heap at a place called Oxyrhynchus, modern-day Bahnasa, Egypt. They were written in Greek and appeared to belong to none of the ancient texts that were then known to have survived. All anyone could do was speculate on what the rest of the text might be. In 1920, Hugh G. Evelyn-White published *The Sayings of Jesus from Oxyrhynchus*, and suggested that the fragments could be part of a text called the *Gospel of Thomas*.

When the Nag Hammadi cache was found, the second codex contained a text called the *Gospel of Thomas*, and after being translated, it was evident that it matched the fragments found at Oxyrhynchus. The *Gospel of Thomas* was made up of sayings, or *logia*, of Jesus, a kind of document that had been theorized to exist by New Testament scholars, but had up until then never been seen.

One of the ways that people passed on Jesus' wisdom in the earliest days of Christianity was through easy-to-remember sayings rather than long stories like the ones contained in the Gospels. Eventually, people started compiling lists of these sayings, and the *Gospel of Thomas* is one example of that kind of document, with 114 separate sayings. Although the Coptic text itself probably dates back to the fourth century, it contains material that could be contemporary to or earlier than the canonical Gospels.

Within Christianity, there have been different "traditions" that honored one particular apostolic figure as patron and revealer of Jesus' message more than others. The best-known examples are Pauline and Johannine Christianity, but there are several others in early Christianity that are less well understood. One of these is the Thomas tradition. Legend holds that Thomas was the founder of the church at Edessa in Syria, which appears to have been the center of the tradition. Many texts written in Thomas' name originated from this region, including the following:

It Is Written

Split a piece of wood; I am there.
Lift up the stone, and you will find me there.

—From the *Gospel of Thomas*

- The *Gospel of Thomas*
- *The Book of Thomas the Contender*
- The *Acts of Thomas*

Mary Magdalene, as we will see, was also the source of an early Christian tradition, something we look at in the next chapter. Within the Thomas tradition, however, there is one very important saying about Mary Magdalene:

> Simon Peter said to Jesus, "Let Mary leave us, for women are not worthy of life."

> Jesus said, "I myself shall lead her in order to make her male, so that she too may become a living spirit resembling you males. For every woman who will make herself male will enter the kingdom of heaven."

This particular saying is number 114, the very last in the collection. It has been suggested that because some of the language in saying 114 is inconsistent with the rest of the *Gospel of Thomas* that it was added to the text at a later date. Regardless of its place within the text, however, I'm sure you will agree the saying is provocative for a couple of reasons. First, Peter is displaying some kind of serious problem not only with Mary Magdalene, but with women in general. Second, what on earth could Jesus have meant by women making themselves males?! (We'll take a closer look at Peter's problem with Mary Magdalene in Chapter 15, but it's important to take a look here at what Jesus may have meant in this controversial saying.)

Although to our modern sensibilities, the notion of a woman needing to become male is reasonably shocking, remember that two thousand years ago the metaphors that were used to describe spiritual states were much different. Jesus wasn't talking about a literal change of sex for Mary Magdalene and all women; he was referring to the common Hellenistic attribution of things that relate to the material world as feminine and things that relate to the spiritual world as male. The saying appears chauvinistic on the surface, but when examined next to other writings of the time, it was a statement of liberation; Jesus was saying that women are included in the group of people who can achieve gnosis and, thereby, salvation. Everyone, including women, must release their material, passionate natures in favor of a more enlightened heavenly, intellectual nature.

Pistis Sophia

In the late eighteenth century, Dr. A. Askew, an Englishman, discovered a Coptic book in a London bookshop. He paid 10 pounds for it and took it home. The British Museum acquired the codex after his death, and thereafter it came to be known as

Lingua Magda

The literal translation of the Greek words *pistis sophia* is "faith-wisdom."

Codex Askewianus. In the mid-nineteenth century the text was translated into German, followed by other languages. A Gnostic scholar named G. R. S. Mead translated it into English in 1896, and although the title mentioned in the books themselves is *Books of the Savior,* it came to be known by its alternate title, *Pistis Sophia.*

The *Pistis Sophia* is made up of four separate books. The first three are clearly meant to go together, but the fourth is older than the others and shows important differences that lead scholars to think that it should stand on its own as a separate book. Still, Mead published translations of all four books together, and so they have all come to be known collectively.

The text itself is based on the premise that after the resurrection, Jesus remained with his disciples for 11 years, teaching them and guiding them in the way of gnosis. They are gathered together on the Mount of Olives, having a conversation. The disciples ask Jesus questions, and through his answers he shares his wisdom with them. His teachings include the idea that humankind possesses a portion of the Divine within themselves, and that his role is to help people realize their true natures and the importance of awakening to the mysteries of salvation.

Illuminations

Medieval mystical Jews, called Kabbalists, had a similar belief to that of Sophia's fallen aspect. To them, the "presence of God," or the *Shekinah,* was personified as female. She was viewed as remaining in exile with the Jewish people. The Kabbalists were influenced by the Gnostics in several areas.

Humans' souls are gendered as feminine, and associated with Sophia in her fallen state, when she was alienated from her true home in the Pleroma. Sophia is seen as living in exile, as are humans; Jesus' task, therefore, is to inspire people to actively pursue spiritual awakening until they have gained gnosis. Then they (and Sophia) will be able to return from their exile in the world of matter.

Mary Magdalene plays an important role in *Pistis Sophia* as a kind of human reflection of Sophia. The text portrays her as one who has gained such wisdom and insight that she surpasses all of the other disciples in understanding Jesus' teachings. Jesus refers to her many times in glowing terms, such as the following:

- Blessed one
- She whose heart is more directed to the Kingdom of Heaven than all her brothers

♦ Blessed beyond all women upon earth

♦ All-blessed Pleroma, who will be blessed among all generations

♦ Blessed one who wilt inherit the whole Kingdom of the Light

These aren't nicknames that were bestowed lightly, to be sure. The text dates back to the third or fourth century; by then there was certainly evidence of a Mary Magdalene tradition, much like the Thomas tradition already mentioned. Mary Magdalene had become a figure of vital importance to Gnostic spirituality.

Mary, by Any Other Name

You may have noticed in the first part of this chapter that there are a couple of texts in the Nag Hammadi Library that give different forms of Mary Magdalene's name.

In many of the Gnostic texts, Mary Magdalene appears by slightly different names. Even in some non-Gnostic Christian texts that weren't included in the New Testament, her name sometimes appears in various forms. This is due in large part to the region where the text was written, local languages, and the way that names were translated. Let's take a look at some of the different spellings that all appear to refer to Mary Magdalene in some places.

Quite Contrary

Mary Magdalene's first name isn't always "Mary" in the Gospels, either. In the Greek copies, it usually appears as "Maria."

Text	Spelling
Pistis Sophia	Maria
Pistis Sophia	Mariham
Pistis Sophia	Mariam
The Dialogue of the Savior	Mariam
First Apocalypse of James	Mariam
The Sophia of Jesus Christ	Mariamne
Gospel of Mary	Mariamme*
Hippolytus	Mariamme*

Mariamme is flagged for your attention in the table for a couple of reasons. First, when you read an English translation of the *Gospel of Mary*, you won't find the spelling "Mariamme." It is only in the Greek fragments of that text where the spelling remains. Most translators only use "Mary" in their English editions.

Second, Hippolytus isn't a Gnostic text, he is a theologian who wrote against the Gnostics as we've already seen. He referred to Mariamme when he wrote about a group of Gnostics called Naassenes. We come back to that in the next section.

> **It Is Written** _____
>
> The issue of her identity in the *Gospel of Thomas* and the *Gospel of Mary* is some-what difficult to determine with so few clues in the text. Part of the justification for believing this figure to be Mary Magdalene draws on parallel controversy dialogues in which the figure in conflict is known to be her, such as the *Gospel of Philip* and *Pistis Sophia*.
> —Ann Brock, *Mary Magdalene, The First Apostle*

Because of the different spellings and the absence of her second name, "Magdalene," some people have wondered whether these really are references to Mary Magdalene. It's an excellent question. Scholars who study Gnostic texts generally agree that these do refer to Mary Magdalene because of the clear roles that she fulfilled; when a different spelling shows up in a place that would normally refer to Mary Magdalene, then it is most likely referring to her. This has been a process of taking a look at all of the known references to Mary Magdalene, comparing them, and then putting the pieces back together.

Other Gnostic Texts

Several other Gnostic texts have surfaced over the years separately from the ones we've already discussed. Let's look at a few that mention Mary Magdalene.

First Apocalypse of James

Two books called the *Apocalypse of James* were contained in the Nag Hammadi Library, and the words "first" and "second" were added just to differentiate them. They are believed to have been written by two different groups independently of one another, so other than the fact that they're both called "*Apocalypse of James*," they aren't really connected.

As one scholar has pointed out, the *First Apocalypse of James* is often overlooked in Mary Magdalene studies for a few reasons. First, the name "Mary" is used only once in the whole text. Second, it doesn't specify which Mary. And third, the text itself is so fragmented that it's hard to put together anything reasonable from the passage that contains her name.

Fortunately, the presence of another, similar text has allowed us to fill in at least a few of the blanks with reasonable certainty. The other text includes a list of women very much like the list in the *First Apocalypse of James*, and it definitely refers to Mary Magdalene. Also, the name Mary appears alongside the name Martha, and in the late second and early third century, when the text was written, Mary Magdalene was already being confused with Mary of Bethany (Martha's sister).

Different traditions grew up around the figures of the apostles who knew Jesus, and the same is the case for James. In the James tradition, he sometimes shared a close relationship with Mary Magdalene, as the two who knew and taught Jesus' message. In the *First Apocalypse of James*, we see a conversation between Jesus and James. Jesus calms James's fears about their upcoming suffering by talking about the return of man to God, who is referred to in this text as "the One Who Is."

Later in the text, Jesus reveals to James a relatively familiar schema of levels that the soul must pass through as it ascends, and gives him secrets for passing by the guardians of each level. It is in this section of the text that seven women of great perception are mentioned. There are a couple discussions of "femaleness" as inferior to "maleness," which as we've already seen is a reference to the common attribution of all things earthly to the feminine and all things eternal to the masculine.

Quite Contrary

If there are seven women of perception mentioned, why are there only four in the list? That would be an unfortunate example of missing text. All that's left of the possible list of three other names is the ending of one: "nna." It has been suggested that the letters were the ending of a name such as Joanna or Susanna.

The seven women aren't named together, but further on in the text Jesus tells James to encourage four women: Salome, Mary, Martha, and Arsinoe. We're led to believe that these four women exhibit some level of understanding that is exemplary. Later in the same paragraph we see this line:

> The perishable has gone up to the imperishable and the female element has attained to this male element.

Antti Marjanen, a professor at the University of Helsinki in Finland, has commented on the *First Apocalypse of James*. He suggests that the text may have been written for groups that included women, and one of the measures to counteract the negativity placed on femaleness was to make heroes of female disciples. In the text, their wisdom appears to be on par with James himself.

Lingua Magda

In the New Testament, mention is made of the **Paraclete**, or "helper," that will come to comfort and aid believers after Jesus departs. Based on the Gospel of John, mainstream Christianity thinks of the Paraclete as the Holy Spirit, part of a triune God. Manichaeans interpreted it differently.

Manichaean Psalms

Manichaeism, which rose in the latter half of the third century, is another religion considered to have its foundations in Gnosticism, and it spread beyond the Mediterranean region as far east as China and Tibet. Founded by a man called Mani, who considered himself to be a prophet and the *Paraclete* mentioned in the New Testament, Manichaeism was a major world religion until about the tenth century in the West.

Few Manichaean texts survive, but among those that do, there is a group called the *Manichaean Psalmbook*, dated to about the middle of the fourth century.

In the *Psalm-book*, there is a group of psalms called the *Psalms of Heracleides*. It is there that we find three psalms that refer to Mary Magdalene. Two of them only mention her name in a list of women disciples, but another includes a dialogue between Mary Magdalene and Jesus outside the tomb. In it, Jesus tells Mary Magdalene (who is called Mariamme in the text) not to touch him. Then he goes on to tell her to go rally the Eleven, who are like lost little orphans without him. Mary answers:

> Rabbi, my master, I will serve thy commandment in the joy of my whole heart.
>
> I will not give rest to my heart, I will not give sleep to my eyes, I will not
>
> Give rest to my feet until I have brought the sheep to the fold.

The text then goes on to glorify her for obeying Jesus and carrying out his instructions with joy in her heart.

Additional Mentions

A few other references that may well have been Mary Magdalene deserve to be mentioned.

Hippolytus, in his writings against the Gnostics, mentioned a group known as the Naassenes, who claimed their teachings were delivered from Jesus to James through a woman named Mariamne. As we've seen, Mariamne is another form of the name Mary, and a name Mary Magdalene has been given in other texts. Hippolytus seems to care about the good name of Mariamne, in that he includes her with Jesus and James when he criticizes the Naassenes for misrepresenting them. In Book 5, Chapter 2 of his *A Refutation of All Heresies*, he says:

> These are the heads of the numerous discourses which the Naassene asserts James the brother of the Lord handed down to Mariamne. In order then, that these impious heretics may no longer belie Mariamne or James, or the Saviour Himself ….

Evidently, Hippolytus knew who Mariamne was and felt that her good name shouldn't be sullied by the Naassenes. We don't know for certain that he was referring to Mary Magdalene, but it's very possible.

Quite Contrary

Some people have suggested that the *Second Apocalypse of James* contains a reference to Mariamne, or Mary Magdalene, also. The first sentence of the text is: "This is the discourse that James the Just spoke in Jerusalem, which Mareim, one of the priests, wrote." We could suppose that the text is somehow related to the Naassenes that Hippolytus mentioned, who received their wisdom from James through Mariamne, but the Mareim in the *Second Apocalypse of James* is later referred to as a man.

We should also visit one last reference, although it tells us little. In his book *Against Celsus* (Book 5, Chapter 61), Christian theologian and teacher Origen (185–254 C.E.) says:

> Celsus knows, moreover, certain Marcellians, so called from Marcellina, and Harpocratians from Salome, and others who derive their name from Mariamme, and others again from Martha.

We know nothing else about this sect that Origen alleges named itself after Mariamme, but there are a couple of clues that could lead us to believe it is Mary Magdalene they're referring to. As we've seen already, Mariamme is the name given to Mary Magdalene in other Gnostic texts, and in this case, her name appears right next to Martha's. At a time when Mary Magdalene was already being conflated with Mary of Bethany, this is a fascinating reference. Unfortunately, we have no other information about sects named in her honor.

The Least You Need to Know

- The Nag Hammadi Library was the biggest and most important discovery of ancient texts in recent history, and teaches us much about Gnosticism.

- The *Gospel of Thomas* is possibly a very early text and contains a controversial reference to women making themselves male.

- In *Pistis Sophia*, Mary Magdalene is the one of Jesus' followers who understands his message better than the rest.

- Mary Magdalene's name appears in many different ways in the Gnostic texts.

- Several small mentions of Mary Magdalene could tell us a lot about what Gnostic Christians thought about her.

Chapter 15

The *Gospel of Mary*

In This Chapter

- ◆ When, where, and how the *Gospel of Mary* came to be
- ◆ First in Coptic, now in English: recent books and translations
- ◆ What the *Gospel of Mary* says
- ◆ Trouble within the ranks

As of the writing of this book, there are at least four different translations of the *Gospel of Mary* available to the reading public, and at least three different books that offer commentary on it. You might be tempted to think that it's only a result of the interest in Mary Magdalene that was generated by the best-selling book *The Da Vinci Code*, but that's not the case. These translations were either published or in the works even before the publication of Dan Brown's thriller.

Why is the *Gospel of Mary* so important? For starters, it is the only known gospel named for a woman, and it speaks volumes about how women were viewed in early Christianity. It also tells us a great deal about why Mary Magdalene in particular was singled out by the Gnostics as an important figure. In this chapter, we take a look at the text and find out why it has created such a stir.

The Berlin Codex

In 1896, a German scholar named Dr. Carl Reinhardt bought a Coptic book in Cairo and brought it back with him to Germany. The book contained four texts:

◆ The *Gospel of Mary*

◆ *Apocryphon of John*

◆ The *Sophia of Jesus Christ*

◆ The *Act of Peter*

Officially catalogued as *Codex Berolinensis 8502*, the collection of texts purchased by Reinhardt is usually just called the Berlin Codex.

An Egyptologist named Carl Schmidt set to work translating the *Gospel of Mary*, and after some initial setbacks finally produced a full translation in German. Unfortunately, the translation was destroyed while sitting in the printer's office when a pipe broke, thus waterlogging the important document. Schmidt was unable to prepare it for publication again due to the eruption of World War I. Before the translation could be published after the war, Schmidt died. And so after many such setbacks it wasn't until 1955 that the *Gospel of Mary* was first published with a German translation.

The copy of the *Gospel of Mary* found in the Berlin Codex isn't complete. In the first part of the book, six pages are missing, and four pages are missing from the middle. We don't know how the pages came to be missing, but the way that the book was constructed can give us some clues. The Berlin Codex, like the texts found at Nag Hammadi, was arranged into a kind of primitive book called a codex. A codex is made up of several sheets of papyrus that are stacked together, folded in half, and then sewn up the middle. They are then placed inside leather covers to protect them and keep them together.

Schmidt's analysis of the Berlin Codex revealed that it was quite probable that the book was found in perfect condition. This led him to believe that greedy people may have torn the pages out, but as we saw in the case of Mohammed Ali Samman's mother in Chapter 14, maybe the reason the pages were torn out was to stoke a cooking fire. We really don't know. But we do know that they probably weren't just carelessly dropped out of the book.

The Coptic copy of the *Gospel of Mary* and two other Greek fragments found in the twentieth century are all that remain of the text. A copy of the *Gospel of Mary* was *not* found with the Nag Hammadi Library in 1945, although it has been published together with the Nag Hammadi texts. Two other texts in the Berlin Codex *were* part of the Nag Hammadi find, though, and it is believed that the *Gospel of Mary* was part of the same religious movement. They are all part of the same class of documents that reveals information about early Christianity.

The Coptic *Gospel of Mary* found in the Berlin Codex dates back to about the fifth century. Many scholars believe, however, that it is a copy of a text that dates back to as early as the first part of the second century. That places it not too long after when the Gospel of John would have been finished.

Recent Translations

There are several translations of the *Gospel of Mary* into English, but a few of them stand out in popularity and accessibility to the general reading public. (See Appendix B for details.)

Karen King

Karen King, a professor of religious history at the Harvard Divinity School, has been studying the *Gospel of Mary* for many years. She published her book *The Gospel of Mary of Magdala: Jesus and The First Woman Apostle* in 2003. It contains an introduction to the text, a history of the Berlin Codex, a complete translation, and 11 chapters of commentary. In her commentary, Professor King illuminates the beginnings of Christianity and places the *Gospel of Mary* in context.

Jean-Yves Leloup

In 2002, a French translation and commentary by a theologian named Jean-Yves Leloup was published in an English edition, simply titled *The Gospel of Mary Magdalene*. Like Professor King's book, his contains an introduction and a full translation of the gospel, but his commentary provides less history in context and more interpretation from a spiritual perspective.

MacRae and Wilson

An older translation of the *Gospel of Mary* is still in wide use. George MacRae and R. Wilson produced an English translation of the text for publication in *The Nag Hammadi Library in English*, edited by James Robinson.

Partial Translations

Several partial translations exist as well, but we only take a look at two. Professor Antti Marjanen from the University of Helsinki in Finland published a partial translation of the *Gospel of Mary* in his book *The Woman Jesus Loved: Mary Magdalene in the Nag Hammadi Library & Related Documents*. His translation appears only as it assists him in describing Mary Magdalene's role in the text.

> **" "** **It Is Written**
>
> In the Gospel of Mary the words of Mary Magdalene are uttered clearly and profoundly to communicate teaching and revelation.
>
> —Marvin Meyer, from *The Gospels of Mary: The Secret Tradition of Mary Magdalene, The Companion of Jesus*

Another partial translation was published in 2004, by Marvin Meyer, a Bible professor at Chapman University in California. His book, titled *The Gospels of Mary: The Secret Tradition of Mary Magdalene, The Companion of Jesus*, presents an easy-to-understand partial translation of the *Gospel of Mary*, in addition to other texts. Professor Meyer's commentary is rarely surpassed in clarity, and is aimed at the general reader.

A Quick Look at the Text

Because the first six pages of the text are missing, the *Gospel of Mary* opens in the middle of a conversation between Jesus and his disciples. As in several other texts, Jesus holds question-and-answer sessions to help illustrate his teachings and to gauge how well his students are learning.

What's the Matter?

The text begins in the middle of a question from an unknown disciple about the nature of matter:

> ... will, then, matter be saved or not?

Jesus' answer is a little hard to understand, but it is usually interpreted as meaning that everything, whether created as a part of nature or not, will return to its original condition. *Platonic philosophy* seems to have some influence on the answer Jesus gives, which makes it complicated for the modern reader. In a nutshell, the idea is that the material world, created from formlessness and nothing, will return to formlessness and nothing. In contrast, things that are of a spiritual nature will return to God.

Lingua Magda

Philosophy is the "love of wisdom." **Platonic philosophy** is based on the ideas of Plato, a philosopher who lived in Greece in the fourth century B.C.E.

What Is Sin?

Peter asks the next question in the text, which I'd like to paraphrase: "Because you've taught us about everything else, what is the world's sin?"

Of course, as you might expect based on his last answer, Jesus' answer to this question is also complicated. He starts by saying that there is no such thing as sin, but that people make sin when they do things that are like adultery.

It would be tempting to take the text at face value, but it's not likely that the teaching is meant to say there's no sin except adultery. More likely, Jesus was saying that sin isn't something that happens when you break laws and moral rules, it's something that happens when you combine things that shouldn't be put together, as in adultery. The things that shouldn't be combined? A spiritual nature and anything of the material world. It would be a little like mixing water with oil.

This interpretation holds up when compared to the next teaching Jesus offers in the text.

Don't Be Misled

After elaborating slightly on his answer about sin, Jesus greets his followers again by wishing them peace. He then tells them to beware of people who would lead them astray, who would tell them to "look here!" and "look there!" The reason not to allow themselves to be led in circles, he points out, is that the Son of Man is *within* them. It makes no sense, therefore, to look high and low for something on the outside when it's inside of you whole time.

He then says that when you find the Son of Man within yourself to follow him, and that those who seek him will find him. His last piece of advice on this subject is that after finding the Son of Man within, to go out and preach the good news.

Illuminations

Jesus punctuates his teachings in the *Gospel of Mary* by saying, "He who has ears, let him hear." This turn of phrase is also used in the canonical Gospels. Matthew 11:15 and 13:9 both record similar sayings of Jesus.

Don't Get Too Attached

Jesus' last teaching in the *Gospel of Mary* is that his followers shouldn't create any rules other than the ones that he himself left for them. He goes on to say that if they create laws, they become bound by them. The implied lesson is that rules and laws are of the material world, and to create them means that they will "tie you down" and prevent you from fully realizing your spiritual nature.

With that, Jesus suddenly leaves them.

Mary Rallies the Disciples

After Jesus' sudden departure, his followers weep and mourn, and fret about going to preach the gospel. If the Gentiles didn't spare Jesus, they reasoned, then why would they be spared? In essence, the disciples were afraid of ending up on crosses, too.

This is when Mary Magdalene enters the picture. She encourages them not to weep and mourn or lose their courage because they will all be kept in Jesus' grace. She then says that they should "praise his greatness" because he has made them all "into men." (Here it is again: Mary Magdalene is associated with a saying about Jesus turning people into men. It's another example of the common way of attributing higher, spiritual concerns as masculine. Later translations of the *Gospel of Mary* render this phrase as "fully human" or "true Human beings.")

Peter then points out that Jesus loved Mary more than other women, and asks her to share something with them that Jesus said to her alone. Mary agrees. She then begins to tell the disciples a story.

Mary's Vision

The story that Mary decides to share is of a vision she had of Jesus. When she saw Jesus in her vision, he commended her for not being afraid; this calls to mind Mary Magdalene seeing the angels at the tomb on the day of the resurrection (see Chapter 9). They told her not to be afraid; in the *Gospel of Mary*, when she sees Jesus in her vision, she isn't afraid at all.

Unfortunately, at this point in the text we run into four more missing pages, so much of Mary's vision is lost to the sands of time. As Karen King points out in her book, all we can do is hope that they are somewhere safe and preserved so they can eventually be discovered.

The text picks up again in the middle of Mary's vision, which describes a somewhat complex *cosmology* and journey of the soul. The soul, in antiquity, was almost always engendered as female, something that is demonstrated in Marvin Meyer's translation of the *Gospel of Mary*. He uses a feminine pronoun when he refers to the soul: "She left" and "she ascended," for example. We return to the contents of Mary's vision in the next chapter.

Lingua Magda

Theories of the way the universe and all of creation works are called **cosmologies**.

Andrew and Peter

At last, Mary is done recounting her vision to the rest of the disciples, and she goes silent. Whenever I read this portion of the text, I imagine that the disciples, too, sit in silence, not entirely sure what to say. If it were taking place on a movie screen, there would surely be crickets chirping merrily in the background.

Indeed, the disciples *aren't* sure what to say, so Andrew, Peter's brother, pipes up and says that people should say what they think about Mary's vision because he, for one, doesn't believe Jesus would have said any of it. Then he calls the content of her vision "strange ideas."

Peter jumps into the conversation then to back up his brother. He asks his fellow disciples whether they think that Jesus really would have given Mary a teaching that he hadn't delivered to the rest of them, and whether they were all now to listen to her. Presumably Peter was questioning Mary's authority to teach them about Jesus' message.

Naturally, Mary is deeply offended, as almost anyone would be in the same situation. She cries, and asks Peter whether he thinks that she's just making it all up and whether he is accusing her of lying about the Savior. The scene is set for a heated confrontation.

Levi to the Rescue

Just as things seem certain to spin completely out of control, another disciple, Levi, enters the picture. He reminds Peter that he is always easily angered. (I imagine Levi patting Peter's arm and saying, "Now, now, Peter, remember your blood pressure!") He points out that Peter is now fighting with Mary like the "adversaries," the negative powers that conspire to keep people trapped in the physical world. Then he says:

> But if the Savior made her worthy, who are you to reject her?

Levi then recommends to the disciples that rather than sitting around and arguing, they should do as Jesus told them to do. They should, in essence, pull themselves together and act like "true Human beings," then go out to preach the gospel. And so they do.

Thus ends the *Gospel of Mary*.

Quite Contrary

No, Levi isn't related to Levi's blue jeans. This Levi was one of Jesus' disciples whom he gathered at the beginning of his ministry. He is mentioned in Mark 2:14: "And as he passed by, he saw Levi the son of Alphaeus sitting at the receipt of custom, and said unto him, Follow me. And he arose and followed him."

Rivalry Between Peter and Mary

As you may have noticed from our look at the gospels of Mary and Thomas, there appears to have been a bit of a rivalry between Peter and Mary Magdalene. Far from being something that shows up only in one or two places, a strong case has been made for the existence of competing factions within early Christianity. Among those factions, there appear to have been two that competed directly: those that claimed Peter as their patron and those that claimed Mary Magdalene. It is believed that the Mary Magdalene tradition represents one in which the apostolic authority of women was recognized and accepted, whereas the *Petrine* ("of Peter") tradition recognized only the authority of men.

Although Peter isn't the first to question Mary's authority in the *Gospel of Mary*, it's no surprise that he should be one of those to question Mary Magdalene's vision. We caught glimpses of some hard feelings between Peter and Mary Magdalene in the Gospel of Luke and the Gospel of John. In both, Peter is singled out as disbelieving Mary Magdalene's message of the resurrection. He needs to go see it for himself, and in Luke, he is one of the first to see the risen Jesus.

Another scene in which Peter complains about Mary appears in *Pistis Sophia:* "Peter leapt forward, he said to Jesus: 'My Lord, we are not able to suffer this woman who takes the opportunity from us, and does not allow anyone of us to speak, but she speaks many times.'"

What does this rivalry mean? First off, it *doesn't* mean that Peter and Mary Magdalene really didn't get along. It's always possible that there is an older oral tradition that supports a real-life clash of personalities, but it's more likely that the texts are reflecting differences within early Christian communities.

You could think of Mary Magdalene as a spokesperson for a community that valued the input of women, and Peter as the spokesperson for communities that didn't. The texts that were produced by these rival communities therefore reflected their disagreements on the role of women within Christianity. Peter and Mary Magdalene were used as mouthpieces for their respective beliefs.

In many of the texts that seem more favorable toward Peter, roles that are traditionally fulfilled by Mary Magdalene are occupied by the Virgin Mary. For example, in a Greek text called *Acta Thaddaei*, the resurrected Jesus appears first to his mother outside of his tomb. In many of the texts where Mary Magdalene is replaced by the Virgin Mary or someone else, Peter is featured prominently.

There are several reasons why this is the case, but it mostly revolves around the desire for an example of female obedience; the Virgin Mary is portrayed as a woman who will submit to the authority of men. I'm not suggesting that this was right or wrong, but this definitely seems to represent some kind of tension between early Christian groups—not just Gnostic Christians, but more orthodox ones as well.

> **It Is Written**
>
> Another strategy, I submit, for curtailing the prominence of Mary Magdalene was to replace her character with another less-threatening figure, such as Mary of Nazareth, the mother of Jesus.
>
> —Ann Graham Brock, from *Mary Magdalene, The First Apostle*

In later years, Mary Magdalene did appear to be taken as the patron of Gnostics to some degree, in opposition to Peter as the patron of the orthodox Church. In other words, Mary Magdalene, as a woman with apostolic authority, may have become a sort of banner that the Gnostics waved as they thumbed their noses at the orthodox Church.

The Least You Need to Know

♦ The *Gospel of Mary* was discovered in 1896 but didn't become widely known until the publication of an English translation of the Nag Hammadi Library in 1977.

♦ There are now several English translations of the *Gospel of Mary*, and many commentaries about what it means.

♦ The *Gospel of Mary* contains a few Gnostic teachings of Jesus and a vision that Mary Magdalene had about the soul.

♦ Gnostic texts, including the *Gospel of Mary*, seem to present a lot of tension between Peter and Mary Magdalene.

Chapter 16

"A Woman Who Knew the All"

In This Chapter

- ◆ Visions of the soul
- ◆ Earning the title "apostle"
- ◆ A close relationship with Jesus
- ◆ Asking questions and interpreting answers

Although the gospel accounts of Mary Magdalene are the foundation of all that is known about her as a historical person, I must admit being completely fascinated by the way she appears in Gnostic literature. Here was a woman who was so admired that she was made second only to Jesus himself in wisdom and understanding.

Four hundred years, which is about as long as Gnosticism lasted, provides a long time for an idea to develop. But it appears to be fairly early on, the early part of the second century, that we see Mary Magdalene being placed into these crucial roles of authority and companionship. In this chapter, we take a look at her most important Gnostic identities.

Visionary

A visionary is a person who has visions. The Jewish scriptures and the Christian Bible is filled with people who have visions, including Jacob, Isaiah, Paul, Peter, and John.

Sometimes, visions come in the form of dreams that people have while they're sleeping. Other times, visions come while is a person is awake, rather like a waking dream. Whatever the case, Gnostic texts also contain many references to visions that help demonstrate teachings.

The Vision in the *Gospel of Mary*

Perhaps one of the most striking roles that Mary Magdalene has in the Gnostic texts is that of a visionary. As discussed in Chapter 15, the *Gospel of Mary* hinges on a vision that she had of Jesus, which she recounts to the disciples. Although many of the pages are missing, we're able to make some educated guesses about what Mary Magdalene's vision was about.

> **It Is Written**
>
> Mary answered and said, "What is hidden from you I will impart to you." And she began to say the following words to them. "I," she said, "I saw the Lord in a vision and I said to him, 'Lord, I saw you today in a vision.'"
>
> —From the *Gospel of Mary*

In essence, Mary Magdalene's vision is about the journey of the soul. The soul begins in the eternal realm, and descends into the world of matter (our physical world). Many Gnostic texts give the impression that when the soul descends into matter, it puts on layer after layer of matter that gradually becomes heavier and heavier. The final layer is the flesh that surrounds it in the form of human beings. In one Gnostic story called *The Hymn of the Pearl*, fancy clothing is used as a metaphor for the "dressing up" of the soul in flesh.

Mary Magdalene's vision, though, is about the soul's ascent back into the eternal realm, heaven, or the Pleroma. As the soul ascends, it passes through all of the different levels of existence that are guarded by certain dark forces. The following illustration shows one possible way to think about the journey of the soul.

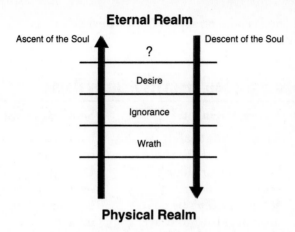

Eternal Realm

Ascent of the Soul   Descent of the Soul

?

Desire

Ignorance

Wrath

Physical Realm

The soul starts at the top, in the eternal realm, and goes down through each level to the physical realm. On its way back up from the physical to the eternal, it must pass by the forces that control each level.

We could look at the different forces rather like the archons that have been mentioned already. In the *Gospel of Mary*, four forces conspire to keep the soul trapped in the physical world. Unfortunately, we only know what the last three are because of the lost pages:

♦ Desire

♦ Ignorance

♦ Wrath

Wrath is made up of seven individual parts, which appear in some ways to echo the four larger powers:

♦ Darkness

♦ Desire

♦ Ignorance

♦ Excitement of Death

♦ Kingdom of the Flesh

♦ Foolish Wisdom

♦ Wrathful Wisdom

Each time the soul ascends to a new level on its way back to heaven, the force guarding that level says something to try

Illuminations

In other Gnostic texts, the soul needs to know certain "pass-words" to get past the rulers of each level.

to befuddle the soul and keep it entrapped. It's worthwhile to take a look at the various deceptions that these forces used.

Attempts to Turn Back the Soul from Its Journey Home

Force	Discouragement	Soul's Response
Desire	Says that the soul never really descended because Desire didn't see it come down, so the soul *can't* be ascending back to heaven	Says that the soul saw Desire, but Desire just didn't see the soul as it descended into matter
Ignorance	Says that the soul is bound in wickedness and cannot judge	Says that it has never judged, and that the barriers between heaven and earth are dissolving
Wrath	Calls the soul "slayer of men" and "conqueror of space"	Says that it has overcome the traps of matter

In the end, the soul is victorious and manages to transcend this earthly realm and return to the eternal. This concludes Mary Magdalene's vision.

At this point, of course, Peter and Andrew get involved in the dialogue and say that they don't want to believe any of it. Levi patiently defends Mary Magdalene, who weeps at their disbelief. Then they all go and begin to tell the world about their risen Savior.

> **Quite Contrary**
>
> One of the Greek fragments of the *Gospel of Mary* contains an alternate ending. In the different version, Levi leaves the rest of the disciples and goes to preach the Gospel by himself.

Some scholars have said that the *Gospel of Mary* indicates a teaching that everything associated with the material world is going to pass away. Rather than end up in a realm of suffering and death, Jesus appears as the Savior to rescue souls and help them return to the Good. Mary's vision, then, is all about how the soul goes about its long journey home.

The Dialogue of the Savior

Another Gnostic text called *The Dialogue of the Savior* presents Mary Magdalene in a visionary role. This time she is experiencing a vision along with two other disciples: Matthew and Judas. Judas is probably actually Thomas (his full name being Judas Thomas).

The text says that Jesus placed his hand on his disciples to show them a vision of how the light of God has been sent into the physical world, and contrasts the eternal realm, a place of fullness, to the realm of matter, which is seen as a place of deficiency. This God did to rescue the spark of divinity that was "fallen" into humanity.

Mary Magdalene's role in *The Dialogue of the Savior* is twofold: She is both visionary and questioner, which we return to shortly. After the disciples, including Mary, have their vision, they spend some time discussing it with Jesus, who helps them understand it better. It is in this text that Mary Magdalene received another of her exalted titles:

> Mariam said, "Thus about 'The wickedness of each day,' and 'The laborer being worthy of his food,' and 'The disciples resembling his teacher.'" This she spoke as a woman who knew the All.

Later translations render the last line as "a woman who had understood completely," but I prefer the poetic quality of the older translation. Understanding is certainly the goal, but the first translation reminds us that she, as a seeker of gnosis, had achieved her goal: *knowledge*. And it wasn't just *any* knowledge, but knowledge of that which was most important.

Apostle

Within the Gnostic texts, there appears to be strong evidence for Mary Magdalene being viewed as an apostle. This goes beyond the designation of Apostle to the Apostles given to her by Hippolytus for the role she played in the resurrection drama.

In Gnosticism, Mary Magdalene preaches, teaches, and leads the other disciples in

> **It Is Written**
>
> [The *Gospel of Mary*] shows us there was a tradition of Mary Magdalene as an important apostle of the church after the resurrection.
>
> —Karen King, quoted in *The Christian Science Monitor* (November 14, 2003)

spreading Jesus' message. These activities themselves place her in the role of apostle. We have much more to consider about Mary Magdalene's apostolic status in the next chapter.

Companion to Jesus

Much has recently been said about how the Gnostic texts support the idea that Jesus and Mary Magdalene were married. This isn't entirely true. The Gnostic texts do say some things that lead us to believe that they could have been married, but their relationship could have been of another character entirely. It could have been a close friendship, or even a spiritual partnership. None of the Gnostic texts explicitly say that Jesus and Mary Magdalene were married; they only say that he loved her and that she was his companion.

We've already had some discussion of the *Gospel of Philip* in Chapter 4, where we took a quick look at the passages in question. One thing is certain: Mary Magdalene is mentioned in very strong terms. She is his companion, and he kisses her often. We don't know exactly where he kisses her, but scholars have suggested that it is on the mouth. The mouth would be a logical place because of what is said of spiritual kisses in the rest of the *Gospel of Philip*.

As we've already seen, the Greek word for "companion" is used: *koinonos*, a word that is used to represent partnerships of all kinds, including marital ones. A Coptic word is also used, *hotre*, which has similar meanings. These terms are sometimes used to indicate marriages, but also sometimes business relationships and other kinds of close associations between two people.

Illuminations

Marvin Meyer, author of *The Gospels of Mary Magdalene: The Secret Tradition of Mary Magdalene, The Companion of Jesus* (see Appendix B), has suggested that the *Noli Me Tangere* scene itself in the *Gospel of John* has erotic overtones, and could support the notion that they were married. At the end of his analysis he concludes that although it's possible, we just can't tell for sure from the texts that are available to us.

Although it can mean something like "spouse," it wouldn't be consistent with the way that the word was commonly used at the time. In fact, *koinonia*, a word that comes from *koinonos*, means "fellowship." The use of the word "companion" in the *Gospel of Philip* has been compared to the kind of association that fellow travelers have with one another more than that between husband and wife.

All of this just means that it's not entirely accurate to claim that because the word *koinonos* was used, "companion" should really be "consort." The fact is that we really don't know *exactly* how it was meant to be used. What we *do* know is that regardless of what kind of companion she was, Mary Magdalene definitely was the person whom the Gnostics believed was most loved by Jesus. It may have been a spiritual love, a close friendship, or a marriage; let's just be content at this point to say that the Gnostics portrayed them as *very close*.

Although the term "companion" is never used as it is in the *Gospel of Philip*, we can assume that the same kind of relationship is implied by the other texts that mention Jesus' love for her. The *Gospel of Mary* says:

> Sister, we know that the Savior loved you more than other women.

and

> Surely the Savior knew her very well. For this reason he loved her more than us.

Although nothing in *Pistis Sophia* refers to Mary Magdalene as Jesus' companion or explicitly calls out the fact that he loved her, the many exalted titles that he gives her tell us that she is special to him, at least in a spiritual way. If we're to believe that Mary Magdalene was Jesus' spiritual complement as an embodiment of Sophia in the flesh, then the wisdom that she displays in *Pistis Sophia* makes sense. Between them, Jesus as teacher and Mary Magdalene as an enlightened student, they're able to further the cause of gnosis.

It is the Gnostic emphasis on Mary Magdalene as Jesus' beloved companion that has strengthened the theory that she could have been the Beloved Disciple in the Gospel of John. The strong Mary Magdalene tradition represented in the Gnostic texts has caused scholars to start looking at the Gospel of John in a new light, and a few have begun making statements and publishing essays that are supportive of the idea.

It Is Written _____

She would have had disciples, her testimony would have formed a community, her accounts not only of the death and resurrection of Jesus, but also of his life and teachings, would have been preserved. But not only that, her words would have been canonized and taught through the ages, and spread over the world.

—Esther de Boer, "Mary Magdalene and the Disciple Jesus Loved," from *lectio dificilior* (on how our perspective of Mary Magdalene would change if she was a candidate for the Beloved Disciple in the Gospel of John)

Questioner of the Savior

Another role emerges from the Gnostic texts that seems a little obvious but it deserves acknowledgement. This is the role of *interlocutor*, or questioner, of Jesus. Because Mary Magdalene was cast as a woman who had understood Jesus' teachings perfectly, she occupies a unique role in which her questions allow him to more fully illustrate his teachings.

In *Pistis Sophia*

In *Pistis Sophia*, the entire text is made up of question-and-answer sessions between Jesus and his followers that evolve into well-rounded conversations. If Jesus in this text was the teacher, then Mary Magdalene could very well have been viewed as a teacher's assistant. Not only does she ask many more questions than all the other disciples combined, but she also sometimes answers questions and interprets Jesus' teachings. Sometimes she even asks questions on behalf of other disciples.

In *Pistis Sophia*, there are a total of 115 different questions and interpretations of Jesus' teachings by his followers. Of those, Mary Magdalene alone is responsible for asking 67 questions. Although we can't look at all of the many questions Mary Magdalene asked, it's definitely worthwhile to see some of the kinds of questions and answers from the first of the four books of *Pistis Sophia*.

- ◆ Will evil magicians be able to prevent good things?

- ◆ Will astrologers and fortune tellers know when the end of the world is coming?

- ◆ How will souls be purified?

- ◆ What is Sophia's place among the Aeons?

An interlocutor, though, is someone who goes beyond just asking questions. They are a real part of a conversation, and as such, sometimes they make statements that aren't questions. In *Pistis Sophia*, sometimes Mary Magdalene offers interpretations of Jesus' teachings. Here are just a few of the subjects where she helps to illuminate what Jesus is saying:

- How Jesus will overturn the power of the archons and destroy them
- The repentance of Sophia
- The importance of Philip, Thomas, and Matthew as witnesses of Jesus' truth
- How Jesus will reward the faithfulness of the disciples
- The true meaning of "the first will become last and the last will become first"
- That Jesus is the source of truth, and Sophia is the source of righteousness
- That mercy descended on Jesus at his baptism in the form of spirit, and that peace was the indwelling Good within Jesus

These may all seem like pretty arcane ideas, and indeed, *Pistis Sophia* isn't an easy book to read. But it is definitely a good way to learn about how some Gnostic groups admired Mary Magdalene as a woman who had understood Jesus' message perfectly and was therefore the best person to pass on his teachings after he was gone.

In *The Greater Questions of Mary* and *The Lesser Questions of Mary*

Mary Magdalene's role as a questioner of the savior is also supported by the mention of texts called *The Greater Questions of Mary* and *The Lesser Questions of Mary*. No copies of these books exist today; we only know about them because of what the fourth-century theologian Epiphanius of Salamis has written about them. In his book *Against Heresies*, Epiphanius says that *The Greater Questions of Mary* contains a story about how Jesus takes Mary Magdalene to a mountaintop and delivers a teaching that shocks her so much she faints.

Illuminations

Interestingly, after reviving Mary, Jesus addresses her exactly as he addressed Peter in Matthew 13:41: "And immediately Jesus stretched forth his hand, and caught him, and said unto him, O thou of little faith, wherefore didst thou doubt?" According to Epiphanius, Jesus' words in *The Greater Questions of Mary* were: "Oh, person of little faith, why did you doubt?"

Because we don't have any copies of the text itself, we don't know exactly what it contains. Because the titles themselves identify Mary Magdalene as one who asks questions, it is most certainly an important indicator of what the authors of those texts thought about her.

In *The Dialogue of the Savior*

In *The Dialogue of the Savior*, Mary again appears in the role of questioner. Let's take a look at the kinds of questions and answers that appear in this text:

Questions and Answers in *The Dialogue of the Savior*

Mary's Question	Jesus' Answer
Where do I take my body when I weep and when I laugh?	(too much text is missing)
To Matthew and Thomas: Where are you going to put Jesus' teachings?	Only someone who has room in his heart can ask about these things [his teachings].
Why have I come to this place?	You make my message clear!
Is there a place that lacks truth?	The place where I'm not.

CAUTION

Quite Contrary

Although many of the Gnostic documents are dismissed as too late to provide any indication of what Jesus may have really said, texts such as *The Dialogue of the Savior* show evidence of having been based on material that was just as early as the canonical Gospels.

As you can see, some of the answers that Jesus gives are almost like puzzles in themselves. They've been compared to the *koans* given to students of Buddhism by their teachers; questions and answers meant to help the student transcend his normal boundaries of thought. Another example of this rather indirect method of answering comes after Mary asks her questions. She exclaims with excitement that she wants to understand things as they really are. Jesus answers that true wealth is found in the search for life.

In some places in *The Dialogue of the Savior*, like many of the other Gnostic documents, portions of the writing are illegible or missing, which leads to gaps in what we can understand of the text. What we can make out, however, reinforces the impression that Mary Magdalene's curiosity and devotion led her to be seen as Jesus' foremost disciple. She had a mature understanding of Jesus' teachings, extending even beyond what an impatient Peter was able to comprehend.

The Least You Need to Know

- ◆ Mary Magdalene had visions that were related to the soul and its place in the eternal realm.

- ◆ Nothing in the Gnostic texts says Jesus and Mary Magdalene were married; there are only some interesting clues about them having a close relationship.

- ◆ Mary Magdalene was Jesus' favorite disciple, and he loved her more than the rest.

- ◆ Because Mary Magdalene had a full understanding of Jesus' teachings, she asked him leading questions and offered her interpretations of what he was saying.

Part 5

Thoroughly Modern Magdalene

Now that we've taken a look at what everyone has had to say about Mary Magdalene in centuries past, it's time to find out what they're saying *now*. You probably have some idea of the modern ideas about Mary Magdalene, or you might not have picked up this book in the first place. But did you know that she now appeals to people across the boundary of faith? You no longer have to be a Christian to find Mary Magdalene interesting. In addition to some of the more traditional ideas about her, and the re-emergence of some very *old* ideas about her, she is, it seems, a new woman for a new age.

Chapter 17

Apostola Apostolorum: The Apostle to the Apostles

In This Chapter

- ◆ What qualified someone to be an apostle
- ◆ Mary Magdalene, woman apostle
- ◆ Mary as an early example of women's leadership in Christianity
- ◆ Remembering an untainted Mary Magdalene
- ◆ What will it take to revise the record?

In 2003, more than 16,000 people worldwide participated in celebrations on Mary Magdalene's feast day, July 22, which honored her as the apostle of the apostles. Due to the activism work of a Roman Catholic organization called FutureChurch, Mary Magdalene is being recognized by more people every year as the woman who preached the good news of the resurrection to the other disciples.

Why would an organization with this purpose exist, anyway? What's the big deal about Mary Magdalene being the apostle of the apostles? In this chapter, we take a look at the rediscovery of Mary Magdalene in her apostolic role and how a movement has been built to restore her good name.

What Does It Take to Be an Apostle, Anyway?

Almost everyone who is familiar with Christianity can tell you how many apostles there were: twelve. Right? It may be hard to believe, but the idea of the twelve apostles didn't start out right away. The earliest Christian writings that we know of aren't the Gospels themselves, but the writings of Paul. Paul applies the term "apostle" to a few people not mentioned in the Gospels:

♦ Paul himself

♦ Andronicus

♦ Junia

Paul tends to define apostleship for himself based on a vision he had of Jesus. In 1 Corinthians 15:3, he includes himself in a list of those who had seen the risen Jesus, as a way to emphasize how legitimate his apostleship was. Among those who he claims saw the risen Jesus were the following:

♦ Cephas

♦ "the Twelve"

♦ "five hundred of the brothers and sisters"

♦ James

♦ "all of the apostles"

Quite Contrary

In 1 Corinthians 15:3, Paul refers to "the Twelve," presumably referring to Jesus' disciples, but he didn't call them the twelve "apostles." References to the "twelve apostles" was a later development.

You might be wondering at this point what the difference is between a "disciple" and an "apostle," and that would be a great question.

A "disciple" is a follower. Jesus' followers were all disciples. The Gospels say that he specifically picked out twelve men to follow him as disciples, but strictly speaking, a disciple is still a term used to refer to a person who is a follower and student of someone else. That would make Mary Magdalene a disciple as well; just not one singled out to follow him as the Gospels say that the men were.

An "apostle," on the other hand, is a person who has met certain requirements. The problem, of course, is deciding whose requirements are the right ones. The earliest person to talk about the requirements of being an apostle is Paul, and as we've already seen, he mentioned people other than the twelve disciples we've come to know.

Based on his writings, Paul seemed to think that there were two main requirements necessary to be considered an apostle:

♦ You had to be a witness to the risen Jesus.

♦ You had to receive a command to proclaim a message from a divine source (called a "commission").

In addition to giving us clues about what he thought an apostle was, Paul makes a distinction between two different kinds of apostles:

♦ People who represent their congregation or Christian community, such as missionaries

♦ People who are commissioned by God, Jesus, angels, or other divine source (called "apostles of Christ")

The New Testament book of Acts, which was almost certainly written by the same person who wrote the Gospel of Luke, restricts the title of "apostle" so only the twelve were able to qualify. After Judas betrayed Jesus, they were left with only eleven, and so a new one had to be chosen. In doing so, they had to decide who could be a candidate to join their group. To be one of the apostles, a person had to be …

♦ A man.

♦ Someone who was with Jesus from the time he was baptized in the Jordan.

♦ Someone who saw the resurrected Jesus in the 40 days between the resurrection and his final ascension into heaven.

This definition would have narrowed down the group of candidates considerably. Before Judas's betrayal, these were the twelve as listed in the Gospels:

Matthew Matt. 10:1–4	Mark Mark 3:13–19	Luke Luke 6:12–16	John
Simon Peter	Simon Peter	Simon Peter	(no list given)
Andrew	Andrew	Andrew	
James (the brother of John)	James	James	
John	John	John	
Philip	Philip	Philip	
Bartholomew	Bartholomew	Bartholomew	
Thomas	Thomas	Thomas	
Matthew	Matthew	Matthew	
James (the son of Alphaeus)	James	James	
Lebbaeus/Thaddaeus	Thaddaeus	Judas (brother Thaddaeus of James)	
Simon the Canaanite	Simon the Canaanite	Simon Zelotes	
Judas Iscariot	Judas Iscariot	Judas Iscariot	

Using this criteria, it was decided that Matthias would replace Judas Iscariot to make them an even twelve again.

Illuminations

Even if Judas had asked for forgiveness for betraying Jesus, he wouldn't have been able to rejoin the Twelve. The New Testament says that he died, either by suicide or by falling down on some rocks.

By the definition in Acts used to choose a new member of the Twelve (which is contradicted by Acts 14:14), Paul himself didn't even qualify to be an apostle, and he is almost universally agreed in modern Christianity to have been one. So it appears that, if Paul qualifies to be an apostle, we need to use Paul's own definition to determine who an apostle can be.

Can you think of anyone else who was a witness to the risen Jesus and received a divine commission to declare the good news?

Was Mary Magdalene an Apostle?

If we use Paul's criteria for apostleship, Mary Magdalene absolutely qualifies as an apostle. This is the reason why Hippolytus and many, many people during the last 2,000 years have referred to her as the *apostola apostolorum.* Apostola apostolorum is usually translated in one of two ways: "apostle *to* the apostles" and "apostle *of* the apostles." The first way of translating the phrase is usually taken to mean that Mary Magdalene's apostleship only extends as far as the other apostles, and that her commission was to tell no one else. "Apostle *of* the apostles," however, recognizes Mary Magdalene as the primary witness who received a commission as legitimate as anyone else's.

Mary Magdalene was part of the first generation of Jesus' followers. She provided for his ministry, and was more faithful than any of the other disciples (except perhaps for John) by remaining on Golgotha to witness the crucifixion. She stayed until he was buried, and was then either the first or one of the first to witness his resurrection. Mary Magdalene played a crucial role in the most central events of the Christian religion. In her role of the first apostle, she is sometimes lauded as the very *founder* of Christianity.

> **It Is Written**
>
> Lest the female apostles doubt the angels, Christ himself came to them so that the women would be apostles of Christ and by their obedience rectify the sin of the ancient Eve ... Christ showed himself to the (male) disciples and said to them: "... It is I who appeared to these women and I who wanted to send them to you as apostles."
>
> —Hippolytus, late second or early third century

In the *Gospel of Mary,* it is Mary Magdalene's behavior that defines what it means to be an apostle, much like it had for Paul in his writings. In the *Gospel of Mary,* we see that the requirements for apostleship aren't based solely on whether or not you were present from the beginning of Jesus' ministry or whether or not you saw him at the resurrection. While those things may have been part of the definition, the very fact that Mary is a woman delivering Jesus' teachings to his other followers takes the issue of apostleship a step further.

Mary's spiritual maturity is what sets her apart from the others, which is the strongest emerging interpretation of why Jesus loved her more than the rest. It was her ability to understand Jesus' message that gave her legitimacy, as shown in Levi's reminder to Peter that Jesus had made them all "truly human." He is reminding

Peter (and Andrew) that the body is part of the material world and will pass away, while the spirit is eternal. Mary might be a woman on the outside, but she's the same as them on the inside.

Why This Idea Is Catching On

There are many reasons why Mary Magdalene's role as apostle of the apostles has been downplayed, the greatest of which appears to be the fact that male apostleship is at the foundation of the Roman Catholic Church's teaching that only men can be ordained as priests.

Illuminations

In spite of the Roman Catholic Church's stance on the ordination of women, Pope John Paul II has himself referred to Mary Magdalene as "apostle to the apostles."

FutureChurch, the organization mentioned earlier in this chapter, was founded in 1990 with the purpose that women should be able to join men in all levels of the Church, and they use Mary Magdalene as a primary example of why that should be so. As an apostle, Mary Magdalene proves that women were important leaders in early Christianity and therefore should be considered equal to men in the Church.

A German group with similar aims called Gruppe Maria von Magdala was formed in 1986.

The ordination of women is a controversial subject within certain branches of Christianity, particularly Roman Catholicism. But the exclusion that women feel from participating fully in their religion extends beyond whether or not they can be ordained; some women have been denied the right to even speak to a congregation, to teach, to encourage, or even to lead in prayer. For these women, Mary Magdalene has become a potent and historical precedent for why their value to Christianity shouldn't be limited to their presence in the pews.

Several feminist scholars have taken up the challenge to restore Mary Magdalene to what many see as her rightful place in Christianity. Some of them have chosen to rely only on the resurrection accounts in the Gospels to prove that she should be recognized as an apostle. Others have brought the newly discovered Gnostic material into the equation as evidence of women's value to early Christianity. The fact that some of the early Christian groups held Mary Magdalene's apostleship as essential and women's leadership as valuable supports the cause of women in modern Christianity.

Quite Contrary

Far from being the only example of women's leadership in early Christianity, several other women have been cited:

◆ In Romans 16:1, a woman named Phoebe is called a deacon (usually translated as "servant").

◆ In Romans 16:7, a woman named Junia is called an apostle.

◆ Cyprian, an African bishop, tells of a woman who administered the Eucharist and performed baptisms (third century).

◆ Pliny, a Roman governor, tells of two women who were deacons (second century).

◆ Pope Gelasius I tells of women who were ordained as priests (fifth century).

Some feminist scholars have even gone so far as to mention the word "successor" in relation to Mary Magdalene. This takes the role of apostle a step further; perhaps, it is said, Jesus not only gave her a commission to spread the good news, he intended that she would carry on his mission. Readings of the Gospel of John support this view, with Mary Magdalene as the Beloved Disciple, with the Gnostic literature again making an appearance as supplemental material.

It often seems, however, that the main emphasis is on what the Gnostic texts, when they're used at all, can reveal about the New Testament. When trying to effect change within Christianity, it's necessary to work within the small group of acceptable accounts of Jesus' life. To go too far outside of bounds into Gnostic territory would negate any radically different message. So for the *apostola apostolorum* view to be widely acceptable, it has to be rooted in the canonical Gospels.

It Is Written

Nevertheless we have heard to our annoyance that divine affairs have come to such a low state that women are encouraged to officiate at the sacred altars, and to take part in all matters imputed to the offices of the male sex, to which they do not belong.

—Pope Gelasius I, in a letter to churches in Southern Italy (494 C.E.)

The Eastern Orthodox Church

The Eastern Orthodox Church, which separated from the Roman Catholic Church in 1054, claims apostolic succession just as the Roman Catholic Church does. But because it branched off at such an early date (or because Roman Catholicism branched off from it, depending on whom you ask), some of its teachings are different from what is more popularly known.

Illuminations

In addition to the Eastern Orthodox feast days for Mary Magdalene and the Myrrhbearers, there is a feast day for the transfer of her relics from Ephesus to Constantinople: May 4.

Mary Magdalene, in the Orthodox tradition, was never associated with the anonymous sinner in Luke, and therefore never became known as a prostitute. She has always been honored as a Holy Myrrhbearer and Equal-to-the-Apostles. Although "equal to the apostles" isn't quite the same thing as "apostle," and several other saints hold the title also, it is still a crucial recognition of Mary Magdalene's importance in the origin of Christianity. Her witness of the resurrection is honored without the taint of her alleged former life.

Setting Things Straight

A few characteristics of the *apostola apostolorum* view round out this approach to viewing Mary Magdalene. Activists who embrace her as the apostle of the apostles tend to focus their energies in three areas where her image could be improved.

No Prostitute

By far, the biggest challenge to those who embrace the *apostola apostolorum* perspective is the fact that Mary Magdalene has been viewed as a prostitute for so long. Even when Mary Magdalene has been honored, she has been subtly maligned in her role as penitent.

So the first characteristic of this movement is getting rid of her false reputation as a harlot. Just get rid of it, throw it out! There is no basis in scripture for calling Mary Magdalene a penitent sinner, and the Catholic Church has officially rescinded its teaching that she was a repentant prostitute, so the notion has no place in Christianity.

On this count, they have their work cut out for them. As mentioned in previous chapters, 1,400 years of tradition doesn't just evaporate when you point out that it's based on faulty information. Centuries of thought has risen up around Mary Magdalene's role as a reformed sinner, some of it very valuable to people, as in the case of those who look to her for hope in changing their own lives. To take away Mary Magdalene's mistaken reputation is to deny her powerful patronage within certain areas of Christian charity work.

It Is Written

Anyone, even today, who wants to see something different in Mary Magdalene is quickly put on the defensive.

—Ingrid Maisch, *Mary Magdalene: The Image of a Woman Through the Centuries* (1998)

Be that as it may, many agree that it's better to rely on inconvenient facts than on meaningful fictions. Mary Magdalene's good name, therefore, should be restored to her after two thousand years of slander.

Acknowledge Apostleship

The second characteristic of the *apostola apostolorum* perspective is that Mary Magdalene's apostleship needs to be recognized. As we saw earlier in the chapter, any Christian church that acknowledges Paul as an apostle depends therefore on his own definition of apostleship. In doing so, they could, if they chose, acknowledge that Mary Magdalene, too, fulfills Paul's requirements for apostleship.

Some have responded to this by saying that the commission that Mary Magdalene received wasn't to spread the Gospel everywhere, but only to Jesus' disciples. Be that as it may, many people believe that the fact that she was singled out to be the primary witness of the resurrection was significant beyond her ability to carry a message to eleven men. In addition, she was recognized as the apostle of the apostles by many of the men who were responsible for the formation of Christianity!

Acknowledge Leadership

Although apostleship refers to the divine commission that Mary Magdalene received to go tell the others that Jesus had risen, there is a step beyond that has been discussed by those interested in the *apostola apostolorum* view. After Jesus rose from the dead and subsequently ascended into heaven, there was much work to be done. Although the canonical gospels are silent on it, early Gnostic Christian tradition

It Is Written

[She] preached to the unbelievers and confirmed the believers in their faith. ... Who among the apostles clung so firmly to the Lord? ... It was fitting, then, that just as she had been chosen to be the apostle of Christ's resurrection and the prophet of his ascension, so also she became an evangelist for believers throughout the world ...

—Anonymous Cistercian author, fifteenth century

holds that Mary Magdalene was among those who took the message out into the world at large.

The very fact that the *Gospel of Mary* is the only Christian text named for a woman goes a long way toward establishing Mary Magdalene as a leader, as does her importance in other Gnostic texts. To the Gnostics, Mary Magdalene was the one people looked to for guidance when the going got tough. In addition, several early legends refer to Mary Magdalene preaching the Gospel outside of Palestine. No matter what, she wasn't a woman content to just sit and let everyone else do the hard work of spreading the good news.

The Least You Need to Know

♦ There are a couple of different ways of defining "apostle"; the definition that extends apostleship to Paul is the least restrictive.

♦ Mary Magdalene meets Paul's requirements for apostleship, and was called an apostle by many of the men who molded the Church into what it is today.

♦ Many people look to Mary Magdalene as an example of women's leadership in Christianity.

♦ The Eastern Orthodox tradition remembers Mary Magdalene as "Equal-to-the-Apostles."

♦ The greatest challenge to restoring Mary Magdalene's good name is overcoming the myth of her sinful pre-Jesus life.

Chapter 18

Still Fallen

In This Chapter

- ◆ A strange fruit in the Garden
- ◆ Sophia's many substitutes
- ◆ Working women in Victorian England
- ◆ Washing your sins away: Magdalene asylums
- ◆ The portrayal of Mary Magdalene as a cultural mirror

With all the accumulating evidence that Mary Magdalene was honored by early Christians rather than despised, it's difficult to understand why she's still saddled with such a bad reputation. If we can back up a little bit from her "bad-girl" image, we can see a pattern begin to emerge where so-called fallen women are concerned.

Mary Magdalene may have been only another example of a religious "type" that was reused many times in many different ways to convey some particular spiritual meaning; in this case, the "fallen" state of humankind.

Eve Started It!

Our journey into the seamy underside of Biblical lore begins with Eve, whom we've already met. She was the famous (or *infamous*, depending on how you look at it) wife of Adam, the first man created by God. They lived a life of peace and harmony in the Garden of Eden, where they enjoyed the fruit from all of the trees except one. God had commanded them to never eat from the tree of knowledge of good and evil; in fact, he told them never to even *touch* it or they would die. This was one dangerous tree.

Quite Contrary

The Bible never says that Adam and Eve ate an apple, it was only said to be "fruit." Because it came off of a tree, though, it was later thought to have been an apple.

Their harmonious existence in Eden evaporated when one day, a snake came to Eve and convinced her to eat the fruit of the forbidden tree. It was the very first act of disobedience. After she ate the fruit, Eve had a knowledge of good and evil, and she didn't die as God had said. Naturally, she convinced Adam to eat the fruit also so they both would know the difference between right and wrong. After eating the fruit, they became aware that they were naked and were ashamed, so they sewed fig leaves together to make little loincloths.

God went for a walk in the Garden of Eden on the evening after Adam and Eve had eaten the forbidden fruit. Knowing that they had disobeyed and would be punished, Adam and Eve hid from God. God finally found them, and Adam confessed what they had done. Then, he blamed Eve:

> The man said, "The woman whom thou gavest to be with me, she gave me fruit of the tree, and I ate.

> (Gen 3:12)

Eve, as eager to shift blame away from herself as Adam had been, said:

> The serpent beguiled me, and I ate.

> (Gen 3:13)

The story goes on to describe how God then cursed all three of them: the serpent, Eve, and Adam, and cast them out of the Garden of Eden. This was, in the Jewish tradition and the Christian tradition that borrowed from it, the fall of humankind.

As we've already seen, Mary Magdalene has been viewed at various points in history as the New Eve. The comparison only works, however, if you assume a sinful past for Mary Magdalene, who is acting as Eve, only in reverse. Where Eve was created in the grace of God, and only afterward became fallen, Mary Magdalene started out fallen, and only afterward came into the grace of God. Eve entered a fallen status of her own free will, and Mary Magdalene, by accepting the teachings of Jesus, left behind her fallen status of her own free will. Eve and Mary Magdalene were thus seen as apt reflections of one another.

Worldly Wisdom

In Gnostic myth, Sophia is the one who is fallen. Her desire to know where she comes from is so strong that she creates another being—the Demiurge—from her yearning (see Chapter 13). This illicit act of creation sets her apart from her brother and sister Aeons in the Pleroma, and she is shamed.

There's more than one way to look at Sophia's sorrows. She could be seen in a fallen state because of her mistaken act of creation, but she can also be seen in a "lower aspect" that could also be considered fallen.

When Sophia sends part of herself into the material world in order to redeem humankind, she herself enters a kind of exile from the divine realm. And as long as humankind is in "exile" from the eternal, so, too, is Sophia.

This is Sophia in her "lower aspect," then, which is inextricably linked with our actions and ability to find gnosis. Sophia's sorrows are our sorrows in this myth, and as we achieve gnosis and return to the divine ourselves, we're also rescuing Sophia.

Mary Magdalene, who in Gnostic texts often appears to be seen as an earthly reflection of Sophia, would then almost certainly have taken on some of her fallen qualities. One of the best pieces of evidence for this comes in the form of a legend about a man named Simon Magus.

Simon Magus was said, by the theologians who wrote against Gnosticism, to have been the father of Gnostic thought, or at the very least a very important Gnostic figure. He was a Syrian teacher whose ideas were probably influenced by early Christian thought, and in many ways, he modeled himself after the Gnostic version of Jesus. He was the savior come to illuminate mankind and rescue them from their imprisonment in matter.

Some people think that Simon Magus may have even been mentioned in the New Testament, in Acts 8:9:

> But there was a man named Simon who had previously practiced magic in the city and amazed the nation of Sama'ria, saying that he himself was somebody great.

Illuminations

According to Simon Magus, in one of Helen's previous incarnations she was Helen of Troy. Helen of Troy was the legendary cause of the Trojan War, and was so beautiful that she was said to have "a face that launched a thousand ships."

Where the legend of Simon Magus becomes important to Mary Magdalene is in his companion, Helen. Simon traveled everywhere with Helen, and told people that she was the embodiment of the "First Principle," who had fallen into the world of matter. Each time she was reincarnated, she had slipped lower and lower in status until finally she was a prostitute in a brothel. Rescuing Helen, Simon Magus said, was why he came to earth in the first place, and he found her on the roof of the brothel.

Clearly, the legend of Helen is meant to be a Gnostic allegory for the fall of Sophia (which is in turn an allegory of the fall of the soul), but the parallels between Simon Magus and Jesus should also make us look more closely at the parallels between Helen and Mary Magdalene.

Both Helen and Mary Magdalene have represented Sophia's presence in the physical world; wouldn't the fact that Helen was incarnated as a prostitute have had some bearing on what was thought of Mary Magdalene's pre-Jesus life as well? This is a question that hasn't been fully explored by scholars, but as the studies of Mary Magdalene's roles in Gnosticism continue, it very well could be the earliest indirect reference to Mary Magdalene as a prostitute.

Prostitution in Victorian England

In 1837, a new queen, Victoria I, took the throne of England. She became the first monarch to live long enough to see her name given to the period during which she ruled; the last 60 years of the nineteenth century came to be known as the Victorian era. Victoria, and the Victorian era with her, died in 1901.

During this time, Victorian England and Western society in general saw many kinds of scientific, technological, and medical innovations toward the advancement of society. The culture of the time was defined by an awareness of civic responsibility, moral fortitude, and proper behavior. In large part, family and public life was inspired by the queen and her husband, whose romance and large family were legendary.

The Great Social Evil

To the Victorian mind, middle-class women were the very models and symbols of virtue and purity. A proper Victorian woman had no carnal desire and only agreed to have sex with her husband for the purpose of having children. What we see now as an unrealistic moral goal created imbalance within the society. This resulted in an incredibly potent double-standard in which it was believed that good women didn't like sex, but men, being creatures driven by sex, still needed it.

Illuminations

In Victorian England, it was believed that women who had not been married by the age of 25 began to physically degenerate. The 1838 *Every Woman's Book* by Richard Carlile says that they "become pale and languid, that general weakness and irritation, a sort of restlessness, nervous fidgettyness takes possession of them, and an absorbing process goes on, their forms degenerate, their features sink, and the peculiar character of the old maid becomes apparent."

What was a healthy, red-blooded, Victorian man to do? Visit a prostitute, of course. Prostitution ran rampant in Victorian England, and some estimates place the number of prostitutes in London at about 40,000 in 1841. It was considered natural for a man to seek out the services of prostitutes to avoid placing undue pressure on his wife for marital relations, so prostitution became a "necessary evil."

It was during this time that a great preoccupation arose with the "fallen woman" theme, which was repeated often in the literature of the time. Mary Magdalene, as a redeemed prostitute, became the model "fallen woman." Her name naturally came to be associated with prostitution as an ever-growing social problem. Prostitutes themselves were euphemistically called "Magdalens," and prostitution itself was sometimes called "Magdalenism."

It Is Written

It is a cruel calumny to call them in mass prostitutes; and as for their virtue, they lose it as one loses his watch who is robbed by the highway thief. Their virtue is the watch, and society is the thief. These poor women toiling on starvation wages, while penury, misery and famine clutch them by the throat and say "Render up your body or die."

—Excerpt from a letter to *The Times* (London) signed "Another Unfortunate," 1858

Harlot with a Heart of Gold

Throughout Western literature and film, a type of character has emerged time and time again: the harlot with a heart of gold. You can probably think of at least one book, film, or television program you've been exposed to that has a character like this. Ground down by poverty or some other unavoidable circumstance, a woman is forced into prostitution. Like Julia Roberts's character in the movie *Pretty Woman*, the harlot with a heart of gold becomes streetwise from pursuing her occupation but somehow manages to avoid losing her soul in spite of her degraded state. She is compassionate and wholesome on the inside, and usually makes some kind of sacrifice to help someone avoid a fate like hers.

It has been suggested that in any given play, the stock character of a harlot with a heart of gold repents, is redeemed, and is dead by the fourth act. This speaks to the fact that Victorians didn't really feel that there was a way for a fallen woman to return to normal society. Once fallen, always fallen. By dying, she could give the ultimate sacrifice without acknowledging the contradictions involved with facing the same social conditions that forced her into prostitution in the first place.

It is Mary Magdalene the penitent who provides the model for the harlot with a heart of gold. She sets her sights on a higher goal, namely Jesus, and leaves behind her tainted life to follow him. Of course, in Mary Magdalene legend she doesn't die at the end, but this was of little consequence. It is the repentance and return to grace that counts.

Magdalen Asylums

In Chapter 3, I mentioned the existence of institutions called Magdalen laundries, which were also known as Magdalen asylums. Today, we imagine an asylum as a place where the mentally ill were sent, but originally it meant an institution where people were cared for who couldn't otherwise care for themselves, or who were in some way in need of care. This was the premise on which the Magdalen asylums were founded. Born to a great extent from the Victorian preoccupation with rescuing destitute and fallen women, the institutions were begun with the best of intentions. Many were able to provide valuable assistance to countless women.

> **CAUTION**
>
> **Quite Contrary**
>
> Magdalen asylums weren't only an Irish phenomenon. They existed, and some still do exist, elsewhere in the world.

In 1998, a piece of property that had been a Magdalen asylum was sold to real estate developers. When the property was excavated for building new structures, 133 unmarked graves were discovered; these were the remains of many women who had died over the years during the operation of the asylum. What began as an institutional system to help women get back on their feet had obviously become a place where women were languishing until the end of their lives. The press found out about the discovery, and for the first time the dark side of the institutional system was exposed. Many of the remains were identified, but some still go without names.

Over the course of about 150 years, approximately 30,000 women were committed to Magdalene asylums for a variety of "offenses," including the following:

♦ Pregnancy out of wedlock

♦ Being a victim of rape

♦ Flirting

♦ Being too lovely to stay out of trouble

Although it's hard to believe that there could have been a systematic removal of young women from society for these reasons, it did happen. Some asylum inmates were orphans themselves and were turned over to the Magdalen institutional system after they had grown too old to remain in an orphanage. Once checked in, a woman couldn't check herself out; she had to wait for a member of her family to come claim her. If it was her family who had hidden her away in the first place, often a woman was destined to spend her whole life institutionalized.

The laundry business wasn't chosen arbitrarily; in the days before automatic washing machines and dryers, someone had to do the laundry. It was a symbolic occupation for women who were supposed to be spending their days repenting for their sexual sins; they were *literally* scrubbing their sins away.

The young women who became inmates were overseen by nuns, who ran the institutions. All would attend mass every day, and religious imagery was vital in the "reform" process. Sometimes the chastity of the nuns was held up against the presumed sinfulness of the inmates, who were seen as ruined.

It wasn't until 1996 that the last Magdalen asylum in Ireland closed its doors. Many women still living are either the children of the "Magdalens," as the inmates were known, or were "Maggies" themselves. To these women, the name Mary Magdalene will always be associated with the pain they suffered at the hands of a cruel institutional system. Although not all Magdalen asylums were like prisons, and some did manage to truly help women in need, it is those that abused their free source of slave labor that will be remembered as Magdalen asylums.

> **It Is Written** _____
>
> Round about that altar will ascend daily to heaven the co-mingled prayer of the consecrated virgin and the penitent girl that no blight of sin or sorrow may ever rest upon you or your children. My brethren, will it not remind you of that last, most touching scene of the life of our Divine Lord, when Mary the sinful but repentant Magdalen, and Mary His Immaculate Virgin Mother, stood beneath His cross.
> —Rev. Dr. Sheehan, *Waterford News,* 1903 (Ireland)

A Cultural Mirror

Across the span of centuries, Mary Magdalene has been portrayed in art in a way that reflects the values of the time and place where the artistic work was created. An artist of fifteenth-century Holland, for example, didn't portray Mary Magdalene in exactly the same way as an artist of fifteenth-century Italy. Likewise, an artist of thirteenth-century Italy wouldn't represent Mary Magdalene in the same way an artist would of sixteenth-century Italy. This isn't a situation unique to Mary Magdalene; that is the case with all art. By nature, it reflects the society that produces it.

When it comes to Mary Magdalene, though, another thing becomes evident. How she has been depicted reflects the cultural values within the society where the art was created. Because we've inherited so many art treasures that portray Mary Magdalene, we've been able to compare the culture that produced the art and the art itself to try to understand why she may have been presented in the way that she has.

Prior to the fourteenth century, for example, Mary Magdalene was rarely pictured at the foot of the cross as she was in later eras. But in the fourteenth century, the presence of monastic orders was on the rise, inspired in great part by Mary Magdalene. Because the monks of certain orders, such as the Dominicans and the Franciscans, placed so much emphasis on devotional activities in which they visualized themselves at the foot of the cross witnessing Jesus' suffering, they began to identify with Mary Magdalene in her role of witness to the crucifixion. Art subsequently began more and more to reflect these ideas and soon Mary Magdalene was a standard fixture at the foot of the cross.

During the Victorian period, with the emphasis on "fallen women," Mary Magdalene was portrayed in *Pre-Raphaelite* art as a romantic and tragic figure. Dante Gabriel Rossetti, one of the leaders of the Pre-Raphaelite movement during the Victorian era, explored the theme of the redemption of fallen women in his artwork and poetry. In one painting of Mary Magdalene, he presents her in a thoughtful and sober pose, with flowing red hair. Behind her is a blossoming plant called Black Hellebore, which the Victorians associated with wrongful accusation and slander.

In the seventeenth century, there was a trend in which it was popular to be painted as Mary Magdalene. Reserved for a wealthy elite who could afford to commission paintings, wives and mistresses of powerful men began to model as Mary Magdalene. Usually the background for these paintings was the grotto, where Mary Magdalene lived in solitude for 30 years; the women would be depicted lounging, Venus-like, in a cave. Some, however, appeared to convey a truly pious reflection on penitence. One of the mistresses of King Louis XIV, for example, eventually identified with Mary Magdalene's penitence to such a degree that she retired to a convent. At least five of his other mistresses were also painted as Mary Magdalene.

Lingua Magda

In 1848, a society of painters broke away from producing the typical art of their day, determined to present their subjects with more beauty, realism, and depth than dictated by the prominent art school of the time. This style was referred to as **Pre-Raphaelite** art. Mary Magdalene was one of the subjects Pre-Raphaelite artists were interested in exploring.

Mary Magdalene continues to be a cultural mirror. In the 1998 movie *The Book of Life*, in which Jesus and Mary Magdalene return to Earth to authorize the end of the world, Mary Magdalene is portrayed by the hip young musician, P.J. Harvey. Harvey's character, Magdalena, wears leather pants and lipstick, and it is she who retrieves the Book of Life (contained, in the film, on a notebook computer) from a trash bin after Jesus tosses it away in a moment of discouragement. In this film, Mary Magdalene is Jesus' companion, his love, and an important part in the eventual fate of the world.

Illuminations

The Book of Life is another movie that wrongly identifies Mary Magdalene as the woman who was caught in adultery.

Strangely enough, Mary Magdalene has gone from being merely a woman who witnessed the resurrection at the beginning of Christianity to an apostle equal to the rest. Then she became a spokeswoman for sexual impropriety, and now is back to a figure who is important in her own right. She is once again being recognized as the apostle of the apostles, and as we see in the next chapter, is the subject of a postmodern fascination with the possibility that she and Jesus were married.

In spite of her many identities, her role as "fallen woman" still gets the most attention. It has been written into our culture from almost the beginning, and as such, it functions as part of our collective identity. Mary Magdalene has become a symbol at the highest level for the many subtleties of class distinction, particularly where it applies to women and where issues of sexuality intersect with issues of morality.

The Least You Need to Know

- ◆ Eve was the original "fallen woman," and her myth had a lot of influence on how Mary Magdalene would be viewed.

- ◆ The Gnostic myth of Sophia seems to have similarities with the legends of Mary Magdalene, and sometimes Mary Magdalene is seen as Sophia in her fallen aspect.

- ◆ Mary Magdalene influenced the ways that Victorian English society viewed prostitutes.

- ◆ One of the solutions for the problem of prostitution was the creation of asylums named for Mary Magdalene, where women who were believed to have used their sexuality incorrectly were incarcerated.

- ◆ We can learn something about a society by how Mary Magdalene is depicted in the art of a given period and place.

Chapter 19

The Holy Grail: The Bloodline Theory

In This Chapter

- ◆ Peering into the Grail's past
- ◆ The mystery surrounding Rennes-le-Château
- ◆ Conspiracy theories and secret societies
- ◆ The confusion one word can cause
- ◆ Sifting through the evidence

Thanks to the movies *Indiana Jones and the Last Crusade* and *Monty Python and the Holy Grail,* most people today are aware of the Holy Grail legend even if they haven't read any of the old Grail stories. Medieval knights go on an honorable quest to retrieve the Holy Grail, a mysterious cup whose original purpose and exact nature no one agrees on. It was the cup used in the first Eucharist at the last supper. It was the cup that was used at the crucifixion to catch Jesus' blood. Or it's simply a magical dish or stone that miraculously serves up food.

In this chapter, we take a look at one more interpretation of the Holy Grail myth, and find out how Mary Magdalene herself has been cast as this elusive vessel.

A Painless History of the Holy Grail

Lingua Magda

Romance in the Middle Ages was a little different than how we think of romance today. A medieval **romance** is a long tale, written as an epic poem or a narrative, of the heroic adventures of a particular figure.

In the last half of the twelfth century, a *romance* writer named Chrétien de Troyes lived in the northeastern part of France. Among his work was a story that was unfinished at the time of his death: *The Story of the Grail*, or as it was sometimes known, *Perceval*. No one is entirely certain of how he came up with his literary ideas, but it's generally thought that he drew heavily from folklore.

The Earliest Grail

In Chrétien's grail romance, a foolish young man named Perceval starts out on a quest to become a knight. He has several adventures, and at one point ends up in a castle nestled high in the hills. The king who lives at the castle is old and feeble, suffering from a wound that prevents him from walking. The king invites Perceval to dine with him and spend the night. As they eat, a strange procession enters the room. Five people holding an array of objects file through and then disappear into another room, without a word being said:

♦ A young man holding a white spear that bleeds from the tip

♦ Two more young men carrying large candlesticks that hold ten candles each

♦ A young woman who carries a magnificent grail that shines more brightly than the candles

♦ Another young woman who carries a silver platter

Illuminations

In Chapter 8, we took a brief look at Longinus, the legendary centurion who pierced Jesus' side with his spear. It is Longinus's spear that figures in some of the medieval Holy Grail stories.

The grail itself is described as "made of fine, pure gold; and in it were set precious stones of many kinds, the richest and most precious in the earth or the sea: those in the grail surpassed all other jewels, without a doubt."

This ends the description of the grail in the very oldest writing about it. The only other thing added about the vessel later in the story is the fact that the procession was taking these items in to an old king, who lived only on the Eucharist that was delivered to him in the grail.

Chrétien's story, although unfinished, was enormously popular, and others added to it until it was deemed finished. Still others wrote their own versions of the grail story, and it is from the others that much of the myth we've learned about today was developed. Most early innovations on grail romances occurred during about a 60-year period between 1180 and 1240.

Later Visions of the Grail

In later stories, the nature of the grail changed, depending on the story and the teller. In Robert de Boron's *The History of the Grail*, written between 1170 and 1212, it became the dish in which Jesus broke the bread at the last supper as well as the dish in which his blood was caught by Joseph of Arimathea at the crucifixion. But to Wolfram von Eschenbach, who wrote another grail romance, *Parzival*, around the earliest years of the thirteenth century, the grail was a stone, not a vessel.

It Is Written

How open a question the physical nature of "the Grail" still was in c. 1200, when Wolfram embarked on his *Parzival*, is shown by the fact that his Grail—he calls it "Grâl"—was a Stone, and that although it had the loftiest spiritual connections it also had some very earthy aspects, since it served up meats hot or cold, wild or tame, and a whole variety of alcoholic beverages to individual taste, so that, as has been wittily observed, it also functioned as "un buffet ambulant."

—A. T. Hatto, in the foreword to his translation of *Parzival*, by Wolfram von Eschenbach

It should be noted at this point that nowhere in the Holy Grail romances does Mary Magdalene figure importantly. She didn't enter into Holy Grail mythology until the twentieth century.

Holy Blood, Holy Grail

As we already saw in Chapter 4, *Holy Blood, Holy Grail* is a book published in the United States in 1983 by Michael Baigent, Richard Leigh, and Henry Lincoln (first published in England in 1982 as *The Holy Blood and The Holy Grail*). In the book, the authors present an argument for how and why the legends of the Holy Grail were really based on a much older truth; that Jesus and Mary Magdalene had been married, and that their family started the Merovingian bloodline in France.

A Little Church in France

Once upon a time, *Holy Blood, Holy Grail* tells us, in 1885, a priest named Bérenger Saunière was transferred to a little country church in the village of Rennes-le-Château in France. The church was extremely old, having been consecrated in the eleventh century, and was in terrible condition. Saunière, only earning six pounds sterling a year, collected donations from the villagers to make some renovations to the church. During the course of renovations, the altar slab was lifted off two stone columns that supported it. One of the columns was hollow.

 Illuminations

If you've read *The Da Vinci Code*, then the name Saunière is probably familiar. Dan Brown named the Louvre curator character Jacque Saunière.

In the hollow column, Saunière found some mysterious documents that had been written by his predecessor. Not knowing what to do with them, he showed them to the bishop. The bishop paid for Saunière to travel to Paris, where he showed them to Abbé Bieil, the director of St-Sulpice. Bieil's nephew just happened to be an accomplished scholar who was familiar with cryptography, and he detected some coded messages in the documents. Among the strange statements was the following:

> To Dagobert II king and to Sion belongs this treasure and he is there dead.

While in Paris, Saunière seemed to make all sorts of connections with people in a certain social circle who were active in Paris's "esoteric subculture." Some say he even became the lover of Emma Calvé, a famous singer of the time who allegedly had connections in occult circles. After his documents were deciphered, he returned to Rennes-le-Château, where he soon began making major renovations to the church that far exceeded his income. Over the space of 24 years, *Holy Blood, Holy Grail* tells us, he spent in the neighborhood of "several million pounds."

Saunière's lifestyle and behavior, say the authors, were lavish and brazen. He appeared to have friends in very high places, including the royal family of Austria, members of which apparently transferred large sums of money into a Swiss bank account in Saunière's name. His new superior became concerned about what was occurring at Rennes-le-Château, and Saunière was disciplined. But after he appealed his sentence to Rome, he was apparently let off without another word.

In January 1917 Saunière had a stroke, and the local priest from a neighboring village came to administer last rites. When he left Saunière's sickroom, however, he was said to have refused to administer last rites because of what Saunière had confessed. Not only had he denied a dying man *absolution*, but according to some legends, "he never smiled again." What was the terrible secret that Saunière divulged on his deathbed?

Lingua Magda

When a person confesses his or her sins to a priest in the Roman Catholic tradition, the priest will then set the person free of those sins. This act is called **absolution**.

This is the basis for the mystery surrounding Rennes-le-Château. The authors of *Holy Blood, Holy Grail* claim to have started investigating the mystery believing that Saunière had discovered some kind of treasure, and were drawn into what became an elaborate hunt for nothing less than the Holy Grail.

Enter Mary Magdalene

It won't be spoiling the end of the story at this point to tell you that the pivotal moment in *Holy Blood, Holy Grail* is when the authors reveal their discovery: that Jesus and Mary Magdalene were married and had children. Today, the idea has solidified somewhat into popular culture due to the success of *The Da Vinci Code*, but in the early 1980s this was a radical notion. Certainly, it had been suggested that maybe Jesus and Mary Magdalene had been married, but no one had ever presented actual "proof" that they had started a dynastic bloodline!

I am, of course, using the term "proof" very loosely. Any evidence that the authors of *Holy Blood, Holy Grail* cited to support the notion that Jesus and Mary Magdalene had children is highly circumstantial and leaves more than a little bit of reasonable doubt. The ideas were based mostly on the French legends of Mary Magdalene's trip to France that erupted from the relics race of the Middle Ages. They were then bolstered by legends surrounding a medieval cast of characters including the Knights Templar and the Cathars (both of which we look at later in this and the next chapter).

> **It Is Written** _____
>
> Perhaps the Magdalen—that elusive woman in the Gospels—was in fact Jesus' wife. Perhaps their union produced offspring. After the Crucifixion perhaps the Magdalen, with at least one child, was smuggled to Gaul—where established Jewish communities already existed and where, in consequence, she might have found a refuge. Perhaps there was, in short, a hereditary bloodline descended directly from Jesus.
>
> —Michael Baigent, Richard Leigh, and Henry Lincoln, *Holy Blood, Holy Grail* (1983)

In short, there is no truly compelling evidence that Jesus and Mary Magdalene were ever married or that they had children. *Holy Blood, Holy Grail* is based on *speculation*, and the authors admit that theirs is a hypothesis for which there is no solid proof.

Orders and Societies

In their breathless pursuit of the secrets of Rennes-le-Château and the mysterious ciphers, the authors of *Holy Blood, Holy Grail* apparently run into information about all sorts of other historical people and groups. Among them are a couple of the "usual suspects" in modern conspiracy theories, as well as an organization that had been previously unknown.

Knights Templar

The Knights Templar were a group of knights originally begun in 1118 C.E. as a monastic order but which grew into a medieval institution all its own. After the First Crusade "liberated" Jerusalem from the control of Islam, the Knights Templar were organized to protect pilgrims on the road to the Holy Land and look after the European interests in Palestine. As the years progressed, the Templars became involved in banking, and were able to organize a primitive form of deposit and withdrawal similar to our modern checking accounts.

With their increasing holdings of money and property, at one time including the entire island of Cyprus, the Knights Templar were naturally an obstacle for the more power-hungry nobles of the time. On Friday, October 13, 1307, Philip the Fair, king of France, had the Knights Templar in France arrested. They were subsequently interrogated and tortured until all sorts of blasphemous heresies were admitted. In other areas, chapters of the Knights Templar were dissolved by local rulers at the pope's command.

Illuminations _____

The notion that the Knights Templar had been the guardians of "grail secrets" is hardly a new one. In the late nineteenth century, a folklorist named Miss Jessie L. Weston speculated that while in Palestine, the Templars had come into contact with a surviving Gnostic sect (the Naassenes, in particular). They came to be in possession of a secret so fundamental to the origins of Christianity that the Church was forced to suppress them in order to survive.

The Priory of Sion

In the national library in Paris, Bibliotèque Nationale, mysterious documents were turning up. Collectively, the authors of *Holy Blood, Holy Grail* began to refer to them as *Prieuré Documents* because they indicated the existence of a secret order called the *Prieuré de Sion*, or "The Priory of Sion." Allegedly, the Priory was an organization that operated behind the scenes in European history to achieve a mysterious goal, which is revealed later in the book: to restore the Merovingian bloodline, descended from Jesus and Mary Magdalene, to the throne of France.

Quite Contrary _____

How do we know that the Priory documents were planted at the national library in Paris? Easy. There are library records that show when the documents were deposited and catalogued. In fact, at least until recently, anyone could even request some of them through the library system.

Among the Prieuré Documents was the infamous *Dossiers Secretes*, a list of all of the supposed leaders, or "Grand Masters," of the Priory since the fourteenth century. Among its illustrious entries were the following:

- Nicolas Flamel (1398–1418)
- Sandro Filipepi a.k.a. Botticelli (1483–1510)
- Leonardo da Vinci (1510–1519)
- Michel de Notre-Dame a.k.a. Nostradamus (1556–1566)
- Robert Fludd (1595–1637)
- Isaac Newton (1691–1727)
- Victor Hugo (1844–1885)

♦ Claude Debussy (1885–1918)

♦ Jean Cocteau (1918–1963)

After establishing the possibility that the Priory of Sion had been founded in 1099, the authors of *Holy Blood, Holy Grail* then assert that the Priory was behind the foundation of the Knights Templar. The Knights Templar apparently functioned as the military and administrative arm, leaving the Priory free to surreptitiously meddle with world events as needed to achieve its goal. (For an organization that's allegedly been around for 1,000 years, it must not be very effective! There is still no Merovingian on the throne of France; indeed, there is no longer a throne in France at all.)

Freemasons

Would any conspiracy theory be complete without the Freemasons making at least a small appearance? In the *Holy Blood, Holy Grail* view of history, the Freemasons are possibly a surviving branch of the Knights Templar.

Freemasons are a secular ("nonreligious") society begun as early as the sixteenth century and as late as the eighteenth century to promote tolerance, morality, and brotherhood. The exact origin of the term "freemason" isn't known. Some suspect it is from working in "freestone," the elaborate stone carving performed in the Middle Ages, whereas others suggest that it comes from the freedom that stonemasons had in moving from worksite to worksite as necessary. Thought by many to have begun as "operative" groups of medieval stonemasons, members who were "nonoperative," or not themselves stonemasons, were gradually admitted to their groups. This eventually led to entire nonoperative groups that used the stonemason's tools and traditions to convey their ideas. Most agree that Freemasonry originates from England, although some insist it started in Scotland.

Robert the Bruce, the King of Scotland in 1317, had been excommunicated by the Roman Catholic Church and therefore could no longer be threatened with any worse ecclesiastical reprisal. Because of Robert's indifference to the Church, many of the Knights Templar fled northward. When the order came from Rome to disband the Templars, those in Scotland were relatively safe from the harsh penalties their French counterparts were suffering.

The Templars' presence in the British Isles has led to speculations about the order's influence on the development of Freemasonry. Many Freemasons themselves claim that their society has Templar roots. The highest degree of the Masonic York Rite is that of Knight Templar, and some associated orders bear the name of the last Knights Templar Grand Master, Jacques de Molay. Most Freemasons, however, decline to speculate on any Templar origins, or deny it outright as mythmaking.

The authors of *Holy Blood, Holy Grail*, however, in pursuing the ever-shifting history of the Priory of Sion, theorized that after the dissolution of the Knights Templar, Freemasonry became the Priory's administrative branch.

Illuminations

The dust jacket of *The Da Vinci Code* contains clues about Dan Brown's next novel. On the flaps, certain letters appear in bold. In order, the bold letters spell "Is there no help for the widow's son?" This is reputedly a Masonic distress call, referring to Hiram Abiff. Abiff allegedly constructed King Solomon's Temple, and was called "the widow's son." Supposedly, he was murdered by one of his workers when he wouldn't divulge an important secret. Joseph Smith, the founder of Mormonism, was believed to have uttered this phrase before being killed, leading to conspiracies about the involvement of the Mormon church with Freemasonry. Incidentally, Smith also taught that Jesus and Mary Magdalene had been married, and that he was one of Jesus' descendents.

The Pun That Changed History

The whole premise of *Holy Blood, Holy Grail* is that it was Jesus' blood, rather than the grail, that was important. As support for this notion, they mention an old French word that was often associated with Holy Grail legend: *sangraal*. Here's the secret: If you divide it as "san graal," it means "holy grail." But if you divide it as "sang raal," it means "blood royal" (or "royal blood," since in French the adjective comes after the noun). Let's look at this one more time for a clear visual:

san graal = holy grail

sang raal = royal blood

This, the authors of *Holy Blood, Holy Grail* assure us, is more evidence for their bloodline theory. The notion has since been picked up by additional authors and cited as a profound revelation.

What most authors writing about the bloodline theory don't say is that many of the people who encountered the word *sangraal* in the Middle Ages were sophisticated enough to know that it was a pun. In addition, there was a widespread cult of the Holy Blood as a Christian relic, much in the same way that other cults grew up around different relics of the Passion and crucifixion. To suggest that our medieval forebears weren't swift enough to appreciate the ambiguity is an insult to their intelligence.

In the fifteenth century, though, the word with a double meaning caused Holy Grail legend to take a new direction. When Sir Thomas Malory wrote his famous works on King Arthur and the knights of the Round Table, he translated it as "sankgreal." Earlier, Robert de Boron, who, acknowledging the vessel as a holy relic because it had held Jesus' blood, still placed the emphasis on the vessel itself. Malory referred to the Holy Blood as the relic, not the vessel. The vessel's only importance was as a vehicle for the blood.

It Is Written

Galahad finds the "sank roiall" in Wales after four years' search. [John] Hardyng, like Henry Lovelich at about the same period, uses the misreading "sang real" for "san greal," so that the Holy Grail becomes the "royal blood."

—Richard Barber, *The Holy Grail: Imagination and Belief* (2004)

Not all of the grail stories use the term, either. The earliest version, Chrétien's, only refers to "the grail" and calls it a "holy thing." He never uses the controversial term. Later romances do use the term, but it is by no means universal in the copies that have survived. The origins of the word "grail" are complicated, and cannot be legitimately summed up with the cursory treatment of "sangraal" given by the authors of *Holy Blood, Holy Grail.*

The sum of all of this is only that it's a mistake to assume that a reading of "sangraal" as "sang raal" is a recent innovation. On the contrary, it has been around for centuries, without ever so much as a hint of it referring to a bloodline.

Breaking It All Down

As attractive as the *Holy Blood, Holy Grail* mythos might be to some, it is based on a complex web of speculation and fraudulent documents. Although very little has been published in English to debunk the whole grand affair, much has been written in French. It is to some of those sources that we now turn to put *Holy Blood, Holy Grail* into perspective.

Bérenger Saunière and Rennes-le-Château

In 1955, the house built by Bérenger Saunière, Villa Bethanie, was acquired and turned into a restaurant. It is believed that in order to generate publicity, the owner concocted an elaborate tale of an errant priest who stumbled across a treasure of inestimable value and secrecy.

In reality, Bérenger Saunière was able to fund his renovations and a lifestyle more lavish than expected of a priest through a practice called *simony*, or the selling of ecclesiastical services. In this case, Saunière was selling masses to people during a time when there was a political rift between church and state. He had taken out many newspaper and magazine ads, and witnesses have even testified to helping Saunière with his correspondence to accomplish this. His financial records still survive and provide documented evidence of this practice.

> **Lingua Magda**
>
> **Simony,** the practice of accepting money for ecclesiastical services, is a term that comes from Simon Magus. Believed to have been the magician named Simon in the book of Acts, he is said to have tried to pay the disciples to teach him how to work miracles.

The mystery at Rennes-le-Château grew in popularity, much the way that many other legends, such as the Loch Ness monster and the UFO crash at Roswell, New Mexico, find their way into everyday conversation. In reality, Saunière's wealth was vastly overstated, and the Church did *not* suspiciously reinstate him to the priesthood. He received last rites on his deathbed as would be expected, in poverty.

Pierre Plantard and the Priory of Sion

What motivation could a person possibly have for claiming to be the last living descendent of a deposed royal family of Frankish kings and the rightful heir to the throne of France? Power, wealth, and infamy? Pierre Plantard's motivations may have been all of those, or merely politically driven, but it is certain that he was a forger of documents, an embezzler, and a fraud who did prison time.

In 1956, an organization called the Priory of Sion was formed in France by Pierre Plantard and another man named André Bonhomme. Named for a hill (Mont Sion) outside the town of St-Julien-en-Genevoise, the Priory of Sion was formed as a group of friends wishing to do nothing more than fight for low-cost housing. They produced a newsletter called *Circuit*, but not much more came of the group.

Pierre Plantard resurrected the Priory of Sion in 1962, when he placed it in the center of an elaborate hoax with the goal of inscribing his own name at the end of the Merovingian bloodline. Rather ingeniously, he made use of legends—both medieval and modern—combined with falsified documents to give the impression that the secret treasure hidden by the Cathars, protected by the Knights Templar, and guarded by an invented list of Priory of Sion "Grand Masters" was the Merovingian bloodline. The bloodline, incidentally, had been started by none other than Jesus and Mary Magdalene.

> **Quite Contrary**
>
> In 1967, one of Pierre Plantard's associates in the Priory of Sion hoax, Philippe de Chérisey, admitted forging the Priory documents himself.

That the authors of *Holy Blood, Holy Grail* apparently accepted the bait, as they say, "hook, line, and sinker," illustrates the depth of their "objective" research. They first presented their findings to the world in 1982, and given that *Holy Blood, Holy Grail* is itself such an impressively spun web of speculation, few readers know where to begin to unwind it for themselves.

Beginning in the mid-1980s, French researchers and civil authorities began to close in on Plantard's fraudulent activity. Finally, in 1993, he admitted to a judge, while under oath, that he had concocted the whole story.

Analyzing the Appeal

There need be no conspiracy to hide some dangerous truth in order for multiple layers of meaning to exist in a legend, in this case that of the Holy Grail. On one hand, the complexity reveals much about the cultures from which legends grow. On the other hand, any holes in a story inevitably lead to speculation that can in turn generate another round of mythmaking. It's important, then, to try to understand what our modern myths reveal about *us*.

Rather than dismissing *Holy Blood, Holy Grail* out of hand as nothing but an unsubstantiated, sensational potboiler, perhaps we should take a look at why it has caused such a stir. I don't claim to have the answers, but I'll wager that the ideas presented in *Holy Blood, Holy Grail* aren't going to disappear anytime soon.

The Least You Need to Know

◆ Holy Grail legends really have little to do with Mary Magdalene.

◆ A book published in the 1980s, *Holy Blood, Holy Grail,* is the source of the modern preoccupation with Mary Magdalene as the literal Holy Grail.

◆ Although the church at Rennes-le-Château does demonstrate a devotion to Mary Magdalene, the fantastic story of Bérenger Saunière is a modern myth.

◆ The Priory of Sion is a hoax.

Chapter 20

The Holy Grail: The Lost Feminine Theory

In This Chapter

- ◆ A brand new vision of Mary Magdalene
- ◆ A geometrical proof
- ◆ Where *The Da Vinci Code* fits in
- ◆ Sorting through some historical laundry

Once upon a time, a young girl slaved away at the hearth, sooty-faced and oppressed. One day, she received an invitation to a royal ball, where she met the prince. He instantly recognized that his life would be incomplete without her. One thing led to another, and eventually, they got married and the kingdom rejoiced. This is the age-old tale of Cinderella, which has been told and retold in many different cultures, in many different ways. But how does it relate to Mary Magdalene?

In the preceding chapter, we explored how Mary Magdalene has been shaped into the literal Holy Grail by allegedly bearing Jesus' children and starting a bloodline. In this chapter, we turn instead to a figurative vision of the Holy Grail, and how Mary Magdalene has again been cast as this mysterious vessel.

Mary Magdalene as the "Lost Feminine"

In 1993, Margaret Starbird published a book called *The Woman with the Alabaster Jar: Mary Magdalen and the Holy Grail.* In it, Starbird details how, although it can't be proved historically, Mary Magdalene and Jesus were married and started a bloodline.

Lingua Magda

A culture or institution that is governed by men is called **patriarchal.** Many people believe that patriarchal cultures place less value on women than on men.

Though unlike Michael Baigent, Richard Leigh, and Henry Lincoln's 1983 book, *Holy Blood, Holy Grail, The Woman with the Alabaster Jar* doesn't pivot on the foundation and survival of a bloodline. It revolves instead around how Jesus' true message was one of balance between masculine and feminine principles, and how that message was crushed by the *patriarchal* Roman Catholic Church. Traces of the truth remain, though, asserts the author, in the form of Holy Grail and "lost feminine" mythology.

The Woman with the Alabaster Jar has been an influential book in some ways, and many people are now drawn to the idea of Jesus and Mary Magdalene as a married couple. All of the figurative Bride of Christ imagery that has existed since the earliest centuries of Christianity has been revisited as a literal truth.

At the same time as claiming a literal marriage between Jesus and Mary Magdalene, though, Margaret Starbird also asserts that the value in recognizing such a union comes in demonstrating a balanced vision of God. Because the patriarchal Church has reigned for so long without the mitigating influence of "the feminine," our culture has become one of severe imbalance. By "imaging God as partners," she writes, healing can take place and balance restored.

The Ritual of the *Hieros Gamos*

At the center of Starbird's theory is a ritual called the *hieros gamos,* or "sacred marriage." The *hieros gamos* was a ritual that was performed in ancient fertility cults throughout Mesopotamia and the Mediterranean region. In the ritual, a priestess who represented the power of a particular goddess and often, the earth, was married to a symbolic and sacrificial king, who represented a particular god and often, the sun.

Although the ritual differed somewhat depending on the place where it was enacted, the main idea was that the priestess and the king were joined in a marriage that was symbolic of the renewal of the land and the community's collective soul. Often the ritual contained references to anointing the king, who was then ritually slain (literally or symbolically) as a sacrifice for his people. In some sacred marriage rituals, the king would then rise again after three days as his bride searched for him in a garden.

In the language of fertility myth, this ritual represented the cycles of the seasons. In the spring fields were tilled and planted, in the summer the fields grew, in the autumn they were harvested, and during the winter everything died off. Then again in the spring, the cycle would begin again. The king represented the presence of the sun at different times of year, and the priestess represented the rich fecundity of the land. Both were necessary in order for the crops to grow, and the people depended on both, in balance, for life.

CAUTION

Quite Contrary _____

Lest you get the impression that fertility cults were just a "flash in the pan" of history, it's worth noting that they were one of the most ancient religious expressions on earth, predating even Judaism. The Sumerians, the Babylonians, and the Canaanites all practiced fertility religions. The *hieros gamos* wasn't the only rite practiced in fertility religions, and many cultures outside of Mesopotamia also held similar beliefs. May Day and the Maypole, for example, are believed to be descendants of ancient spring fertility celebrations.

There is some proof that the ritual had meaning on another level not completely connected with the well-being of the land—that is, with the priestess representing the individual soul and the king representing God. The concept of the soul has been different depending on the time and place, however, and it's difficult to draw a direct line between sacred marriage rituals and the relationship between humans and the Divine. Certainly, it's likely that more indirect connections do exist, but this probably wasn't a ritual that was being practiced regularly during the first century. Although there were mystery religions that were active during the Roman Empire that employed some of the same ideas and figures as older fertility cults, there isn't a direct correlation.

Margaret Starbird theorizes that, whether or not similar rituals were still enacted during the Roman Empire and within its borders, references to it would have been recognizable. Therefore, the anointing scene in the Gospels that we explored in earlier chapters was actually a *hieros gamos* ritual meant to convey already-familiar ideas of masculine and feminine, sun and earth, in balance. As a *hieros gamos* ritual,

Mary Magdalene would have been a representative of a goddess, or in this case, "the sacred feminine."

You might be wondering now why Mary Magdalene would have been involved in the anointing scene; the woman who anointed Jesus wasn't ever named as Mary Magdalene. Starbird subscribes to the unity theory; that is, she believes that Mary Magdalene, Mary of Bethany, and the anonymous woman in Luke were the same person. By combining the three women, she has written, Pope Gregory the Great was only solidifying as doctrine what was already acknowledged as fact.

Saint Sarah

So what happened after Jesus died? In *The Woman with the Alabaster Jar*, Mary Magdalene was pregnant. Jesus' uncle, Joseph of Arimathea, smuggled the pregnant Mary out of Palestine because, as the wife of a man guilty of sedition (Jesus' alleged crime), she would have been in danger. In Alexandria, she gave birth to a daughter whom she named Sarah, which means "princess" in Hebrew. After a number of years, Mary Magdalene, Joseph of Arimethea, little Sarah, and some others undertook a voyage that brought them to the shores of southern Gaul.

Is this beginning to sound familiar? Now the medieval legends started by the monks at Vézelay take over for a while. But another innovation takes place; instead of landing at Marseilles, they landed at a little village that is now called Stes. Maries de la Mer, or "Saints Marys of the Sea." This little village claims that it was on their shores where Mary Magdalene and the others landed. To this day, they recognize the patronage of a woman called Saint Sarah, who is dark skinned and honored as the mother of the gypsies. Margaret Starbird believes that the Saint Sarah of the gypsies was actually Jesus and Mary Magdalene's daughter.

> **It Is Written**
>
> She might be symbolically "dark" for reasons associated with the "hidden" bloodline of the princes of Judah, whose appearance, described as "brighter than snow and whiter than milk," is now "blacker than soot, they are unrecognized on the streets" (Lamentations 4).
>
> —Margaret Starbird, from "Mary Magdalene: The Beloved" (1999 article for Magdalene.org)

In one medieval legend of Mary Magdalene's voyage to France, Sarah is said to be a servant girl with dark skin. Knowing that she is represented with dark skin by the villagers of Stes. Maries de la Mer, Starbird has drawn an association between that which is known to the world as "light" and that which is hidden from the world as "dark." Whether Sarah was hidden from the world for her protection or because she was simply lost because she wasn't a male heir is irrelevant; Starbird believes that her dark skin is somehow a metaphor for her lack of recognition.

She goes further and suggests that the many "Black Madonna" statues, so called because of their black skin, are actually statues of Mary Magdalene holding a baby Sarah. Although the Black Madonnas or Black Virgins have been the subject of controversy and veneration since before *The Woman with the Alabaster Jar* was published, many people have picked up on this symbolism. Today you can take guided tours of the Black Madonna sites in southern France to explore their supposed connection to Mary Magdalene and the sacred feminine.

The Cathars

Centuries passed, and France held an ancestral memory of the "true" lineage of Jesus and Mary Magdalene. The truth erupted, Starbird writes, in the heresies of the Cathars in medieval France.

The Cathars were people who lived in the southern region of modern-day France (then known as Languedoc), and practiced a religion called Catharism. This offshoot of Christianity flourished in the twelfth century. It was deemed heretical by the Roman Catholic Church, which took drastic measures to stamp it out. In the early part of the thirteenth century, a full-fledged crusade was launched against the Cathars, and tens of thousands of people were slaughtered. In 1245, 200 Cathars were burned beneath the fortress of Monsegur. The last known Cathar clergy-member died in the beginning of the fourteenth century.

Illuminations

"No one expects the Spanish Inquisition!" These words have become a staple of *Monty Python*, a British television comedy, humor. But few people know that the Inquisition was formed in response to the Cathar heresy. Because it was so difficult to squash Cathar ideas, what's known as the Medieval Inquisition was formed in the thirteenth century to root out heresy with more delicacy and precision than all-out war. (The *Spanish* Inquisition didn't start until the fifteenth century.)

What did the Cathars believe that was so heretical? Very little survives of their beliefs, actually, which makes them a prime target for speculation. Basically, they held some notions that are quite similar to Gnostic ideas; a radical dualism between the material world and the spiritual world, and a need to separate oneself from the material world as much as possible to find salvation. To avoid becoming more a part of the material world, for example, they tried to refrain from the following:

- Eating meat

- Having children (when possible)

- Taking vows or oaths of any sort

The Roman Catholic Church, they taught, was part of the material world. The Cathars elected their own religious leaders, called *perfecti*, which means "the Perfect." Anyone, man or woman, could become one of the Perfect. The body was part of the corrupt material world, and it was the spirit within that was part of the eternal. The spirit, they believed, was neither male nor female.

The Perfect led lives of unblemished purity; they were vegetarians, celibate, and poor. They were maintained by the faithful to whom they ministered, and were generally seen as a breath of fresh air compared to some of the medieval Church's bejeweled bishops, who appeared to be concerned only with filling church coffers. The irreproachable behavior of the Perfect, in fact, may have had at least some influence on the formation of the monastic orders in the Middle Ages.

But there was another thing that made the Cathars controversial, according to one of the documents written against them. They held docetic beliefs; Jesus was just a man, they taught, who was overshadowed by the eternal Christ. After the crucifixion, Christ had accomplished his mission and left Jesus, who survived. Jesus, the man, then went on to marry Mary Magdalene.

There are some contradictions here. The Cathars apparently did hold Mary Magdalene in high esteem; they built churches in her honor and observed her feast day. But why, if they spurned the material world, would they have honored a human man and woman? The answer, according to Margaret Starbird, was that they knew the "truth" about Jesus and Mary Magdalene's mission to restore balance and love to the world. It's difficult to believe a report, after all, that comes from a source that considers them heretical.

After the Cathars' last stand at Montsegur, Starbird theorizes, the surviving Cathar sympathizers were forced underground, where they found innovative ways of preserving their beliefs and passing them to new generations. One of these ways was through medieval watermarks in paper, and another way was through the images on the *Tarot* trump cards. The Tarot trumps, she suggests, were actually a "flashcard catechism" meant to teach children and converts about Jesus and Mary Magdalene. Because the origins of Tarot cards have been lost to time, they, too, have been a subject ripe for speculation. Margaret Starbird's idea is only one of many suggestions for their original purpose.

"Fossils" of the heresy also survived, she writes, in the form of Holy Grail legend and "lost feminine" fairy tales such as Cinderella. The Fisher King in Holy Grail legend, for example, is the tale of a king who is wounded and his kingdom has become a wasteland. It isn't until the Holy Grail is found that he will be healed and his land restored. To Starbird, this is an allegory for the state of Christianity today; Jesus, the wounded king, won't be whole until his bride, Mary Magdalene, is restored. In the meantime, his kingdom has become a desert wasteland.

Lingua Magda

Today, **Tarot** cards are often associated with fortune telling and the occult, but when they first appeared around the fifteenth century in Italy, they were apparently just playing cards. The Tarot "trumps" are a subset of the 78-card Tarot deck that bear highly symbolic images. Among them are The Lovers, The Chariot, The Hermit, The Hanged Man, and The Tower.

More Sacred Numbers

In Chapter 1, I mentioned that Margaret Starbird has used the numerical value of "the Magdalene" as evidence that it is an epithet. Let's explore this a little bit more. In her second book, *The Goddess in the Gospels: Reclaiming the Sacred Feminine* (see Appendix B), she presents the basics of her idea that Mary Magdalene's name is a hidden code that reveals her *true* role in the Gospels.

Greek and Hebrew characters serve a double purpose; they represent both language and number. As such, it is possible to calculate the numerical value of words; this is called *gematria*. We know that gematria was practiced in the first century, but we don't know to what extent. Starbird has determined that the numerical value of how "the Magdalene" appears in Greek is 153. She believes that this was done intentionally.

Illuminations

In the Gospels, there is a story about Jesus appearing to the disciples after the resurrection. The disciples are in their boat, but they aren't catching any fish. Jesus tells them to cast their net in a certain place and they'll find many fish. They do so, and Peter pulls in an enormous catch. The exact number of fish they caught? According to the *Gospel of John*, it was 153.

Strangely enough, the number 153 is also associated with the shape of the *vesica piscis*, which means "bladder of the fish" or "vessel of the fish" because of its shape. If you have two circles of the same diameter with an overlapping radius, the shape between them is a vesica piscis, as shown in the following illustration. The ratio of the height to width is 265/153; in antiquity, Starbird writes, the term for the shape was abbreviated and called simply "the 153."

A vesica piscis is made by overlapping two circles of the same diameter. The shaded area shows the vesica piscis.

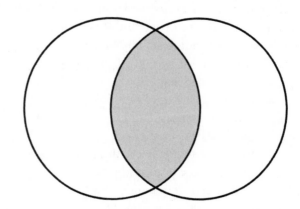

So now, Mary Magdalene's name has become associated with the vesica piscis through gematria. Why should this be important? Starbird goes a step further: The vesica piscis is a shape that has maternal and feminine connotations, and was therefore associated with "the Earth Goddess." As such, Mary Magdalene, through gematria, is now associated with ideas of the sacred feminine. Also, because fish were such a big deal in early Christianity, Jesus himself being associated with fish in his own gematria, Mary Magdalene is thus intended to be his complement, his "vessel."

CAUTION | Quite Contrary

Some people have asked me if the height-to-width ratio of the vesica piscis is equal to PHI, the "golden ratio" discussed in *The Da Vinci Code*. It's not. PHI is roughly 1.618. The height-to-width ratio of the vesica piscis is the square root of 3, or about 1.732.

The Da Vinci Code

Dan Brown's book *The Da Vinci Code* (see Appendix B), which I've mentioned a few times already, took Margaret Starbird's ideas about Mary Magdalene into the mainstream. Even though Brown mentioned two of Starbird's books in the text of *The Da Vinci Code*, few people realize that her ideas were included in the plot.

There are several ways that *The Da Vinci Code* turns into a quest for the Holy Grail, but ultimately, it says:

> The quest for the Holy Grail is the quest to kneel before the bones of Mary Magdalene. A journey to pray at the feet of the outcast one.

The crux of the book isn't on the bloodline, although it is certainly an important part of the story. It is the absence of the sacred feminine in Christianity that is the primary theme throughout *The Da Vinci Code*, and it is directly related to Margaret Starbird's writings. In reference to the "lost feminine," Dan Brown wrote:

> The Grail is literally the ancient symbol for womanhood, and the *Holy* Grail represents the sacred feminine and the goddess, which of course has now been lost, virtually eliminated by the Church. The power of the female and her ability to produce life was once very sacred, but it posed a threat to the rise of the predominantly male Church, and so the sacred feminine was demonized and called unclean. It was *man*, not God, who created the concept of "original sin," whereby Eve tasted of the apple and caused the downfall of the human race. Woman, once the sacred giver of life, was now the enemy.

A Cup of Myth (and a Dash of Fact)

The Holy Grail, of course, no matter how you would like to interpret its legends, is a powerful myth. I have received innumerable e-mails from people since the publication of *The Da Vinci Code* asking, "Is it true?" And to ask about the truth behind *The Da Vinci Code* is to ask about the truth behind the whole "lost feminine" branch of Holy Grail-Mary Magdalene interest. Perhaps the best way to answer this question is to say that I remain a skeptic. Although my own spiritual leanings don't rule out a belief in Jesus and Mary Magdalene as a married couple, I have to admit that I'm just not convinced.

The Ring of Truth

Here is where we get into a discussion about the philosophical meaning of "truth" versus historical "fact." For many people, *The Da Vinci Code* has that vague, elusive "ring of truth," that gut feeling that something about it is just "right." For many other people, though, the reaction is just the opposite, hence all the "debunking" books that have been published since *The Da Vinci Code* hit bookshelves.

Whatever your feelings about the book, you can't deny that it has been a phenomenon all its own, and it has stimulated an unparalleled interest in Mary Magdalene. In fact, it's quite likely that there hasn't been this much fascination with Mary Magdalene since the Middle Ages, when her bones were "discovered" at Vézelay! Since the publication of *The Da Vinci Code*, I would be interested in knowing how many tourists have arrived at the Louvre Museum in Paris asking whether there is a secret chamber beneath *la Pyramide Inversée* that contains her bones.

Lingua Magda

At the Louvre Museum in Paris, there is a modern pyramid structure built of glass and steel in front of the main building. When you go into the Louvre, beneath the courtyard, there is another pyramid of glass and steel hanging from the ceiling. *La Pyramide Inversée* is French for "the inverted pyramid." In *The Da Vinci Code*, we're led to believe that Mary Magdalene's bones are buried under a third tiny pyramid that stands beneath the point of la Pyramide Inversée.

Why *has* the notion of the "lost feminine" in the form of Mary Magdalene found such appeal for so many people? With more than a year on the New York Times Bestseller List, one has to wonder whether it's worth examining the reasons why *The Da Vinci Code* is having such an enormous impact on the reading public. Is it simply because it's a great yarn? Is it because people are interested in a good conspiracy theory? Is it merely effective marketing techniques by the publisher? Is it because many people feel that something is missing from their religion, and this is as good an explanation as any? Although we can't explore all of those questions here, this should provide more than enough material to inspire an ambitious student of sociology.

Whatever the answer, *The Da Vinci Code* has inspired a change in religious thought. In some places in the United States and beyond, a new mode of spiritual exploration is opening to include Jesus and Mary Magdalene as married partners. She isn't his housewife in this new spirituality, and she isn't defined by him; she is being recognized as the embodiment of a healthy feminine principle that hasn't had a face for thousands of years. In this new kind of spirituality, called Grail Christianity by some, Jesus and Mary Magdalene are complements to one another, just as the sun is to the earth and the earth is to the sun.

Separating Fact from Fiction

If balance between the masculine and feminine is so important, as theorized in the "lost feminine" view of Mary Magdalene, then it is probably also crucial to balance emotion and spirit with reason and intellect. In doing so, it's necessary to recognize that the "lost feminine" spirituality that has been initiated by Margaret Starbird (in respect to Mary Magdalene) is based largely on speculation, and many of the ideas don't hold up to rigorous scholarly inquiry. *The Da Vinci Code*, therefore, although it may have the "ring of truth" for many, is really just a good novel.

Separating the facts from the fiction can sometimes be a challenge. Let's take a look at some of the claims made in *The Da Vinci Code* that might need some further clarification.

Claim: A Gospel of Mary Magdalene exists.

True. We've already seen an entire chapter (in this book) about the text.

Claim: The Diaries of Mary Magdalene exist.

False. Nope. Nada. Nothing of the sort has ever been found.

Claim: Jesus loved Mary Magdalene more than the others and kissed her often.

Maybe. As we've already seen, the *Gospel of Philip* is the text that claims Jesus kissed Mary Magdalene. Several Gnostic texts refer to her as the one Jesus loved more than the rest.

Claim: Jesus left instructions with Mary Magdalene on how to build his church.

False. There is no text that included instructions from Jesus to Mary Magdalene about how to set up or continue his church. Perhaps an argument could be made for Jesus imparting a higher wisdom to her so she could lead the others, but they weren't "instructions" as such, and it wasn't a "church" as such. In the Gnostic texts, it was the goal of helping people attain gnosis, not setting up an institution.

Claim: The Roman Catholic Church killed 5 million women and children as witches.

False. The number of people killed as witches in the Middle Ages has often been placed as high as 9 million, which was close to the entire population of Europe at the time. These high numbers have been shown to be a modern myth started in the late nineteenth century. The number closer to reality is between 40,000 and 100,000.

Claim: The modern Priory of Sion is a secret society that has guarded the truth about Mary Magdalene and Jesus for centuries.

False. The Priory of Sion (Prieuré de Sion) was founded by Pierre Plantard in the 1950s, and it was he who contrived a mythical origin for the organization to support his own claim to French royalty.

Claim: Mary Magdalene was of royal blood from the tribe of Benjamin.

False. There is absolutely no evidence whatsoever that she was from the tribe of Benjamin, or any other tribe for that matter. Any suggestion that she is from one tribe or another is conjecture.

Claim: Jesus and Mary Magdalene had a daughter named Sarah, who started the Merovingian dynasty.

False. Again, there is no real evidence that Jesus and Mary Magdalene had a daughter named Sarah, or *any* child for that matter.

It would take a whole other book to really pull apart the threads of legend and myth that Dan Brown has woven into his story, but again, it's beyond the scope of this book to examine all of them. Several books on the market already attempt to do just that.

Is *The Da Vinci Code* without value because of the many fictions it contains? Absolutely not. It is still an excellent jumping-off point for discussions of religious history, the development of doctrine, and associated spiritual explorations. The fact that so many people are fascinated by it proves that there is healthy dialogue to be had on these subjects. And if, in the process, it breaks down some of the barriers between scholars, theologians, clergy, and the faithful who sit in the pews, that can only be a good thing.

The Least You Need to Know

- The second branch of the Holy Grail myths of Mary Magdalene is that she represents the "lost feminine" in Western culture.

- The Cathars may have believed that Jesus and Mary Magdalene were married, but we don't know whether that was central to their belief system.

- Margaret Starbird has associated Mary Magdalene with the *vesica piscis* shape through gematria and the number 153.

- Many of the ideas about Mary Magdalene contained in *The Da Vinci Code* come from Margaret Starbird's books.

- As meaningful as they are to some people, many of the ideas that underpin the "lost feminine" theory are highly speculative.

Chapter 21

More Modern Mythology

In This Chapter

- ◆ A representative of the Goddess
- ◆ Mary as a co-redeemer
- ◆ Mary Magdalene from the beyond
- ◆ A small but meaningful ritual

We've seen how Mary Magdalene has become, in the past 20 years, an exalted example of apostleship, and how she has become the Holy Grail, both literally and symbolically. Would it surprise you to know that there are still *more* ways of viewing Mary Magdalene today? It shouldn't. In a culture in which everyone is permitted their own way of viewing just about everything, Mary Magdalene isn't exempt from efforts to create something tailor-made for a specific group or individual.

What is astonishing, though, is that very few people claim to be creating a new mythology; everyone attempts to base their visions of Mary Magdalene on some kind of suppressed history. Unfortunately, in many cases, there is very little hard evidence to back up the new ways of seeing her. What occurs instead can only be judged subjectively; either it's a hodge-podge of disparate ideas crammed into an unlikely container, or a colorful array of diverse possibilities that, taken together, create a woman of unparalleled wisdom, beauty, and humanity.

Temple Priestess

In 1983, a writer named Barbara Walker wrote a book called *The Women's Encyclopedia of Myths and Secrets* (HarperSanFrancisco, 1983). A large volume, *The Women's Encyclopedia* has entries on many particulars of history that are reinterpreted from Walker's women-centric perspective. Now considered a classic in some circles, *The Women's Encyclopedia* is, unapologetically, a pinnacle of revisionist history. It also appears to be the source of several controversial ideas about Mary Magdalene that have refused to fade away.

> **Lingua Magda**
>
> In many Mesopotamian religions, a practice known as **sacred prostitution** occurred, in which a woman who was an initiate of a particular temple provided certain sexual services. This wasn't an ordinary brothel; the practice was performed as a religious devotion. Some people believe that Mary Magdalene may have been such an initiate, leading to her later identification as a prostitute.

The most prominent of these disputed suggestions is the suggestion that Mary Magdalene was a priestess in some kind of pagan temple. Although there is evidence that temples devoted to goddesses did exist in the Roman Empire and that *sacred prostitution* was practiced occasionally, there is no evidence that Mary Magdalene was one of them. This again is based on a liberal reading of the anointing scene in the Bible. Where author Margaret Starbird asserts that the anointing scene is a reenactment of a *hieros gamos* ritual in order to convey a ubiquitous idea of union with the Divine (see Chapter 20), Walker suggests that it was a *literal* ritual with Mary Magdalene acting as priestess and Jesus as the sacrificial king.

Although there is about the same amount of evidence for each, which is to say it's circumstantial at best, the temple priestess view of Mary Magdalene has remained. Many people who are involved in the newer goddess-oriented religions such as Wicca and other Neo-pagan expressions of spirituality have found a great deal of appeal in the temple priestess perspective. To them, Mary Magdalene as a temple priestess becomes a woman in charge of her sexuality and spirituality. She uses her body as a sacrament, in service of herself, her people, and the Divine.

Problems with Walker's Mary Magdalene

As positive as some people have found Barbara Walker's encyclopedia to be, any reference work would be remiss to not point out its inaccuracies.

Claim: Jesus called Mary Magdalene the apostle of the apostles.

False. Jesus never said that. As far as we know, Hippolytus is the first person to give Mary Magdalene that title.

Claim: Jesus told Mary Magdalene that she would excel beyond the other disciples in the Kingdom of Light, where she would rule.

Maybe. This is a reference from *Pistis Sophia*.

Claim: Origen called Mary Magdalene "the mother of all of us."

False. Walker bases this statement on a book by Marjorie Malvern, called *Venus in Sackcloth: The Magdalen's Origins and Metamorphoses* (see Appendix B). In reality, Origen was calling *the Church* the "mother of all of us," and was referring to Mary Magdalene as a symbol for Ecclesia.

Claim: The *Gospel of Mary* said all three Marys of the canonical books were one and the same.

False. It is the *Gospel of Philip* that makes a reference to the three Marys in Jesus' life, but it never says that they were one and the same. It could be read that way, but many scholars believe it is a reference to three different people.

It Is Written

Why, you who hate me, do you love me,
and hate those who love me?
You who deny me, confess me,
and you who confess me, deny me.
You who tell the truth about me, lie about me,
and you who have lied about me, tell the truth about me.
You who know me, be ignorant of me,
and those who have not known me, let them know me.

—From *Thunder, Perfect Mind* (a Nag Hammadi text, translated by George W. MacRae)

Claim: A Gnostic poem merged the Virgin Mary and Mary Magdalene:

> I am the first and the last.
> I am the honored one and the scorned one.
> I am the whore, and the holy one.

False. That excerpt is taken from a Nag Hammadi text called *Thunder, Perfect Mind.* No one knows exactly who it is about or who wrote it. It doesn't contain any direct references to the Virgin Mary or Mary Magdalene, and nothing to lead us to believe that it's about them. It is frequently thought to refer to Sophia, to illustrate her divinity through paradoxical statements (something that occurs in other, unrelated, texts of the time). Only insofar as Mary Magdalene was viewed as an embodiment of Sophia could the text possibly refer to her.

Claim: Magdalene means "she of the temple tower."

False. "Migdal," which means "tower," is the root of "Magdalene," but there is nothing in the word that means "temple."

> ### Illuminations
>
> In yet another take on the word "migdal," Margaret Starbird has written, in *The Woman with the Alabaster Jar*, that another reason why Mary may have received the epithet "Magdalene" is in reference to Micah 4:8: "And thou, O tower of the flock, the strong hold of the daughter of Zion, unto thee shall it come, even the first dominion; the kingdom shall come to the daughter of Jerusalem." In Hebrew, "tower of the flock" is "migdal-eder." In this verse, Starbird writes, the "tower of the flock" is another symbol for the people of God, collectively.

Claim: The seven demons sent out of Mary Magdalene were Sumerian "spirits of the nether spheres."

False. The Gospels don't say what the spirits were, and there's no documented reason to believe that they were Sumerian spirits more than any other kind of spirit. It's entirely possible that this is what was meant, but there are no direct references or links that can be established to prove it's so.

Claim: The Gospels say that no men went to Jesus' tomb, and that the resurrection was announced only to women.

False. As we've already seen, Joseph of Arimathea and Nicodemus were the ones who put Jesus into the tomb, and wrapped his body in cloth and spices. In the *Gospel of Luke*, the first resurrection appearance is to Cleopas and perhaps Simon Peter, not Mary Magdalene or any other woman.

Although I've listed a number of items here, it is by no means a complete list. Almost every line of Walker's entry on Mary Magdalene is based on a misreading of her source material, taken out of context, or otherwise mistaken. I urge you not to depend on Walker's entry for any factual information about Mary Magdalene or her legends. If, on the other hand, you are merely looking for a creative exploration of modern myth, the book has served many well.

A Sacred Marriage

Few books have been written in support of the temple priestess view, but among them is Clysta Kinstler's novel *The Moon Under Her Feet* (see Appendix B), in which Mary Magdalene is taken as a child to a temple to be trained as a priestess. She grows up in the ways of the goddess, and eventually becomes the high priestess, called "the Magdalene." She follows Jesus, called Yeshua in the book, and eventually performs the most sacred rite, the *hieros gamos*, with him. After the ritual, he sacrifices himself for his people. She later bears his child and travels to Gaul.

For many people, Kinstler's vision of Mary Magdalene is liberating, and for some, it has opened an inroad back into the Christian faith with which they were raised. This time, however, Christianity has a woman with whom they can identify rather than holding themselves up against what they see as an impossible virginal ideal.

> **⚠ CAUTION**
>
> **Quite Contrary**
>
> Although it is a great fictional device, there is no evidence that "the Magdalene" has ever been a title, for priestesses or anyone else. There is some small amount of evidence to show that the New Testament women named "Mary" do have some subtle things in common with Moses' sister, "Miriam," from the Jewish scriptures. However, there isn't any basis for the use of "Mary" (or "Magdalene") as a formal title.

Celtic Witch-Druid

On the outskirts of standard portrayals of Mary Magdalene in fiction is Elizabeth Cunningham's Celtic pagan Mary Magdalene, whom she calls Maeve, in *Daughter of the Shining Isles* (see Appendix B). Raised by nine warrior-weather-witches on the Isle of Women, she grows up to be utterly irrepressible and innocently self-assured, something she soon learns is an unwelcome trait in women. She is accepted into a coed school of druids where she meets her soul mate, Esus (Jesus), who is on something like a study-abroad program from Palestine.

Esus is reserved, intelligent, and quiet, serious about his studies and about discovering the path best suited to serving his people. His character is an incredible contrast to Maeve, who is something more like a friendly, if tempestuous, wild-haired force of nature. The book appeals to a Neo-pagan audience eager to see how Jesus and Mary Magdalene may fit into a completely different worldview, which is done by accounting for Jesus' so-called lost years as time spent studying in northern Europe.

Mary as Co-Redemptrix

There are so many small groups carving out new spiritualities involving Mary Magdalene that it's impossible to list all of them. But among them is a very interesting idea that Mary Magdalene, as Jesus' wife and equal, acts as a *co-redemptrix*. Some groups even believe that when the second coming occurs, Jesus won't be alone; he'll bring his beloved wife with him.

Lingua Magda

A redemptrix is a female redeemer. A co-redemptrix is a female who shares the role of redeemer with someone else; in this case, Jesus. Some Roman Catholics view the Virgin Mary as a co-redemptrix.

This is an idea that occurs primarily in association with certain groups that are difficult to define precisely. Some could be described as Neo-Essenes, Neo-Nasoreans, and Neo-Mandaeans, or all of the above. They incorporate ideas from the ascetic Jewish sect, the Essenes, who were responsible for the Dead Sea Scrolls, along with the Gnostic thought present in Hippolytus's description of the Nasoreans and the Mandaeans, who are still in existence today. (It's not known when the Dead Sea Scrolls were written, but most scholars agree that they predate Christianity. They are Jewish texts that don't tell us anything about Jesus or Mary Magdalene.)

The interesting thing is that none of these groups, the Essenes, the Nasoreans, or the Mandaeans, teach that Jesus was married to Mary Magdalene. At most, they hold her sacred as evident in other Gnostic texts; as an apostle, a wise disciple and a beloved follower. It is in a modern combination of ideas, interpreted afresh and elaborated upon that this startling image of Mary Magdalene emerges.

Although very few hold this perspective on Mary Magdalene, it is quite deserving of documentation among her rapidly evolving modern legends.

The New Age Movement

Defining the term "New Age" is like trying to scoop one particular drop of water out of a lake. Although all the new perspectives on Mary Magdalene described so far could legitimately be classified as "New Age," it is the specific inclusion of certain practices that caused me to create a new section for this category. Here we approach two of the most commonly held New Age beliefs: reincarnation and channeling.

Reincarnation is the belief that, after death, a person's soul, spirit, or "energy" survives and is reborn into another form, usually human, time after time. The goal is to grow in wisdom and/or compassion until finally the soul is released from the cycle. There are many world religions that hold some belief about reincarnation, including New Age spirituality. "Past-life regressions" have become a staple of this new spirituality, to discover who you were once in order to better understand who you are now.

Channeling is a common New Age oracular practice whereby a person goes into an alternate state of consciousness (a trance) and claims to have contact with people who are no longer living or with entities that have never been human. This is a practice that also has occurred in many different religions at many different times, though it has been called by many names. Perhaps it was inevitable that Mary Magdalene would "make contact" with someone given how incredibly popular she has become in the past decade.

Certain New Age organizations teach that Mary Magdalene was Jesus' "twin flame," or his cosmic "other half" with whom he will spend eternity. Mary Magdalene, it is alleged, was reincarnated as a woman who lived in the early part of the twentieth century, Aimee Semple McPherson. McPherson was the founder of the "Foursquare Gospel" Christian evangelical movement in the United States, and held no such belief. McPherson was never part of the New Age movement. She taught a down-home, Bible-based form of Christianity that deviated very little from the very conservative Protestant values of rural America at the turn of the last century. She died in 1944.

The claim that McPherson was Mary Magdalene reincarnated comes from a "channeled" revelation to Elizabeth Clare Prophet, the one-time leader of a New Age apocalyptic church, The Church Universal and Triumphant. Prophet purports to have channeled many "ascended masters," and refers to Mary Magdalene as "the Ascended Master Lady Magda."

Tom Kenyon is a therapist, author, and researcher whose primary work has been to study the effects of sound on human consciousness. In 2002, however, he and his partner, Judi Sion, published a book called *The Magdalen Manuscript: The Alchemies of Horus & the Sex Magic of Isis* (see Appendix B). The book contains a "received text": one that was dictated, allegedly, by Mary Magdalene through Tom Kenyon. Judi Sion recorded the message.

> **Lingua Magda**
>
> **Alchemy** usually refers to the practice of trying to turn one substance into another substance. You've probably heard about Renaissance alchemists trying to turn metal into gold. The term "alchemy" is now used loosely to indicate all kinds of transformative processes, particularly those that are spiritual, emotional, or psychological in nature.

In the book, "Mary Magdalen" delivers the story of her love for Jesus, who is called Yeshua. As a priestess of Isis, she had been trained in techniques of sacred sexuality, in which she engaged with Yeshua. Together, they experienced and developed a method of "sexual *alchemy*," which she outlines in her message via Tom Kenyon.

The "received" portion of the book is actually quite short. The remainder of the book is comprised of an explanatory text by Tom Kenyon and "One Woman's Story," the account of Judi Sion's life. Both Kenyon and Sion add their own introductions to each section of the book.

This represents a quite literal take on the *hieros gamos* myth popularized by Margaret Starbird (see Chapter 20). Although it has much in common with the temple priestess perspective that we've already covered, it extends into a new territory of "internal alchemy" as taught by Tom Kenyon. Additionally, it addresses the "lost feminine" aspect of Mary Magdalene myth. It emphasizes the perceived imbalance in ourselves and our society, and a lack of ecological regard as a result of a lopsided way of thinking.

The Mantle of Mary Magdalene

In Palo Alto, California, a woman named Rosamonde Miller is the bishop of a church called the Church of Gnosis (Ecclesia Gnostica Mysteriorum). Ordained by Stephan Hoeller of Ecclesia Gnostica, Miller branched out with her own organization that was associated with, but not part of, Hoeller's group. What sets Rosamonde Miller's Gnostic church apart for our purposes is the fact that she claims to hold another ordination in a lineage of female apostleship dating back to Mary Magdalene.

In 1962, she has written, Rosamonde Miller was contacted by members of a group from Paris called the Holy Order of Miriam of Magdala. The secretive group has allegedly only ever performed ordinations on women, and not only invited Miller to take an ordination, but to become the successor of the Lady bishop, as well as the last "Marashin," an honor which apparently has no parallel in other religious traditions. The order traces its line of apostolic succession back to Mary Magdalene herself.

In the 1970s, she became involved with the Ecclesia Gnostica, and some years later founded her own church in Palo Alto. The two churches have suffered some confusion because of their similar names and ecclesiastical ties, but they remain separate organizations.

Every year on the day when Mary Magdalene's feast day is celebrated, a special ritual takes place. Anyone wishing to enter into a "communion" of Mary Magdalene may approach the altar from which Miller presides over the service. Then, in a very short ritual, Miller puts each person who approaches under a mantle, or veil, that she wears. By so doing, the celebrant is able to establish a connection with Mary Magdalene through Miller.

The church stresses that it follows no dogma and is not a membership-based organization. It claims to incorporate the wisdom present in many of the world's religious traditions, with an emphasis on gnosis, or innate knowing, as a higher spiritual truth.

The Least You Need to Know

- Other than a liberal reading of the New Testament anointing scene, there is no evidence that Mary Magdalene was a temple priestess.

- The temple priestess mythology tends to appeal to people who pursue a goddess-oriented religion.

- Some small sects view Mary Magdalene as a co-redeemer who will return with Jesus at the second coming.

- Some people are now claiming to be Mary Magdalene reincarnated or to have contact with her through "channeling."

- Small groups throughout the United States have begun to incorporate Mary Magdalene into their religious observances.

Part 6

Exploring Mary Magdalene

Since very early in Christianity, believers have honored martyrs and saints who led exceptionally holy lives, and who were close to Jesus. Mary Magdalene is no different, and by virtue of her ability to survive such misrepresentation for so long, maybe she is even more deserving of acknowledgement. Regardless of your reasons, if you want some ideas for further study and thought, this section is full of them.

Be sure to read this section before the next time you visit an art museum; you'll want to be able to identify Mary Magdalene in any Christian art you see!

Chapter 22

Mary Magdalene in Fine Art

In This Chapter

- ◆ Clues for identifying Mary Magdalene in fine art
- ◆ The usual cast of characters
- ◆ A persistent little jar
- ◆ Clearing up some questions

While at the Metropolitan Museum of Art in 2002, I was astonished at the array of Mary Magdalene art in one museum. If this is what it's like at one museum, I thought, how much art must there be around the world? The realization was staggering. She appears in paintings, sculpture, architecture, and sketches. She is young, old, blonde, brunette, and red-headed, incredibly beautiful and agonizingly weathered. What a woman she must be to inspire such a variety of depictions!

There is, perhaps, no better way, save reading about her in the source texts, to explore how Mary Magdalene has been appreciated over the last 2,000 years than to take a look at art in which she appears. In this chapter, let's take a look at the different Christian scenes in which she traditionally appears and what she often brings to the story being conveyed in pictures.

At Jesus' Feet: The Anointing

Assumed for so long to have been the woman who anointed Jesus before the crucifixion, the natural place to begin our journey through Mary Magdalene art is with the anointing pictures. This subject wasn't commonly depicted until the later Middle Ages and Renaissance, and it is usually a somewhat romantic and emotional scene.

In it, Jesus is often reclining at the table of Simon the Pharisee, and at his feet is a woman who is wiping his feet with her hair. She is often crying, and the other guests at the dinner sometimes appear in an array of startled poses, gesturing their surprise and indignation at having a sinner at their table. Jesus sometimes is holding his hand up in a gesture of absolution (his first two fingers raised, the other fingers and his thumb down against his palm), forgiving the woman for her sins because she loved him so much.

Courage and Love: The Crucifixion

Studying Mary Magdalene in the crucifixion images has been one of my favorite pastimes. Developing an understanding of how the images have evolved through time and location has been important to understanding how Mary Magdalene has been viewed. Before the fourteenth century, when she appeared in crucifixion images at all, she was usually standing in the distance, often with a group of other women. Occasionally she was grouped with a number of women who were supporting the Virgin Mary, who was collapsing in grief. In these cases, she wasn't singled out at all, but was one of a supporting cast of characters. It wasn't her story; it was a scene in which she only played a small part.

It Is Written

The immediacy of the Magdalene's eyewitness account evokes the viewer's emotive response.

—Diane Apostolos-Cappedona, *In Search of Mary Magdalene: Images and Traditions* (on Mary Magdalene's presence in crucifixion images)

During the fourteenth century, images of Mary Magdalene at the foot of the cross became much more prevalent, and here she became a much more important element of crucifixion compositions. She placed herself below Jesus' feet, over the "grave of Adam," where Jesus' blood flowed to pay the price for sin. I've already mentioned that her presence at the foot of the cross was in response to the rise of medieval monasticism, but in a way, her presence near Adam's grave was also a crucial indication of her traditional place in Christianity. She represented the taint of the world and the redemption of humankind.

How can we recognize Mary Magdalene in images of the crucifixion when she isn't at the foot of the cross? There are a number of ways, and these apply to the other scenes in which she appears as well. Consider it a cheat sheet for identifying Mary Magdalene. Often she appears with any number of the following characteristics:

♦ A jar of some kind; it can be small or large, round, square, or oddly shaped, open on top or with a lid. This is her primary symbol.

♦ Long hair, usually worn loose or at least uncovered. It can be any color.

♦ Nice clothes. Mary Magdalene is often dressed sumptuously because she was believed to have been wealthy. In a scene with a number of women who are otherwise unidentifiable, look for the woman dressed in bright colors and/or gold brocade. You can almost always count on that being Mary Magdalene.

♦ The color red. If she isn't wearing expensive-looking clothes, look for the figure dressed in bright red. This isn't always dependable, but sometimes it's the only thing that distinguishes her from the rest of the women.

♦ Postures of intense grief; often she is wringing her hands or throwing her arms up in the air as if wailing.

♦ She is either directly beneath Jesus' feet or clinging to the cross; although she sometimes appears in other places, if there is a woman in this spot, it's almost always Mary Magdalene.

We take a look at more identifying characteristics later in this chapter as we explore her presence in more scenes.

Enduring the Aftermath: Post-Crucifixion Scenes

A number of artists, exploring the piety of the figures who were present at the crucifixion as well as the Easter narrative, depicted the events that followed the crucifixion. In these also, Mary Magdalene is a frequent subject. Again, she is sometimes difficult to identify with certainty, but there are a few more tricks for spotting her.

Deposition

The deposition is the scene in which Jesus' body is taken down, or "deposed," from the cross. Although this isn't a strictly scriptural scene in that the Gospels never gave the particulars of how this was done, everyone knows that he must have been taken down from the cross to have been placed in a tomb.

Some of the fairly common themes you see in deposition pictures are men atop ladders that lean against the cross as they struggle to descend with Jesus' lifeless body. Another commonly appearing item is a large pair of pliers, with which the nails were removed from Jesus' hands and feet. Because most deposition images are from the later Middle Ages and the Renaissance, as in the crucifixion images, Mary Magdalene is one of the women at the foot of the cross. Sometimes she is still clinging to the cross itself, and sometimes she is huddled together with a group of women that includes the Virgin Mary.

> **CAUTION**
>
> **Quite Contrary**
>
> It has been suggested that Mary Magdalene is almost always pictured at Jesus' feet in these paintings, but I've found that to be untrue. Although Mary Magdalene is often seen cradling Jesus' feet, she is almost just as often depicted at his head, and sometimes, she's just standing nearby.

Lamentation

The lamentation is sometimes also called the deposition, and sometimes the terms are combined because this scene takes place immediately after Jesus is taken down from the cross. Often the lamentation is also called Pietà, an Italian word that means "pity." Although some believe the Pietà is strictly an image of the Virgin Mary mourning over her son, it very often includes "the Holy Women" as well as John and, sometimes, Joseph of Arimathea and Nicodemus.

The Deposition of Christ
by Fra Bartolomeo, c. 1515.

(Photodisc)

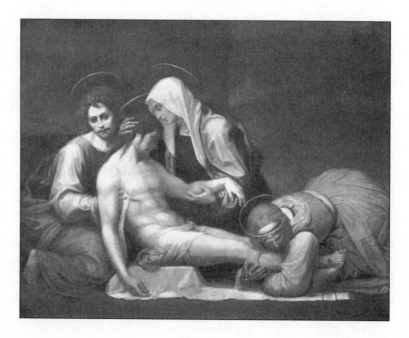

So the lamentation and the Pietà are essentially the same thing; a scene of tearful mourning over Jesus' dead body. *The Deposition of Christ* is an excellent example of a lamentation scene. (Notice that it is referred to as the deposition, though; the terms are quite often used interchangeably.)

Most of Mary Magdalene's symbols already listed are still applicable in this scene: the jar, the fine clothes, the loose hair, and the wild gestures of grief. Occasionally she holds a hankie of some kind to dab her tears, but not frequently or exclusively enough to count that among her symbols.

Entombment

As with our previous two scenes, the deposition and the lamentation, the entombment is sometimes blurred with the rest of the post-crucifixion activities. In the entombment scenes, however, Joseph of Arimathea is almost always present because he was primarily responsible for putting Jesus into a tomb.

> **Illuminations**
>
> What if, in an image of the deposition, lamentation, or entombment, a man is holding the jar instead of a woman? Well, it depends. First, find John. He'll be the young man with no beard. Then, if there is only one other man and he's holding a jar, it's Joseph of Arimathea. If there are two other men and one is holding a jar, then it is probably Nicodemus, who brought "a hundred pounds" of spices with which to wrap Jesus' body.

Joseph of Arimathea is usually depicted as an older man, and because he was believed to have been wealthy, he often appears in fine clothing as well. Very often Nicodemus is present with his big jar of spices, but just as frequently, it is Mary Magdalene with her ointment jar. Occasionally more than one woman is depicted with a jar, as they were sharing the responsibility for anointing his body; in this case, look for the woman with the long hair and expensive clothing.

In the entombment, Jesus is very often being lowered down into a sarcophagus, or stone casket. This casket makes another appearance in many of the resurrection images as artists show him rising out of it.

A Picture of Hope: The Resurrection

The mood of the scenes up until this point has been somber at best. With the resurrection, the darkest part of the Easter narrative has passed and a new day is dawning. It is in the resurrection scene that we see Mary Magdalene in her most famous role.

> **It Is Written**
>
> … the women's testimony of the empty tomb became one of the most frequently depicted images in early Christian art.
>
> —Susan Haskins, *Mary Magdalen: Myth and Metaphor* (1993)

Myrrhbearers

The role of myrrhophore is Mary Magdalene's oldest identity, and it is in this role that she first appears in art. Throughout the centuries she has continued to be portrayed in this role, usually appearing with the other women who accompanied her to the tomb.

Sometimes there is no way to distinguish between the women. There are usually three, all dressed pretty much the same, all carrying jars. Occasionally one of them is dressed in red or has long, loose hair visible, which would lead us to believe that figure is supposed to be Mary Magdalene. But usually this isn't a role in which Mary Magdalene is intended to stand out; she is just one of a number of faithful women who are expressing love and devotion to their slain teacher.

"Touch Me Not"

We've already gone over the *Noli Me Tangere* scene a number of times, but let's approach it again strictly from an artistic perspective. There are a few extremely common motifs in depictions of this scene:

♦ Mary Magdalene is kneeling or lurching toward Jesus, her arms stretched out toward him.

♦ Jesus is recoiling from her touch, and/or holding one or both hands in a "stop" gesture.

♦ Jesus is often wearing a big hat or other gardener disguise, and is sometimes holding a gardening implement such as a shovel.

♦ Jesus sometimes holds a banner showing a cross of the resurrection: a red cross on a white field.

In addition to these, sometimes either or both Jesus and Mary Magdalene gesture toward heaven, as if to remind the viewer of Jesus' words that he has "not yet ascended to [his] Father." Occasionally, too, Jesus is seen touching Mary Magdalene's forehead, which calls to mind the medieval relic piece of skin on Mary Magdalene's skull at St. Maximin.

This scene is Mary Magdalene's time to shine. She shares the frame with no one else but Jesus, and it is a profoundly personal, almost intimate, moment captured in time. Her grief has suddenly ended, and she has just realized that her beloved *Rabboni* has risen from the grave. Naturally, she reaches out to touch him, but he, for some reason that no one has entirely been able to agree on, advises her to curb her enthusiasm. In a way, it's tragic; there is, at that moment, nothing more that Mary Magdalene wants in the world than to embrace Jesus. But Jesus, as Christians *have* agreed for the last 2,000 years, apparently had bigger things to attend to.

Cameo Appearances

We've now covered the most famous and popular Gospel scenes in which Mary Magdalene is an important figure. There are, however, a few more scenes and settings in which she appears, and for anyone wanting to do more research on her, it's important to cover a few more areas.

Raising of Lazarus

Under the assumption that Mary Magdalene was the same person as Mary of Bethany and therefore Martha and Lazarus's sister, images of the raising of Lazarus sometimes include a very Magdalene-like figure. This scene also tends to foreshadow Jesus' own resurrection, so it's extremely fitting that Mary Magdalene would be present.

Usually images of Lazarus's resurrection include a large number of people; the Gospels say that there were a great many onlookers present. They had gathered to grieve with the family as well as to see what Jesus was going to do. This was a very public miracle. Jesus is most often the central figure, holding his hands out in a commanding gesture as he calls Lazarus forth from the tomb. Lazarus, in his grave clothes or wrappings, sits up in a stone casket or emerges from a tomb.

Martha and Mary are usually kneeling nearby, and there is another curious element to these paintings: many of the onlookers, Martha and Mary included, are sometimes holding their noses, or holding a cloth up to their faces. The gospel narrative includes a detail that Lazarus had been in the tomb for four days, and that his body had surely begun to decompose. So in the depictions of this story, everyone is naturally either prepared for the inevitable scent of death or reacting to it; it's difficult to tell which.

Illuminations

Sometimes, only some of the onlookers in the raising of Lazarus are shown shielding themselves from the odor. In some cases, this is meant to convey their superficial understanding, and identifies them as disbelievers.

Distinguishing between Martha and Mary is often difficult, because Mary is not typically holding her jar. Here are a few other ways to separate Mary from Martha:

- If one woman is obviously older and one is younger, the younger one is Mary.

- If one has her hair loose, that's probably Mary.

- If one of them is at Jesus' feet, that's probably Mary.

Just as often, though, it's very difficult to tell which woman is Martha and which is Mary. It's possible that in those particular images, Mary Magdalene/Mary of Bethany's identity isn't important; it is the miracle that should be the whole focus.

At the Grotto

The next category of portrayals grew in popularity during the Renaissance, when a romantic vision of a lovely, but penitent, Mary Magdalene, alone in her grotto, took hold of imaginations. The former courtesan never aged, never starved, never showed any signs of hardship in spite of living in the wild. Somehow her long hair remained combed.

The grotto pictures are interesting for other reasons, though; they often reflect a contemplative Mary Magdalene. She appears in the grotto with a number of symbols that we hadn't seen in other images:

- A skull, to represent death and the impermanence of the physical world, as well as to act as a reminder of Golgotha

- Books, which she is frequently reading

- Her ever-present jar

Often in the grotto images, she is shown reclining, sometimes reading a book. Often she is also shown clutching her hands to her bosom and looking heavenward, as if to show the depth of her repentance. In some, she looks as if she is in agony, and in others, she looks quite content. Often, she is nude or semi-nude.

It has been suggested that some of the grotto pictures were appreciated on a level not quite intended. In the sixteenth century, at a time when nudity in art was considered in poor taste—particularly when it came to the saints of God—Mary Magdalene was still depicted without clothing, or at least partially clothed, because of the strength of her legends. Both her past sinful life and the legends of her nakedness covered only by hair during her time in the grotto had a lasting effect on how she was to be portrayed.

The Jar

If one wished, there would probably be enough material to fill an entire coffee-table book on the subject of Mary Magdalene's jar. The different styles represented are as varied as the cultures and time periods in which the art was created. At times dainty and smooth, at other times cumbersome and sharply edged, the jar is Mary Magdalene's primary emblem.

In a sixteenth-century painting by Bernardino Luini called *The Magdalen*, a lovely woman is pictured in rich green with a hint of a smile on her lips. In her left hand she holds a small white jar, and with her right hand she is grasping the lid, which is only partially covering the jar. The painting is reminiscent of Pandora, who in Greek legend set free all the evils in the world when her curiosity led her to open a box, leaving only one virtue at the bottom. But rather than focusing on all the evils in the world, in Luini's painting Mary Magdalene seems to be indicating that the healing balm contained therein is Hope.

It Is Written

The naked and penitent Magdalen, in her Provençal grotto, was too far rooted in the popular imagination, and in Catholic dogma, to be discarded for the sake of veracity and decorum, and duly became an object of legitimized voyeurism.

—Susan Haskins, *Mary Magdalen: Myth and Metaphor* (1993)

Quite Contrary

In certain recently published books, the jar shown in so many depictions of Mary Magdalene is called "the Marian Chalice," supposedly her ointment jar turned into the Holy Grail, the vessel used to collect Jesus' blood. On the contrary, there is very little to suggest that anyone during the last 2,000 years acknowledged her ointment jar as anything but an ointment jar.

In Saint Mode

The last important category of art in which Mary Magdalene appears is simply as a saint who is portrayed alone or among other saints. Often this is the result of someone commissioning a work that contains a specific Biblical scene or their own patron saints (or the patron saints of a group they represent).

> **Lingua Magda**
>
> A **triptych** is a painting that's done on three separate panels. Usually the center panel is larger and contains the main subject, such as the crucifixion. Often patron saints are painted on the side panels.

For example, the crucifixion *triptych* done by Perugino mentioned in Chapter 4 was commissioned by the church San Domenico at San Gimignano. It depicts St. Jerome as well as the Virgin Mary, John, and Mary Magdalene, even though Jerome lived centuries after the others. This presented no inconsistency, though; the subjects were meant to display a devotion, not a realistic scene.

The presentation of different saints who lived at very different times together in the same image was common practice. In fact, there are several paintings of the Virgin Mary with a baby Jesus that also has Mary Magdalene and other saints watching over them. This isn't a suggestion that Mary Magdalene was present when Jesus was a baby, it's an indication of who commissioned the painting and who their patron saints were.

Likewise, there are many images of saints in an otherwise plain scene, either together as a group or pictured individually in sets in which Mary Magdalene appears. She almost always has her primary emblem, or attribute, the ointment jar. In these kinds of images, her jar is the best way, and sometimes the only way, to identify her.

The Power of Suggestion

Because we are separated from much of the art that we see today by centuries and even continents, it's important to remember that sometimes we may interpret what we see much differently now than how it was intended by the artist. Much the way that Leonardo da Vinci portrayed young men with very feminine qualities, we should remember that the art we look at was produced in a culture different from our own. Let's take a look at a few areas where misunderstanding sometimes takes place.

Eve's Influence

In medieval alchemy, a pursuit that used symbols and images to represent chemical and spiritual processes, there is a curious image that appeared in a couple of texts. It's a picture of Jesus as the "New Adam," resurrected and triumphant. He is often shown with a woman who has traditionally been interpreted as Eve: she stands nude with extremely long hair flowing over her body. There are enough other images from the Middle Ages of Mary Magdalene portrayed nude, Eve-like, covered only by her long hair, that it makes one wonder if the alchemists weren't intending to depict the "New Eve" along with the "New Adam."

> **It Is Written**
>
> The conception of the Magdalen as a second Eve survives, with all its ambiguous implications, to affect the figure of the Magdalen in literature and art. We have seen one example of the conception's survival in the account of the transformation of Jen Cousin's *Eva Primera Pandora* into a representation of the Magdalene.
>
> —Marjorie M. Malvern, *Venus in Sackcloth*

Regardless of who was intended, it was, one way or another, Eve. And Mary Magdalene, as the "New Eve," has been portrayed many times in poses reminiscent of the traditional depictions of the first Eve. Often this goes along with her presence in the grotto, naked and penitent, but occasionally there is no context to identify whom the figure is meant to be; it is left to the title of the work to distinguish between them.

Ecclesia and the Cup

One very important thing to know about Mary Magdalene in pictures of the crucifixion is that she shouldn't be confused with another figure who is often called only "Ecclesia." *Ecclesia* is a term for the collective group of believers, the Church. The Church itself has been characterized as female since very early on.

In some images of the crucifixion, some nothing more than crude drawings, there is a figure standing below the cross whom we haven't yet met. Usually she is present with Longinus, who has just thrust his spear into Jesus' side, opening a wound from which blood and water flow. Ecclesia is a woman standing beneath the wound catching the blood and water in a large cup or dish.

Illuminations _____

In many crucifixions that include Ecclesia, another mysterious woman appears on the opposite side of the cross. Often she is blindfolded and turning away. She is called *Synagoga*, after the traditional place of Jewish worship. Many Christians looked at these crucifixion images as a way to indicate that Ecclesia was the "true" church of God. (Ecclesia = Christian church, Synagoga = Jewish synagogue.)

By now I'm sure you can anticipate some of the reasons why Mary Magdalene is sometimes confused with this figure:

 ◆ Mary Magdalene has been a representative of Ecclesia.

 ◆ Mary Magdalene is portrayed with a jar, which can easily be confused with a cup or dish.

 ◆ Mary Magdalene is often positioned beneath the cross.

If you factor in that the Ecclesia figure was also important to the development of the cult of Holy Blood, which in turn contributed to the Holy Grail myth, there is another dimension of association. But still, there is no reason to believe that it was Mary Magdalene who was intended to be portrayed catching Jesus' blood. There is a well-documented progression in crucifixion art that depicts Ecclesia in this role, and it evolves eventually into Joseph of Arimathea himself catching the blood or even the Virgin Mary in her own role as the representative of the Ecclesia. Crucifixion images with Ecclesia predate Mary Magdalene's standard presence at the foot of the cross.

Is She Pregnant?

Author Margaret Starbird has recently suggested that Mary Magdalene looks, in some paintings, as if she is pregnant. Indeed, there are several paintings in which the modern observer would look at the Mary Magdalene figure and agree: wow, she has a big abdomen! How could it be anything *but* pregnancy?

To the casual observer, certainly, that looks like the answer. But if you do a careful study of the other art produced during the same period, by the same artist and others of the same school or locale, you will always find an explanation. In medieval works, it is a case of the fashions of the time; often a woman wore several layers of skirts, and it was common to gather some of them up over her midsection. This often creates the illusion of a large abdomen.

In other cases, the artist, for reasons perhaps known only to the artist, appears to prefer to depict women with disproportionately large abdomens. Sometimes even the "virgin" saints are depicted in the same way, which makes a representation of pregnancy a highly unlikely intention. In the case of Georges de la Tour, whose *Penitent Magdalene* paintings have gotten many people wondering, there are a couple of reasons why we can rule out pregnancy.

First, in some of these paintings, Mary Magdalene is depicted with her blouse off of her shoulders, and a scourge lies on the table. A scourge is a small whip made for punishing oneself, which was sometimes a method of penitence. It's highly unlikely that Georges de la Tour would have painted a Mary Magdalene, allegedly pregnant by Jesus, who felt a need to scourge herself. In those where a scourge does not appear, the symbols of vanity, such as jewelry and a mirror—which appear in many other paintings of Mary Magdalene—lie on the table instead.

> **CAUTION**
>
> **Quite Contrary**
>
> Often mirrors have multiple layers of meaning. Usually, in Mary Magdalene paintings, a mirror is symbolic of vanity, which she left behind. Often, though, as may also be the case in Georges de la Tour's *Penitent Magdalene* paintings, mirrors can represent introspection.

Second, in another painting by Georges de la Tour called *Woman Catching a Flea*, we see a woman who also has a large abdomen, but who does not otherwise look pregnant. In the high-waisted skirts that were in fashion at the time, it's easy to see how the illusion of pregnancy could have been created. In any case, not all large abdomens indicate pregnancy; sometimes it's a distortion by the artist, and sometimes it's the model herself, with a hereditary shape molded by motherhood.

I write this not to discourage anyone from looking for interesting themes in Mary Magdalene art; I'm only advocating the careful investigation of all the possibilities before landing at the conclusion that something highly unlikely is being depicted. By all means, have fun exploring the symbolism surrounding Mary Magdalene; there is much to be learned about the cultures and artists who depicted her, and how they felt about her. Just remember the old adage: If it sounds too good to be true, it very well might be.

The Least You Need to Know

- There are a number of different clues for identifying Mary Magdalene in art.
- Mary Magdalene appears in several different New Testament scenes often depicted in art.

◆ Some art portrays Mary Magdalene as she appears in legends rather than in the Gospels.

◆ It's sometimes easy to misunderstand the intentions of an artist who lived in a different time and culture, so careful study is needed to make sense of certain images.

Mary Magdalene in Popular Culture

In This Chapter

◆ Mary Magdalene gets some ink

◆ A star is born: Mary on stage and screen

◆ The music that celebrates Mary

◆ Portrayals on television (and even in comic books)

We've taken a look at the different ways Mary Magdalene has been appreciated by artists during the past two centuries, but what about her most recent appearances? Mary Magdalene continues to mystify and intrigue us even now, especially after the suggestion in the 1980s that she may have been Jesus' wife. Imaginations have been pouring over her legends and images, and she has consequently been worked into some incredibly powerful works of modern artistic expression.

The one thing that has remained consistent throughout the modern era, in spite of changing attitudes toward religion and culture, is that Mary Magdalene has remained an important subject. She continues to inspire even the most cutting-edge writers and artists.

The Printed Page

Since the appearance of the printing press, Mary Magdalene's name has been appearing in typeset, and before that, she appeared at the tip of a scribe's sharpened quill. One of the first books ever to be printed was the Bible, in which, of course, her name appears in the Gospel narratives. In the last century, however, she has become a figure of both religious and secular cultural interest. (For details on the books mentioned in the following sections, as well as others, see Appendix B.)

Nonfiction

The amount of nonfiction writing that has been devoted to Mary Magdalene has been truly staggering. The term "nonfiction" should be taken with a grain of salt, however, because many works that have attempted to detail Mary Magdalene's life have succumbed to a great deal of speculation. Just the night before writing this chapter, in fact, I came across a nonfiction book that inexplicably defined Magdala as meaning "the town of the doves." There are so many misconceptions floating around out there that it's quite easy to write a nonfiction book that's filled with inaccuracies. Many books claim to be nothing more than "speculative nonfiction," which is to say, nonfiction that asks "what if?"

If you were to look at a historical bibliography of nonfiction works about Mary Magdalene, you would see a steady increase in titles during the twentieth century, culminating with the 1990s and exploding after 2000. A few relatively recent titles are definitely worth looking at if you're ever in search of a good, truly nonfiction approach to Mary Magdalene.

> **" " It Is Written**
>
> I realized that her image embodied the perceptions of every era, being refashioned again and again to suit the needs and aspirations of the times.
>
> —Susan Haskins, *Mary Magdalen: Myth and Metaphor*

Mary Magdalen: Myth and Metaphor by Susan Haskins is always the first book I recommend to people who are looking for a historical perspective. Published in 1993, the book went out of print for a number of years until the resurgence in interest due to *The Da Vinci Code*. Susan Haskins has, by far, gathered the most information accumulated over the longest span of time, and the book is the equivalent of a good survey course on Mary Magdalene. Although the later chapters are written from a distinctively feminist perspective, her treatment of the subject is even-handed and expert.

The Making of The Magdalen: Preaching and Popular Devotion in the Later Middle Ages by Katherine Ludwig Jansen is absolutely *the* book to read if you're interested in the complex medieval view of Mary Magdalene. Drawing a great deal from the wealth of liturgical material from the Middle Ages, Jansen assembles a Mary Magdalene as complicated and sometimes paradoxical as the culture that appreciated her so much. She also sheds more light on the Magdalene cult in France and the back and forth over her relics that took place between Vézelay and St-Maximin.

The Resurrection of Mary Magdalene: Legends, Apocrypha, and the Christian Testament by Jane Schaberg is a fascinating approach to Mary Magdalene studies. In Schaberg's skillful hands, Mary Magdalene the woman is extracted from the myriad legends that have accumulated over the past 2,000 years and is restored to an unprecedented brightness. Concluding that Mary Magdalene may have been intended as a successor to Jesus, much as Elisha was to Elijah, Schaberg's unflinching and deft examination of Mary Magdalene is both scholarly and poetic.

Fiction

The top of the Mary Magdalene fiction list currently has to be Margaret George's epic novel *Mary, Called Magdalene*. George's Mary Magdalene is no prostitute, but is instead plagued by demon-induced madness that drives her away from her beloved family and hometown. She is finally healed by her childhood acquaintance, Jesus, and after learning that she is no longer welcome at home, she carves out a new life for herself as a disciple. Grand in scale while still moving on an emotional level, *Mary, Called Magdalene* is probably the most widely accessible piece of Mary Magdalene fiction currently in print.

> **Illuminations**
>
> In *Mary, Called Magdalene*, Mary Magdalene's troubles with demons begin as a child, when she picks up a small carved idol from the dirt on a journey to Jerusalem. The statue is an image of Ashara, a Caananite goddess who was worshipped widely in the ancient world.

One year before the exquisite success of *The Da Vinci Code*, another mystery novel based on a similar premise was released. Because six million people haven't yet read *La Magdalena*, by William M. Valtos, I won't ruin the ending, but by now even the description of the book will give it away for many readers. A private investigator vacationing in Spain meets a young nun called La Magdalena, whose identity is a well-kept secret. Those who want to conceal the secret, which could change Christianity at its core, put La Magdalena and her private-investigator bodyguard in grave danger.

Mary Magdalene fiction has usually taken three different shapes: stories that extol her piety, stories that capitalize on her erotic and sinful past, and stories that focus on her relationship with Jesus. Rarely do any authors put her in the middle of an entirely new universe, but this is exactly what David Niall Wilson does with his vampire thriller *This Is My Blood*. Of all the odd ways that Mary Magdalene has presented herself in the imaginations of artists and writers, never before has she been conceived as a vampire! This strange book goes to show just how deeply Mary Magdalene has been embedded into our postmodern culture, for better or for worse.

Children's Books

Growing up, I remember reading Bible stories with my grandmother. I don't remember any books about Mary Magdalene from my childhood, but there are two books today that will make sure other children grow up knowing about the woman who was closest to Jesus.

For the preschool age group, there is *Mary & the Empty Tomb*, by Alice Joyce Davidson. A sturdy board book with bright and energetic pictures, it tells, in rhyming verse, the story of Mary Magdalene as she discovers Jesus on the morning of the resurrection.

Geared toward older school-aged children, *Mary Magdalene: A Woman Who Showed Her Gratitude* by Marlee Alex is a more detailed look at Mary Magdalene. Richly illustrated by José Pérez Montero, the book is part of the Outstanding Women of the Bible series by Wm. B. Eerdmans Publishing Company.

On the Stage

The dramatic stories of Christianity that include Mary Magdalene were acted out in theaters by live actors long before movies were introduced. Today many theater productions are eventually translated onto film, but in a few cases, the only way to appreciate a play is in written form.

Jesus Christ, Superstar

How can we even begin to look at Mary Magdalene's appearance in the spotlight without first remembering her role in *Jesus Christ, Superstar?* Andrew Lloyd Webber's famous stage production debuted in 1971, and has found a loyal following since. First produced as a soundtrack, the play was made into a film in 1973. Mary Magdalene's shining moment in this modern rock-opera is a song devoted to exploring her conflicting feelings about Jesus, called "I Don't Know How to Love Him."

 **Illuminations**

The Broadway stage production of *Jesus Christ, Superstar* ran for more than 700 performances before closing in 1973.

Many people credit *Jesus Christ, Superstar* with renewing their interest in Christianity during the 1970s. Where their previous experience had been with a difficult-to-read King James Bible, the play and later the film made Jesus more accessible to a modern audience. In addition, the rock format brought in a new generation who had previously seen Christianity as un-hip.

Mary Magdalene

In 1910, a play called *Mary Magdalene* by Belgian writer Maurice Maeterlinck was published in English. A masterful piece of work, it was never granted a license to be produced on stage, and so it has circulated in book form. In the play, Mary Magdalene is a pampered courtesan whose lover, Lucius Verus, is a Roman military tribune. Verus loves her passionately, but she doesn't seem to return his affections in more than a business relationship. One day, Jesus rescues her from an attack by a crowd and her life is changed.

Finally, she decides to give in to Verus's love for her, but she still questions him and his men about what they know of Jesus. Then Lazarus visits Mary and summons her to Jesus. She leaves Verus. In the last act of the play, Jesus has been arrested and is soon to be executed. Mary Magdalene and the others try to plan a daring rescue, and she calls upon Verus to help them. When Verus arrives, he sends everyone else away and reveals his plan for saving Jesus.

Because he views Jesus as his rival for Mary Magdalene's affections, Verus offers her a deal: He will intervene with Pilate and rescue Jesus if Mary Magdalene will finally give herself to him. But because she is a changed woman, and she understands Jesus' mission, she can't bring herself to agree to such a compromise.

In a fit of rage, Verus calls everyone else back into the room, including Martha, Joseph of Arimathea, and several people who had been healed by Jesus. He tells them that Mary Magdalene could have saved their teacher, but that she had refused. Everyone's confusion turns to chaos when they hear the sound of a procession outside; it is Jesus carrying his cross through the city streets. Verus offers once more to save Jesus, and Mary Magdalene, resolute and apparently in a state of ecstasy, refuses again by telling him simply to "Go."

My Magdalene

In the late 1990s, playwrights David Tressemer and Laura Lea Cannon wrote and produced a play called *My Magdalene*, based on research they had done about Mary Magdalene and their vision of the sacred feminine. It follows the story of a young woman named Clara, who discovers a Mary Magdalene who has been maligned and misunderstood. Eventually her experience of Mary Magdalene leads her on a journey toward a kind of gnosis. Throughout, Mary Magdalene appears as a priestess of Isis. In places, the stage is a jubilant flurry of color, dance, and celebration of the mysteries of Mary Magdalene as Tressemer and Cannon imagine them.

> **Illuminations**
>
> In yet another vision of Mary Magdalene's jar, *My Magdalene* presents it as a sacred artifact that is given to Mary Magdalene after she reaches a certain level of wisdom and initiation within the mysteries of Isis.

We can, unfortunately, only experience plays when and where they are produced, but the story behind *My Magdalene* has been preserved in a video production called *ReDiscovering Mary Magdalene* (see Appendix B). It includes interviews with David Tressemer and Laura Lea Cannon as well as the members of the cast and crew behind the play.

Magdalene's Mind

A relative newcomer to the stage is a work by Gloria Amendola, a Connecticut playwright, called *Magdalene's Mind*, which was produced for the first time in 2004. In the play, Mary Magdalene returns to Earth to tie up some loose ends and prepare for the age to come. She visits three different people in New York during the course of one night, teaching them about themselves and learning from them as well. At the end, she is reunited with Jesus, her beloved, and together they prepare to usher in an era of forgiveness, balance, and peace. *Magdalene's Mind* is dramatic, with some unexpected revelations of personal truth, punctuated by poignant humor and ultimately, love.

On the Big Screen

Ever since the dawn of moving pictures, Mary Magdalene's name has appeared. Some of the earliest films made explored her role as a legendary temptress, some merely nodded to her inspiration:

- *The Magdalen* (1912)
- *Remember Mary Magdalen* (1914)
- *A Factory Magdalen* (1914)
- *A Modern Magdalen* (1915)
- *A Magdalene of the Hills* (1917)
- *The Soul of a Magdalen* (1917)

Although she has been portrayed on film many times over the last hundred years or so, it is only a few modern pictures that really set the standard for her cinematic depiction.

The Last Temptation of Christ

The Last Temptation of Christ is a 1951 book (translated into English in 1960) by Greek author Nikos Kazantzakis. Adapted for film by Paul Schrader and directed by Martin Scorcese, the movie has been both lauded as "a bold and triumphant re-imagining of The Scriptures" and derided as blasphemous. It opened in theaters in 1988 amid protests and violent opposition because of the unconventional storyline; theaters were firebombed, screens were slashed, moviegoers were attacked.

The controversy revolved around a portion of the story in which Jesus, who was crucified after a conflicted ministry, has a dream in which he is rescued from the cross and goes on to lead the life of an ordinary man. He weds Mary Magdalene, a former prostitute, and after she

> **Quite Contrary**
>
> Many people think that Jesus gets married in *The Last Temptation of Christ*, but really, he is *tempted* with a vision of marriage, children, and ordinary life. The entire dream sequence, in which he lives an entire lifetime and finally accepts his mission, takes place only within seconds while he is dying on the cross.

dies in childbirth, he goes on to take both Martha and Mary of Bethany as wives. Together the three of them raise a number of children, and he lives into old age.

Mary Magdalene is played passionately by Barbara Hershey. A fiery but profoundly sad character, Hershey's Mary Magdalene loves Jesus deeply but has been stung by his rejection when he chose to follow God instead of settle down with her. This is the emotional wound that forced her into prostitution, and she blames him for her situation. As his ministry gets off the ground, she becomes a follower after he saves her from being stoned for adultery. It isn't until Jesus' dream sequence that we see Hershey's Magdalene experience happiness; dressed in white with a laurel crown on her head, she meets him beneath green trees as a joyful bride. Back in real life, she stands below the cross as the ever-faithful disciple we have come to know.

Lingua Magda

In the New Testament, the **book of life** is a book in which all of the righteous have their names inscribed. At the end of time, it says in Revelation (otherwise known as the Apocalypse of John), every person will be judged, and only those with their names in the book of life will enter paradise.

The Book of Life

Another recent portrayal of Mary Magdalene that merits mention is P. J. Harvey's Magdalena in *The Book of Life*. I've already pointed out that Harvey's character is a street-smart Mary Magdalene, a woman who would look at home in any urban setting. If the actual book of life in the movie itself is any indication, though, *The Book of Life* is a different kind of film; in this picture, the Lamb of God opens the seven seals on a Macintosh PowerBook!

The Passion of the Christ

In 2004, Mel Gibson's much-hyped movie *The Passion of the Christ* opened in theaters. Widely criticized for its graphic depictions of the violence surrounding Jesus' arrest, trial, and crucifixion, it nonetheless found a wide following among Christians wishing to contemplate the magnitude of Jesus' sacrifice.

A fixture in the film is a trio formed by the Virgin Mary, John, and Mary Magdalene, who is played by Monica Bellucci. Although she has as few spoken lines as most of the others in the film, she brings to the movie an ability to convey deep sadness and grief without words.

Although she is never referred to as a prostitute, in one scene she is shown as the woman whom Jesus rescues from being stoned, presumably the adulteress. When her face appears on camera in that scene, she is wearing heavy black eye makeup and fine jewelry; we can only assume that, because she is dressed plainly at the crucifixion, the implication is that she had been a sinful woman of some kind. *The Passion of the Christ* includes several references to popular, but noncanonical, Christian legends, so it is highly likely that Gibson intended to portray Mary Magdalene as a prostitute.

The Passion of the Christ isn't based strictly on scripture. Much of its imagery comes from *The Dolorous Passion of Our Lord Jesus Christ,* a book of the visions that eighteenth-century Christian mystic Anne Catherine Emmerich had about Jesus' last days.

The Matrix

Some might think it's a stretch to say that Mary Magdalene figured into *The Matrix,* the dark 1999 hit that combined a martial arts and post-apocalyptic action film with references to timeless mythology. However, much of the philosophy underlying the first movie in the trilogy is Gnostic in nature, with a messiah figure and even a John the Baptist figure. It's only natural that we should also look for a Mary Magdalene figure, and we find her in the character Trinity, played by Carrie-Anne Moss.

> ## Illuminations
>
> The Trinity character isn't the only connection that the *Matrix* trilogy has with Mary Magdalene. In the second installment, *The Matrix: Reloaded,* we meet a character named The Merovingian who is a gatekeeper of sorts guarding the "Holy Grail" that Neo and his friends seek. The Merovingian's girlfriend is named Persephone, who is played by Monica Bellucci, the same actress who played Mary Magdalene in Mel Gibson's *The Passion of the Christ.*

Trinity is the woman who falls in love with the savior figure, Neo. Although there are subtle clues through the film that point to Mary Magdalene, it is the climax of the movie that really solidifies the connection. Neo is killed in what appears to be a sacrificial death that must occur before he is really recognized as the messiah. She waits on the "other side" for him, weeping. With her kiss and her love, she appears to bring him back from the dead. It is a completely new take on the resurrection scene: Through the intense and faithful love of a woman, Neo is restored to life.

Musical Magdalene

Although this chapter is devoted to Mary Magdalene in modern art forms, this section is the exception. Because there isn't as much music about Mary Magdalene as other kinds of art, it clearly makes more sense to present it all in one place. Here we take a look at some of the music, from the early Middle Ages until now, that has celebrated Mary Magdalene.

Gregorian Chant

Some of the oldest music devoted to Mary Magdalene that survives today is in the form of Gregorian chant. Named, interestingly, for Pope Gregory the Great, who if you'll remember was the pope who combined Mary Magdalene's identity with those of Mary of Bethany and Luke's anonymous sinner, Gregorian chant is a very old sacred musical form.

It Is Written

O mundi lampas et margarita praefulgida, quae resurrectionem Christi nuntiando apostolorum apostola fiiri meruisti, Maria Magdalena, semper pia exoratrix pro nobis adsis ad Deum qui te elegit.

(O light of the world and shining pearl, who announced the resurrection of Christ, and so became apostle of the apostles: Mary Magdalene, may you always lovingly plead for us to God, who chose you.)

—Chant for Mary Magdalene's feast day, pre-800 C.E.

Recordings of Gregorian chant devoted to Mary Magdalene include *Historiae: The Offices of St. Lawrences and Mary Magdalen's (Gregorian Chants)* by Laszlo Dobszay and Janka Szendrei, and *Eastertide*, on the Solesmes label, which includes a track called "Appearance to Mary Magdalene, Gospel Antiphon of the Resurrection."

Classical

There are many time periods that can be lumped together under the heading "classical," which doesn't always do justice to the different forms being represented. But in the interest of simplicity, we'll just refer to all music that can't be otherwise classified into an easy-to-remember genre.

Many pieces of music were composed in Mary Magdalene's name during the Renaissance, that incredible cultural flowering that occurred during the fifteenth and sixteenth centuries in Europe. Among the pieces that have been recorded are a performance for lute called *La Magdalena*, by Christopher Wilson, and *Missa Maria Magdalene*, by the sixteenth-century Spanish composer Alonso Lobo, and performed by the Tallis Scholars.

Classical music from the last 200 years includes the 1873 oratorio by French composer Jules Massenet, *Marie-Madeleine*, and the 1889 *Cantata to Mary Magdalen* by Vincet d'Indy.

Folk and Pop

No musical subject is able to truly reach the masses today, though, if not through more popular musical forms that receive radio play. Perhaps one of the most poignant is Richard Shindell's *The Ballad of Mary Magdalene*, as performed by Dar Williams, but Kris Kristofferon also showed fascination with Mary Magdalene in his two songs *Magdalene* and *Lights of Magdala*. Other artists who have performed songs about Mary Magdalene include the following:

- Me'Shell NdegeOcello

- Perfect Circle

- Lenny Kravitz

- Tori Amos

- P. J. Harvey

Many lesser-known performers have also included some devotion to Mary Magdalene in their work, including Ani Williams. Williams is a Sedona, Arizona, harpist and documentary filmmaker, whose album *Magdalene's Gift* reflects the more modern views of Mary Magdalene's role as beloved and priestess.

Illuminations

Although it is fairly well known that Jimi Hendrix wrote *Wind Cries Mary* after a breakup with his girlfriend, some Mary Magdalene enthusiasts believe that it perfectly reflects the new "lost feminine" mythology of Mary Magdalene.

A New Generation

Mary Magdalene has, so far, been incorporated into every art form in Western civilization. So would it be any surprise that she should also appear in popular media as well?

Television

In 1999, a two-part miniseries called *Jesus* aired in the United States as well as in other countries. Jesus is played by Jeremy Sisto, and Mary Magdalene by Debra Messing, of *Will and Grace* fame. In a strange twist compared to other modern versions of the Gospels, Mary Magdalene and Mary of Bethany are two different women, and Jesus has a romantic interest (that he sets aside in the name of his mission) in Mary of Bethany. Mary Magdalene, on the other hand, is Jesus' "most loyal" disciple.

The Mary Magdalene in this miniseries is, unfortunately, a prostitute, as well as a defensively independent woman who is distrustful of all men. She spends most of her time on the margins of Jesus' followers and is pulled into the fold by Jesus' mother. She weeps at the crucifixion and, when she sees that the tomb is empty, she runs and tells the disciples that Jesus' body had been stolen. After Peter and John check out the tomb, she has an emotional *Noli Me Tangere* scene, in which she fully embraces Jesus. Only then does he explain that she shouldn't hold on to him. She goes back to the disciples and announces that she has seen the Lord.

On the positive side, *Jesus* didn't portray Mary Magdalene as the woman caught in adultery. That was a different woman this time, and it was Jesus' attitude toward her that interested Mary Magdalene in his message.

In total contrast is a strange and ethereal Mary Magdalene in the equally strange cult-classic television program *Millennium*. The television show deals with many religious and conspiracy themes, and was brought to us by the man behind *X-Files*, Chris Carter. In an episode called "Anamnesis," five girls are having visions of Mary. Only it turns out that the visions aren't of the Virgin Mary, but Mary Magdalene.

The girl at the center of the phenomenon has DNA that matches the blood on the Shroud of Turin, which many believe was the cloth used to wrap Jesus in the tomb. She is, it turns out, a descendant of Jesus and Mary Magdalene. The episode comes complete with references to Gnostic texts as well as a Priory of Sion-like guardian who knows about the girl's bloodline.

The producers of *Millennium*, if anything, must be praised for translating the subject of the sixteenth-century painting, *St. Mary Magdalene Approaching the Sepulchre*, by Gian Girolamo Salvaldo, for the television screen. The painting itself shows Mary Magdalene wearing a shiny, metallic cloak, from under which we can just barely see her face. In a couple of very quick vision sequences, this painting is brilliantly brought to life.

Comic Books

You might think of comic books as nothing more than Superman and Batman, but many modern comics are extraordinary works of art and literary creativity. In 2003, a comic company called Top Cow debuted their timely comic *The Magdalena*. It is in this modern art form that Mary Magdalene becomes something that few saints have even dreamed of becoming: a superhero.

Perhaps that isn't entirely accurate; it isn't Mary Magdalene herself who becomes a superhero, it is her successors, who work as vampire hunters. They possess uncanny martial arts abilities and are backed by the oldest institution on Earth, the Vatican. One of her primary weapons is the Spear of Destiny, which we've already encountered under another name, the spear of Longinus. Not to be taken *too* seriously, *The Magdalena* falls into the category of "interesting ways that Mary Magdalene has entered popular culture."

The Least You Need to Know

- Mary Magdalene's name has been appearing on the printed page since the invention of the printing press, but in the past century she has become more popular than ever.

- Modern theater continues to celebrate Mary Magdalene's life, presenting the most recent views on who she may have been.

- Mary Magdalene has been a presence in cinema since the beginning of moving pictures.

- From Gregorian chant to rock, Mary Magdalene has been mentioned in almost all musical forms.

- Many forms of popular art are picking up on Mary Magdalene's most recent legends, those of her as the beloved of Jesus and their foundation of a bloodline.

Chapter 24

Devotional Ideas

In This Chapter

♦ Pouring out your heart and soul through prayer

♦ Finding some quiet time for contemplation

♦ Helping others by volunteering

♦ Other ways to honor Mary Magdalene

It is a unique challenge to present suggestions for honoring Mary Magdalene in a real, tangible way. Although you might have a different religious approach than another person who reads this book, in this chapter I offer some ideas that appeal to people of many backgrounds. What works for one person won't necessarily work for the next, so feel free to adapt these ideas to your own personal spiritual expressions.

The suggestions I make here come from the many years that I have been exploring ways of including Mary Magdalene in my own spiritual life. Although a majority of my time has been spent in studying what is known of her history, there is still something luminous about her that inspires my devotion.

Dedication to Prayer

Although it may seem like a simple thing, there are many ways to pray and many reasons why people pray. Among the different ways to pray are simply speaking words to reciting memorized prayers, sometimes using devotional tools such as rosary beads to aid in the process. People pray to seek guidance from God, to express thankfulness, and to practice their faith.

Some people think that speaking words to God opens a direct line of communication, whereas others think that intercession on their behalf by ancestors or saints is a better way to approach it. Still others have a more internalized view of prayer as a method for organizing their thoughts on a certain matter through the language of their faith.

Mary Magdalene often intersects with prayer in two ways: either as an example of some virtue that is extolled in prayer, or as a saint who can intercede on a person's behalf through prayer.

Prayers About Mary Magdalene

As you might imagine, some prayers of Mary Magdalene have included the fervent desire to be like her in that she left behind her worldly life for one of religious devotion. Another angle is praying for the faithfulness that she displayed at the crucifixion, and for which she was rewarded by seeing the risen Jesus first. Prayers of this type usually are addressed to God or Jesus, and refer to Mary Magdalene as his faithful servant or apostle.

Prayers to Mary Magdalene

For Roman Catholics and some others, Mary Magdalene is often asked to intercede for them in certain matters on which she is usually consulted. For example, Mary Magdalene has recently been cited as the patron saint of the maligned; if a person was suffering because of a lie someone had told about them, they might pray to Mary Magdalene for assistance. In this way, her role in the Gospels as well as her many legends and even the way that people have thought about her have affected her perceived area of influence.

It Is Written _____

Saint Mary Magdalene, you came with springing tears to the spring of mercy, Christ; from him your burning thirst was abundantly refreshed; through him your sins were forgiven; by him your bitter sorrow was consoled.

My dearest lady, well you know by your own life how a sinful soul can be reconciled with its creator, what counsel a soul in misery needs, what medicine will restore the sick to health.

It is enough for us to understand, dear friend of God, to whom were many sins forgiven, because she loved much …

… This is my reassurance, so that I do not despair; this is my longing, so that I shall not perish.

—From *Prayer to St. Mary Magdalene,* by Anselm of Canterbury (twelfth century)

Peaceful Contemplation

Contemplation itself is defined in a few ways, including "meditation on spiritual matters." Although that is certainly a fitting description, contemplation can also include thoughtful reflection and study on a subject. Ironically, study and meditation are usually viewed as opposites; in one your mind is fully engaged, and in the other your mind is fully disengaged. Although these are the common perspectives, there are many ways to approach both.

Study

Perhaps the easiest way to explore Mary Magdalene more fully is to simply read and learn about her. As we've already seen, there is two thousand years' worth of material just waiting to be examined. Art, literature, poetry, and music are excellent ways to learn more about Mary Magdalene, but reading what has been written about her is one of the most instantly gratifying experiences when you have a thirst to know more.

Illuminations _____

Contemplation through reading and study has a long tradition in Christianity. Called *lectio divina,* or "sacred reading," reading the Bible and other sacred literature with reverence and a contemplative attitude is sometimes seen as a form of prayer.

"Study," however, isn't always merely reading. Try this exercise:

1. Find two books about Mary Magdalene by two different authors. (See Appendix B for a good selection.)

2. Read the first book, taking time to appreciate everything it says, even if you don't immediately understand everything. Take notes if you feel like it.

3. After you're finished, take a week to think about the book. Write down what you feel you learned from it, what you liked and what you didn't like about it.

4. Then do the same with the second book. At the end, try writing down a comparison of the two without opening either book.

This isn't a book report, it's just a personal exercise to understand what you've learned. Afterward, you'll have a good idea of what areas you are most interested in, and what things you'd like to learn more about.

Remember that "contemplation" is "thoughtful reflection" on something. Try just sitting and thinking about what you read and learn about Mary Magdalene, and allow yourself to reflect on why she is interesting to you.

Meditation

Meditation is, in essence, quiet time. Although "thoughtful reflection" is a kind of a quiet time, it is more a quiet time of the body. You have to sit yourself in one place for a while to read a book. Meditation, on the other hand, is a quiet time of the body *and* the mind.

> **CAUTION**
>
> **Quite Contrary**
>
> Many people have a view of meditation as something that Buddhist monks do in monasteries, but at its most basic meditation has been practiced in many of the world's religions, including Christianity. It is, basically, just trying to focus your thoughts on a particular subject and spending some time just thinking about it.

To enjoy some quiet time of the mind, you need not sit in any special positions, chant special words, or do any funny breathing. You don't really even need to try to make your mind "blank." To meditate as a devotional activity, all you need to do is the following:

1. Find a comfortable place to sit, and make yourself comfortable.

2. Breathe deeply if it helps you relax, but breathe normally if that is how you are most comfortable. Your eyes can be open or closed, but if they're closed, you'll have fewer distractions.

3. Bring into your mind one particular thing you would like to take time to think about, and try to focus your thoughts on only that thing.

4. If you notice that your thoughts are straying to other topics, bring them back to the one thing you've decided to think about.

5. When you feel your thoughts straying too often, or when you've meditated for a particular length of time (or you've fallen asleep), then you're done!

You could meditate on many things about Mary Magdalene. From the Gospels, you could meditate on how she would have felt to be relieved of seven demons, whatever they were, or her joy at discovering that the gardener outside Jesus' tomb was really Jesus! Ideas on meditation topics from the Gnostic texts include specific parts of her vision from the *Gospel of Mary*, or how she may have felt being the disciple with the most mature understanding of Jesus' teachings.

> **It Is Written**
>
> Let the words of my mouth and the meditation of my heart be acceptable in thy sight, O LORD, my rock and my redeemer.
> —Psalms 19:14

Mary Magdalene's legends, of course, are a treasure-house of ideas for meditation. You could think about Mary Magdalene compared to Eve, or compared to the Shulamite woman in *Song of Songs*. You could spend some time meditating on the anointing scene in the Gospels and even purchase some spikenard oil to give an extra dimension of scent to your thoughts. You could try imagining yourself in Mary Magdalene's place in the grotto in France, or even try to understand her new role as a symbol of the sacred feminine.

Whatever subject you choose, try to define it well before you sit in meditation. Don't make it too complicated, just pick one little thing to ponder, and then allow yourself to ruminate. There are no goals, necessarily; you don't have to come to any new understanding or awareness. This is a devotional act. The idea is just to give yourself in thought, for a little while, to Mary Magdalene.

Helping Others

There are few better ways to commemorate a person's life than by engaging in activities that they themselves might have cared about. Based only on her presence in the Gospels there are a number of areas in which volunteering your time and energy could be a fitting tribute to Mary Magdalene. You need not spend all your free time devoted to volunteer activities; any commitment of time, however small, is usually welcomed by charity and nonprofit organizations.

Religious Charities

Perhaps the best place to start is with religious charities, because most people who would care about donating their time in Mary Magdalene's name will do so out of some amount of religious devotion. If you attend a church regularly, see what activities your church is involved in within your community; there might be something that is appropriate for your skills and commitment level.

> **Illuminations**
>
> Consider volunteering for religious charities outside of your own faith, with the goal of learning about traditions other than your own. This kind of community involvement promotes interfaith dialogue that brings neighbors closer together.

You may also be interested in volunteering at your church. If you are inclined, you may make an excellent Sunday School teacher, or even a member of the lay clergy. Perhaps you could volunteer to give a talk to your church about Mary Magdalene, or organize for a guest speaker to come and deliver a presentation about her. Remember that Mary Magdalene was the "apostle of the apostles," so teaching or preaching, if possible in your church, would be a perfect way to honor her!

Women's Causes

In the canonical Gospels as well as the Gnostic texts, Mary Magdalene was the foremost among Jesus' women followers. In addition, she was evidently very independent and found herself at odds with Peter in the Gnostic sources. With that in mind, why not spend some time encouraging other women to find their voices and restore their lives?

Mary Magdalene's name, as we've seen, has been invoked as the patron for "fallen women" for centuries, and it still continues. The most obvious place to start considering volunteer work for women is in safe houses and ministries devoted to women who are escaping from prostitution. Many places will also cater to the needs of women who are trying to get out of abusive relationships, are homeless or poverty-stricken. Many also have children in their care. These women desperately need a safe, warm place to stay, food to keep them going, and assistance in finding resources to rebuild their lives. Any time devoted to helping them would be well spent.

Remember the story about Mary Magdalene in the *Golden Legend*, in which she helped a couple conceive, and then saved the mother and child from death? Throughout the Middle Ages, Mary Magdalene was one of the saints called upon to protect women during childbirth, and this suggests another worthy volunteering opportunity. Many hospitals welcome volunteers in their obstetric wards, especially those with experience in nursing and childcare. Some women just need someone to talk them through their labor when they have no one else, and some babies need someone to rock them when their families have, for whatever reason, become unavailable.

Illuminations

In the Middle Ages, there is evidence that in some areas, women wore "childbirth girdles," a special kind of garment that was supposed to make birthing easier. Some places kept childbirth girdles said to have belonged to the Virgin Mary, relics which were borrowed by women in labor to assist them in birthing their babies. Mary Magdalene was, during the later Middle Ages, very well known for her maternal and childbearing miracles, and thus there was at least one birthing girdle that was also under her patronage.

Hospices

Perhaps the most fitting volunteer opportunity is the least likely to appeal to most people. Hospice is care provided to those who are in the last stages of a terminal illness. It is becoming more and more common as people decide to die with dignity rather than to draw out the inevitable for as long as possible. In contrast to the emotionally sterile atmosphere of a hospital, many free-standing hospice centers have homelike environments where the families of patients can gather around their dying loved ones.

To care for someone as he or she dies is a noble, and very difficult, thing to do. Often training is available for hospice volunteers to help them learn how best to serve the patients and their families. This is an opportunity that presents itself in Mary Magdalene's memory because of the role she played during

Quite Contrary

Volunteering at a hospice center doesn't mean you have to come into contact with people who are dying. Some volunteers believe in the cause but are still uncomfortable with patient situations. Often there are plenty of other ways to help: in administration, bookkeeping, food service, janitorial, and other areas.

the crucifixion; she was the most devoted of Jesus' followers, always staying near Jesus until his final moments were past. As a witness to the crucifixion, we always remember her as she appears in the larger picture of Christianity, but let's not forget that it's also a story about a woman standing by faithfully so her loved one doesn't die alone.

Other Ways to Acknowledge Mary Magdalene

There are, of course, countless ways to perform a devotional act. At the most basic level, almost anything you do with the intention of honoring or remembering Mary Magdalene could be considered a devotion, so let yourself explore the ways that she captures your imagination. Here are a few more ideas.

Create a Devotional Shelf

A more fitting name for this would, of course, be an "altar," but we aren't actually worshipping Mary Magdalene here, and "altar" tends to have worshipful connotations. Consider this only an idea for setting aside a space in your home for some objects that help you think about Mary Magdalene. Your reasons for doing this will be your own, but they might include a desire to keep her faithfulness in your thoughts as you go about your everyday life or making a "sacred space" where you can sit to do your other devotional activities.

A devotional shelf can be anything you'd like it to be. It should be a reflection of your personal interest in Mary Magdalene.

A devotional shelf can fit whatever requirements you set for it. It can be on a book-shelf or the top of a cabinet, or a small table. The devotional shelf pictured here is on top of a wooden cabinet. If you intend to put candles on it, be sure to keep it out of reach of children and pets and make sure it's sturdy. (And never leave the candles burning unattended!) You could even set aside a corner of your desk for an object or two that make you think about Mary Magdalene. Do whatever works best for you.

Many people like to put a nice cloth on their shelf. The most historically appropriate color would be red, of course, but feel free to use any color and fabric you like. Even a length of lace or a table runner will work. Remember that Mary Magdalene is also portrayed in deep green or gold brocade in many paintings, so consider those colors, too.

Candles have been used in religious devotion since long before Christianity, and they continue to be used in many world religions, including Christianity, to this day. In many Roman Catholic Churches, you can light a votive candle when you say a prayer; this is to indicate the solemnity of prayer and is a way to keep vigil. *Novena* candles are another appropriate kind of candle to use on a devotional shelf.

You might want to put candles, votive, novena, or other kinds, on your devotional shelf. As I mentioned already, though, be sure to keep them out of reach of children and pets, and make sure they can't be tipped over!

Lingua Magda

Novena candles are those in the tall, slender glasses that you can find in many places, including some grocery stores. Often novena candles are associated with special novena prayers or readings, which are recited over the space of nine days. You can find an Internet address for a novena to Mary Magdalene in Appendix B.

Other objects you might want to consider for your devotional shelf include pictures and statues. You can find many pictures of Mary Magdalene in books, and local Christian bookstores might carry religious cards with her picture on them. If they don't carry anything, be sure to ask. Sometimes a store won't bother carrying an item if no one asks for it, but with the recent increase in interest in Mary Magdalene, you might be surprised!

There aren't many statues of Mary Magdalene available, but a lovely one, a reproduction of a statue of Mary Magdalene at Vézelay, has recently become available from a company called Sacred Source. You will find more resources for Mary Magdalene–related items, which are sometimes difficult to find, in Appendix B.

So now you have a shelf with a cloth, some candles, a picture of Mary Magdalene, and maybe a statue. What else? Here is where you use your imagination and draw on the stories of her that are meaningful to you. If you're interested in her association with the anointing scene, you may want to put a small perfume bottle on your shelf. If it is Mary Magdalene's role as apostle that captures your interest, perhaps a wooden egg that is painted red would be a good addition. More ideas include the following:

- Seashells, for her legendary journey to Gaul

- Stones, for her 30 years in the grotto

- A book, for her contemplative life

- Some myrrh, because she was a myrrhophore

- A jar of some kind, of course!

You are limited only by your imagination. I once knew a woman who decorated her devotional shelf with shiny red Christmas garland, and a number of people who placed chocolate on it on a regular basis, though I couldn't imagine why. When I asked about it, one woman replied, "because it just seemed like Mary Magdalene would have needed some chocolate sometimes, too."

Go on a Pilgrimage

In the Middle Ages, one of the most popular ways to express a devotion to God and certain saints was to go on a pilgrimage to sacred locations. A few places were more popular than others; it just depended on what any particular pilgrim wanted, or needed, to do. Some pilgrims went because they were forced to do so to make penance for some crime or mistake, but many more went for their own reasons.

> **It Is Written**
>
> With naked feet and sack-cloth vest,
> And arms enfolded on his breast,
> Did every pilgrim go.
> —Sir Walter Scott, *The Lay of the Last Minstrel*

The most obvious way to do a pilgrimage of your own is to buy a plane ticket, book a hotel, and take a guided tour of a location that is associated with Mary Magdalene. Although it's expensive, there really is nothing like seeing a place with your own eyes, and if you're so inclined, it can be an immensely rewarding experience.

If you can't manage to get the time off work, pony up the thousands of dollars it would cost to take a vacation, and spend a few days in a distant and exotic location, there is another option. Pilgrimages are, or should be, spiritual exercises. If you find yourself with an earnest desire to make a major commitment that a pilgrimage entails, you shouldn't let the obstacles dissuade you. Consider taking a pilgrimage *in spirit.*

When I first heard of this devotional act, I thought it was brilliant, and hopefully you'll see the value in it, too. Before planes, trains, and automobiles, the only way to get from Point A to Point B was by the power of your own two legs. Okay, you could ride a horse if you were lucky, but on medieval pilgrimages the emphasis usually wasn't on comfort, it was on the serious spiritual dedication necessary to walk all the way from, say, England to Spain.

> **Illuminations**
>
> Although there is evidence that early Christians visited the places sacred to their faith during the first two centuries, it was Queen Helena's highly successful trip to the Holy Land in the fourth century, and her discovery of so many relics, that made the pilgrimage a more common practice.

If you want to take a pilgrimage in spirit, you first need to decide where you want to go. Say, for example, you want to visit Vézelay, France. Estimate how many miles it is from where you live to Vézelay. How many miles a day would you have to walk to get there in a year? Five years? Ten years?

It could be that you live halfway around the world from Vézelay, so perhaps you will want to pick an arbitrary number that will satisfy your need for a serious commitment. Or perhaps you are already accustomed to walking or running five miles a day. Whatever your situation, the idea is to spend some time each day walking, jogging, running, or however it is that you get yourself around, and that you do it with the mindfulness of pilgrimage.

My friend walked five miles every day and kept track of her accumulated miles until she had walked the entire distance from the United States to Vézelay, France. That's not something you can do in a year. In fact, it was a five-year commitment that she made to exploring Mary Magdalene's importance to her. If you are so inclined, you can do that same thing, too, and you might get more out of it than a seven-day vacation.

After covering the accumulated distance to a distant place, you will have spent many hours on the devotion. Although you haven't literally walked to France, you have covered the same distance (perhaps) and completed a pilgrimage "in spirit."

The Least You Need to Know

- Prayer can take many forms; to pray to, or about, Mary Magdalene is a practice that is well established within Christianity.

- Contemplation and meditation are ways of quieting your mind and body so you can spend time thinking about a certain thing, in this case, Mary Magdalene.

- There are many volunteer opportunities that would be excellent ways of honoring Mary Magdalene's memory.

- Acting on a devotion to Mary Magdalene doesn't have to be a huge investment of time or money; there are very simple ways to remember her every day.

Chapter 25

Celebrate Her Feast Day

In This Chapter

- ◆ Narrowing down the identities
- ◆ A day of devotion, a day of celebration
- ◆ Celebrating with others
- ◆ Joining hands for a global celebration
- ◆ Baking some sweet treats

It's safe to say that you now know a lot more about Mary Magdalene than you did when you started reading this book. You've learned about the roles she played in the Gospels, how her legend grew and changed through the Middle Ages, how she figures in Gnosticism, and what the most recent perspectives on her are. We've also explored some things that you can do to honor Mary Magdalene.

The last thing that remains is to learn about ways to celebrate her feast day on July 22, if you choose to do so. Again, the way that you observe her feast day will depend entirely on your view of her and how she is meaningful to you. As a result of the many different ways of looking at her, I include many different suggestions here so that you can take what sounds appropriate and leave the rest.

A Personal Observance

The best place to start when thinking about how to celebrate Mary Magdalene's feast day is assuming that you'll be observing it on your own. This is, after all, probably a personal interest for you, so perhaps there is no one else interested in celebrating with you, or you choose to observe it alone, in your own way.

Which Mary Magdalene to Celebrate?

The first thing to ask yourself is, what do you want to get out of this? Are you wishing to just explore her more fully, or do you have a very specific perspective in mind? For example, if Mary Magdalene has always interested you, and you are open to the many ideas of her that are in circulation, you might want to try a variety of things. If you're certain that she was nothing more than an important apostle, on the other hand, that narrows down the number of possibilities, which could be preferable.

Before we jump right into some fun things to do to celebrate, let's summarize all the different roles that Mary Magdalene has played during the past 2,000 years:

- Myrrhophore
- Demoniac
- Breadwinner/financial supporter
- Disciple
- Anointer

- Mourner
- Witness
- Apostle
- Visionary
- Questioner
- Teacher
- Courtesan/"fallen woman"
- Penitent
- New Eve

> **Illuminations**
>
> Why would anyone want to celebrate Mary Magdalene as a demoniac? Good question. If we consider the demons that plagued Mary Magdalene as figurative, then anyone who has been troubled by ailments might find that he or she has something in common with Mary Magdalene.

- Bride of Christ (figurative, as Ecclesia)

- Evangelist

- Healer

- Contemplative hermit

- Patron/protector

- Jesus' wife (literal)

- Holy Grail

- Symbol of the sacred feminine

We could break her legends down even further and come up with more minor identities, but you get the idea. The more time you spend thinking about her legends, the more evident her subtle characteristics will become. If you aren't like me and you don't mind writing in books, feel free to make a mark next to the identities in the preceding list that you'd like to focus on when commemorating Mary Magdalene on her feast day.

The next step is to think about the individual roles and come up with ways to remember them in a formal observance. I give you some ideas to help get you going.

Readings

One of the best ways to acknowledge a saint on a feast day is to read the Biblical passages that are related to that saint. In Mary Magdalene's case, this might be passages from the Gospels that mention her name, or it might be passages from *Song of Songs*, with which she has traditionally been associated.

Just spend some time looking up the passages you'd like to read, and then read them. This is a particularly nice thing to do if you are usually too rushed to appreciate a reading, or if you don't often read the source material associated with her. Even now, after doing so much work related to Mary Magdalene over the past seven years, I find it intensely moving to go back to the traditional material one more time.

> **It Is Written**
>
> And you, O Magdal-eder [Tower of the Flock], hillock of daughter Zion! Unto you shall it come: the former dominion shall be restored, the kingdom of daughter Jerusalem.
>
> —Micah 4:8

Devotional Activities

In the preceding chapter, I covered many ways you could exercise a devotion to Mary Magdalene. Perhaps you can't do it every day or make it a regular part of your life, so making it an important part of her feast day is a great alternative. The most fitting activities are prayer, contemplation, and meditation.

Set aside some time on her feast day to just think about Mary Magdalene. After all, that's what a feast day is all about!

Take the Day Off

For several years, I worked for an employer that allowed employees two *floating holidays.* They acknowledged that their employees come from vastly different cultural backgrounds, and that the regularly observed American holidays sometimes aren't those that are celebrated by everyone. The floating holidays were designed specifically for people to take a day off for a religious observance that wasn't otherwise a day off.

Lingua Magda

Many modern employers will allow employees to take a **floating holiday,** a day off to observe a special religious observance that isn't otherwise covered by the usual American holidays.

I took full advantage of the floating holidays by requesting July 22 off every year so that I could spend the day thinking about Mary Magdalene and doing devotional activities. It has been an important personal tradition, and it's one that you might be able to do as well if it is important to you.

If you can't take the day off, don't worry! It is the spirit of a feast day that's most important, and you can still remember that the day is a special one even while working. Maybe you can just set aside some time in the morning before you go to work, or in the evening after you get home, to do something out of the ordinary. Sometimes it's just enough to keep it in mind. You can also choose to observe the feast day on your next available day off.

Wear Something Special

One thing I've noticed over the years is that when people get together to talk about Mary Magdalene, they often show up wearing shades of red. This isn't an accident. One of the easiest ways to celebrate Mary Magdalene is by wearing her colors: red, deep green, and gold brocade.

I have to be honest and admit that I wear red on Mary Magdalene's feast day about as faithfully as other people wear green on St. Patrick's Day. Sure, green really doesn't have anything to do with St. Patrick, and when it comes down to it, red has nothing to do with Mary Magdalene. It is a traditional color, though, and if you are interested in creating a new tradition for yourself, you could do worse than to tap into something that has been around for centuries.

> **Illuminations**
>
> What good is wearing red on Mary Magdalene's feast day if no one else knows why you're wearing it? Well, perhaps it doesn't matter what other people think. *You* will know why you're wearing red (or any other color you choose), and it is a personal expression of spirituality. You could always volunteer the information!

Visit a Special Place

July 22 falls in the middle of summer, making it an excellent time to take an outing. It might be something as simple as a picnic on the beach or a visit to a museum. Or perhaps there is a place that has always been special to you that you rarely have the chance to visit. If Mary Magdalene is your patron saint, there is no better time to visit your sacred places than on her feast day.

Make Scents

One of my favorite suggestions for Mary Magdalene's feast day is making perfume, or otherwise doing something related to scents. Because she has been so closely associated with scents, perfumes, and ointments for so long, it's entirely fitting that you would celebrate by stimulating your olfactory system.

> **It Is Written**
>
> While the king was on his couch, my nard gave forth its fragrance.
> —*Song of Songs* 1:12

One of the easiest ways to express this interest is to go purchase some new perfume, if you wear it. However, there are now some places where you can go and have them mix your own special blend of perfume at very reasonable prices. The Body Shop, for example, is a store where you can go in, smell a large number of different natural scents, then pick some out and have them mix it for you. You then get to go home with a bottle of your very own scent. What better way to remember Mary Magdalene's feast day than by creating a personal scent that you can wear all year?

Another alternative might be visiting an herb farm and cutting an array of fragrant herbs for your home, or bringing home some small herb seedlings to plant in your own garden. And because essential oils have become so easily available, you might want to try a new scent in a diffuser, which releases the fragrance through your whole house.

Lingua Magda

Henna is an herb that is crushed and mixed into a paste, then applied in artistic designs on the hands and feet of brides in some Middle Eastern countries, as well as India. The henna stains the skin a reddish color for about two weeks. This art is often called mendhi. Some Hebrew brides in first-century Palestine used henna to stain their hands and feet.

Make a Feast

How could we have come this far without actually mentioning *food?* A feast day is designed for feasting! Although this is normally an event that brings communities together, which I discuss in a moment, you might, for whatever reason, want to feast alone. This is perfectly acceptable.

One year, I decided to celebrate Mary Magdalene as the Bride of Christ. I dressed in something that had a "bridal" feel to it, and put *henna* on my hands and feet. I made myself what I thought would be an excellent "bridal feast": wine, cheese, bread, and fruit. I put fresh flowers on the table, including some very fragrant lilies. As I ate my feast, I read *Song of Songs* from beginning to end. It was a solitary observance, but deeply meaningful to me nonetheless.

Celebrating with Others

What happens if you're all alone in your admiration of Mary Magdalene and you'd like to share your interest with others? In a group of two or more people, everyone can learn from one another, encourage each other, and enhance the experience. There is nothing quite like having some fellowship with those who share your interests.

One way to do this, of course, is to ask around your church, if you attend one regularly. It's possible that several other people share your interest and would like to celebrate a feast day with you. You might include an announcement in the weekly program, or put up a notice on a bulletin board.

Likewise, places in your community will often have free community message boards where such a notice would be welcome. Be sure to include your name and telephone number so people can get in contact with you, but it's best not to put up your address for anyone to see. The best way to meet people with whom you aren't acquainted is in a public place; you might want to meet your new friends in a coffee shop or a library the first time.

If you have a computer and Internet access, you can also go online to find others who share your interest in Mary Magdalene. It's easy: Just visit http://groups.yahoo.com/groups/magdalene-list and follow the instructions to subscribe to the Magdalene.org e-mail list. Soon you'll receive e-mails from other members of the list and can join in all of the discussions. The same rules of caution apply: Never give out your home address to strangers, and if you do want to meet your cyberfriends in person, arrange to do so in a public place.

Quite Contrary

Some people have the impression that Mary Magdalene only appeals to women, but this is absolutely not true. *Many* men have an interest in Mary Magdalene, so you may want to include them if you're trying to form a community.

A Discussion Group

So now that you have some friends who share your interest in Mary Magdalene, what do you do with them? One of the best ways to explore a subject with people who come from different backgrounds is to form a discussion group. Have everyone read the same book and be prepared to discuss it when you all meet in person. See Appendix B for some recommended books to start you off.

A Guest Speaker

If you're already part of an established community or discussion group, you might want to invite a guest to speak to your group on Mary Magdalene's feast day. Perhaps there is someone in your area doing some important work related to Mary Magdalene, or perhaps their work is only indirectly related. Use your own judgment in choosing a guest speaker, but it can never hurt to ask! There might be someone who is eager to share his or her experience, but isn't sure where to start.

Song and Dance

If your group is a more festive type, try incorporating music and a truly celebratory atmosphere. You might want to try listening to some of the music mentioned in Chapter 23, or even finding some songs that you could sing together.

> **Illuminations**
>
> If you're not sure what kinds of songs to look for, but you'd like to do some singing, try looking for Easter hymns. Often they include a reference to the women finding the tomb and meeting the risen Jesus.

At the Mary Magdalene feast day celebration I organized in 2004, two people who are experienced in leading circle dances attended. After all of the main presentations, those who were interested met out in the lobby, where we joined hands and danced in a circle, singing a song about Mary Magdalene. Those who participated in the dance said it was the one thing about the event that really made it feel like a celebration.

More Feasting

There is nothing like a holiday for cooking for a crowd. Perhaps your feast day celebration will feel more like a Christmas dinner, or a potluck-type event, where everyone brings a dish to share with everyone else. Whatever form it takes, sharing food with a community to celebrate a particular event is one of the most ancient practices on Earth; it rejuvenates our connections within our community and introduces us to new neighbors. In fact, depending on where you have your feast day, you might want to start a new tradition in your area by inviting people to participate who wouldn't otherwise know about Mary Magdalene. It's entirely up to you!

FutureChurch

A Catholic organization called FutureChurch has worked for many years to help local community churches organize Mary Magdalene feast-day events. They do this to encourage the recognition of Mary Magdalene as the first apostle, and they might be a great resource for planning your event. There are some excellent ideas on their website (www.futurechurch.org), and they can also send you a packet with more information.

A Global Observance

Whether you are celebrating Mary Magdalene's feast day alone or with others, you can try to also make a connection with other people around the world who are observing the day as well.

The Internet is a valuable tool for connecting with other people with similar interests. As the founder of Magdalene.org, I've done extensive work related to Mary Magdalene online, and continue to do so. One of the most important aspects of my work has been to create an online community of many hundreds of people who share an interest in Mary Magdalene. People from all walks of life, very different religious and political backgrounds, and from many different countries can all exchange messages and learn from one another.

You can connect with this global community as a way to encourage people to remember Mary Magdalene's feast day. Every year during the week of July 22, many messages are exchanged in a spirit of brother/sisterhood and fellowship, wishing each other a blessed feast day. Although it's about as simple a thing as could be imagined, it's just as meaningful as receiving a card in the mail at Christmas. We remember one another during our holidays because we're sharing in an important cultural tradition. Many people with a devotion to Mary Magdalene are merely reviving Christian traditions that have been forgotten.

Sweet-Tooth Recipes

I can't set you loose to celebrate Mary Magdalene's feast day without first suggesting some appropriate dishes. Although you could certainly cook any food that sounds good to you, it adds an extra dimension to the festivities if you include dishes that are named for Mary Magdalene.

Although I've only included a couple here, many dishes could be prepared in an acknowledgement to Mary Magdalene. In most cases, the recipes are named after women called Madeleine, but as the French version of the name "Magdalene," many people like to try these recipes on Mary Magdalene's feast day.

> **CAUTION**
>
> **Quite Contrary**
>
> If you think that baking French pastries is difficult, think again. These recipes have been written for American cooks and tested in my very own kitchen. I'm no pastry chef, but if the speed with which these delectable desserts disappeared is any indication, the recipes were a success. I'm sure you'll be able to do it, too.

There are three kinds of cookies that are uniquely appropriate for Mary Magdalene's feast day, all of them French. The first is the extremely popular Madeleine cookie, which comes in about as many different varieties as you can imagine. The second is the navette, or "little boat" cookie, which is actually more like a sweet biscuit. I've included recipes for Madeleines and navettes here.

The third kind of cookie is very difficult to find a recipe for: colombe. Prepared by an Italian bakery in Milan called Le Tre Maries ("The Three Maries"), the colombe is a dove-shaped cookie traditionally prepared for centuries during the Easter season.

Madeleines

Madeleines are small, seashell-shaped butter cookies. Made famous by Marcel Proust, who mentioned them in his autobiographical novel, *Remembrance of Things Past*, the little cakes have been around for centuries. No one really knows who they are named for. Although the most rational choice is the name of the woman who first baked them, some believe that the seashell represents the ocean voyage undertaken by Mary Magdalene and her companions.

To make these cookies, you need Madeleine pans, which are available at most kitchen stores. These cookies are a little slice of heaven when consumed with tea. This recipe makes about 14 cookies.

> 1 cup sugar
>
> 2 eggs
>
> 1 tsp. lemon juice
>
> 1 tsp. vanilla extract
>
> 1 cup all-purpose flour
>
> ½ tsp. baking powder
>
> 6 oz. butter or margarine, softened (not melted)
>
> Powdered sugar (optional)

Grease and flour the Madeleine pans extremely well, or the cookies will stick. Preheat the oven to 350 degrees.

In a large bowl, whisk together the sugar and eggs until creamy. Add the lemon juice, vanilla, flour, and baking powder and stir gently until ingredients are combined. Stir in the butter. The final batter will be a little springy.

Add only 1 tablespoon of batter to each Madeleine mold. Bake for 12–15 minutes, until the edges of the Madeleines are golden brown and the tops are light gold.

Let the cookies cool slightly in the pan, and then place on a cake rack to cool completely. Be careful as you remove the Madeleines from the molds. If you try to remove them before they've cooled enough, they will break apart. If desired, sprinkle powdered sugar on top.

Madeleines will keep in a sealed container for about a week.

Navettes

Produced by one bakery in Marseilles, France, since the eighteenth century, navettes ("boats") commemorate the landing of Mary Magdalene and the others on the shores of Gaul. There are two different shapes for navettes; some are rather puffy and boat shaped, and the more traditional ones are cylindrical, with a little slash on top. This recipe is for the more boat-shaped variety. Because recipes for navettes don't call for baking powder, the resulting pastry is dense and biscuit-like. They do, however, have a subtle citrus flavor, and are excellent when served warm. This recipe makes 12 to 14 cookies.

> Zest from one orange
>
> 2 tbsp. warm water
>
> 3 cups all-purpose flour
>
> 1 cup sugar
>
> 2 oz. butter or margarine, softened slightly (but not melted)
>
> 3 eggs
>
> 1 tsp. milk
>
> 1 egg yolk

Combine the fresh zest from one orange with the warm water and set aside.

Mix the flour with the sugar, and cut in the butter. Make a well in the center and add the eggs. Strain the orange zest from the water and pour the water in with the eggs. Mix well until a dough forms. Allow the dough to sit for 1 hour in the refrigerator.

Roll dough into 1½- to 2-inch balls, and then roll them so they are slightly elongated and oval. Place on a buttered cookie sheet. Pinch the ends to make them boat shaped.

With the backside of a butter knife, make a lengthwise indentation on each "boat." Allow to sit for 2 more hours in the refrigerator.

Preheat the oven to 350 degrees. Mix the milk with the egg yolk, and paint the top of each "boat." Bake for 15 minutes or until they are golden brown. Remove from the oven and allow to cool, in the pan or on a rack. Navettes aren't as fragile as Madeleine cookies, so you can transfer them right away if you'd like.

Navettes keep very well in a sealed container for a week or more. Just pop them in the microwave for a few seconds to heat them up for a warm treat. These little biscuits are excellent with fruit preserves.

Endlessly Fascinating Mary

As we've seen, Mary Magdalene has held our attention almost since the beginning of Christianity, and continues to do so even today. While other saints have come and gone in the popular imagination, Mary Magdalene has remained one of the most commonly venerated saints and inspirational figures in the Gospels. Her reputation as a sinner has been all but erased officially, but her pre-Jesus life remains the subject of curiosity and speculation, as does her life after Jesus was gone.

Whether or not Mary Magdalene was any of the things that she has been imagined to be, she continues to find a place in every era. She reflects to us what we think of ourselves and inspires a continual re-examination of what may have been left unsaid in the Gospels and the earliest days of Christianity. After all is said and done, Mary Magdalene remains a mystery—and it truly seems that we like her that way.

The Least You Need to Know

◆ There are many things you can do to observe Mary Magdalene's feast day on your own.

◆ One of the best ways to pass Mary Magdalene's feast day as a community is with a discussion group of some kind.

◆ The Internet is a great tool for meeting others around the world with whom to share Mary Magdalene's feast day.

◆ Mary Magdalene's feast day is a *feast* day, so preparing and sharing food is an excellent way to celebrate.

◆ Madeleines and navettes are French pastries that are frequently associated with Mary Magdalene.

Mentions of Mary Magdalene: A Quick Lookup

Unfortunately, it would take a much longer appendix to present all the references to Mary Magdalene (if that would even be possible!), so please remember that this isn't an exhaustive list. Some of these can be found in books that are easily available, and most can be looked up online as well.

New Testament

Many of these references are only to Mary Magdalene's name; you can find many more references to her by reading each passage in context with the rest of the chapter or section.

Matthew

27:56

27:61

28:1

Mark

15:40

15:47

16:1

16:9

Luke

8:2

24:10

John

19:25

20:1

20:18

Gnostic Texts

Many different Gnostic texts refer to Mary Magdalene, but not always by the name "Mary Magdalene." In the passages listed here, look for a variant of the name "Mary," as I mentioned in the table in Chapter 14. Some of the Gnostic texts don't have chapters and verses numbered like the New Testament. In those cases, I've just included the number that will enable you to find the right spot in the text rather than a full reference.

Dialogue of the Savior

126

131

134

137

139–144

146

First Apocalypse of James

40

Gospel of Mary

The whole central portion of this text consists of a vision that Mary Magdalene is describing to the other disciples. Listed here are only the references to her by name.

5:2

5:4

5:5

5:7

9:1

9:5

Gospel of Philip

59

63

Pistis Sophia

The references in *Pistis Sophia* are far too many to list here, so I'm only listing the chapters in which she is referred, in Books 1 and 2.

Chapters 17–21

Chapters 24, 25

Chapter 30

Chapters 33, 34

Chapter 43

Chapter 45

Chapter 50

Chapter 52

Chapters 60–62

Chapters 72–74

Sophia of Jesus Christ

98

114

Gospel of Thomas

114

Manichaean Psalm-Book

Psalms of Heracleides 187:1–35

Noncanonical, Non-Gnostic Texts

Many, many Christian texts aren't classified as "Gnostic," and are not included in the New Testament. Several of these texts also refer to Mary Magdalene.

Acts of Philip

8:94

8:101

9:107

9:109

9:115

9:126

9:137

9:142

9:148

Diatessaron

16:19

51:30

52:21

52:33

52:45

53:25

53:31

53:32

Epistula Apostolorum

Verse 9

Gospel of Nicodemus: Acts of Pilate

Chapters 10 and 11

Gospel of Peter

12:50

Writings of the Church Fathers

Many of the early Christian writers mentioned Mary Magdalene. Again, this is by no means a complete list, just something to provide some further study.

Aurelius Augustin (St. Augustine)

The Harmony of the Gospels: Book III

21:58

24:61

24:63

24:65

24:68, 69

25:70

25:75

25:79

Tractates on John: Tractate CXXI

Section 1

Section 3

Section 4

On The Psalms: Psalm LXIX

Section 23

Jerome

The Perpetual Virginity of Blessed Mary: Against Helvidius

Sections 13–15

Letter XXXIX to Paula

Section 6

Letter LIX to Marcella

Section 4

Letter CXXVII to Principia

Section 5

Eusebius of Casaerea

Demonstratio Evangelica

Chapter 8

Origen

The reference here isn't to Mary Magdalene by name, but as "a half-frantic woman."

Adversus Celsus: Book 2, Verse 54

Papias

Fragment X (quoted by Irenaeus)

Tertullian

A Treatise on the Soul

Chapter 25

Against Praxeas

Chapter 25

Appendix B

Resources

If you're interested in learning more about Mary Magdalene, the following books (both fiction and nonfiction), websites, and videos are a great place to start.

Books

Alex, Marlee. *Mary Magdalene, A Woman Who Showed Her Gratitude.* Eerdmans Publishing Company, 1988.

Apostolos-Cappedona, Diane. *In Search of Mary Magdalene, Images and Traditions.* American Bible Society, 2003.

Ashcroft, Mary Ellen. The Magdalene Gospel: Meeting the Women Who Followed Jesus. Augsburg Fortress Publishers, 2002.

Baigent, Michael, Richard Leigh, and Henry Lincoln. *Holy Blood, Holy Grail.* Dell, 1983.

Barber, Richard. *The Holy Grail: Imagination and Belief.* Harvard University Press, 2004.

Brock, Ann Graham. Mary Magdalene, The First Apostle: The Struggle for Authority. Harvard Divinity School, 2003.

Brown, Dan. *The Da Vinci Code*. Doubleday, 2003.

Cunningham, Elizabeth. *Daughter of the Shining Isles*. Barrytown Limited, 2000.

Davidson, Alice Joyce. *Mary & the Empty Tomb*. Zonderkidz, 1998.

De Boer, Esther. *Mary Magdalene: Beyond the Myth*. Trinity Press International, 1997.

Finnegan, Frances. *Do Penance or Perish: Magdalen Asylums in Ireland*. Oxford University Press, 2004.

Fisher, Trevor. *Prostitution and the Victorians*. Sutton Publishing Limited, 1997.

Freke, Timothy, and Peter Gandy. *The Jesus Mysteries: Was the "Original Jesus" a Pagan God?* Three Rivers Press, 1999.

George, Mary. *Mary, Called Magdalene*. Viking Press, 2002.

Grassi, Carolyn M., and Joseph A. Grassi. *Mary Magdalene and the Women in Jesus' Life*. Rowman & Littlefield Pub. Inc., 1986.

Haskins, Susan. *Mary Magdalen: Myth and Metaphor*. Harper Collins Publishers, 1993.

Ilan, Tal. *Jewish Women in Greco-Roman Palestine*. Hendrickson Publishers, 1995.

Jansen, Katherine Ludwig. *The Making of the Magdalen: Preaching and Popular Devotion in the Later Middle Ages*. Princeton University Press, 2001.

Kenyon, Tom, and Judi Sion. *The Magdalen Manuscript: The Alchemies of Horus & the Sex Magic of Isis*. ORB Communications, 2002.

King, Karen. *The Gospel of Mary of Magdala: Jesus and the First Woman Apostle*. Polebridge Press, 2003.

Kinstler, Clysta. *The Moon Under Her Feet*. HarperSanFrancisco, 1991.

Layton, Bentley. *The Gnostic Scriptures*. Doubleday, 1987.

Leloup, Jean-Yves. *The Gospel of Mary Magdalene*. Inner Traditions International, 2002.

Maisch, Ingrid. *Mary Magdalene: The Image of a Woman Through the Centuries*. Liturgical Press, 1998.

Malvern, Marjorie M. *Venus in Sackcloth.* Southern Illinois University Press, 1975. (Out-of-print.)

Marjanen, Antti. *The Woman Jesus Loved: Mary Magdalene in the Nag Hammadi Library and Related Documents.* Brill Academic Publishers, 1996.

Meyer, Marvin. *The Gospels of Mary: The Secret Tradition of Mary Magdalene, the Companion of Jesus.* Harper Collins, 2004.

Murphy, Cullen. *The Word According to Eve: Women and the Bible in Ancient Times and Our Own.* Houghton Mifflin Company, 1998.

Murray, Peter, and Linda Murray. *Oxford Dictionary of Christian Art.* Oxford University Press, 1996.

O'Shea, Stephen. *The Perfect Heresy: The Revolutionary Life and Death of the Medieval Cathars.* Walker Publishing Company, 2000.

Pagels, Elaine. *The Gnostic Gospels.* Vintage, 1989.

Partner, Peter. *The Knights Templar and Their Myth.* Destiny Books, 1990.

Picknett, Lynn, and Clive Prince. *The Templar Revelation.* Touchstone, 1998.

Robinson, James M., ed. *The Nag Hammadi Library in English.* HarperSanFrancisco, 1990.

Rudolph, Kurt. *Gnosis: The Nature & History of Gnosticism.* Harper & Row, 1987.

Schaberg, Jane. *The Resurrection of Mary Magdalene: Legends, Apocrypha, and the Christian Testament.* Continuum International Publishing Group, 2002.

Starbird, Margaret. *The Woman with the Alabaster Jar: Mary Magdalen and the Holy Grail.* Bear & Company, 1993.

———. *The Goddess in the Gospels: Reclaiming the Sacred Feminine.* Bear & Company, 1998.

Valtos, William M. *LA Magdalena.* Hampton Roads Publishing Company, 2002.

Wilson, David Niall. *This Is My Blood.* Terminal Fright Publications, 1999.

Websites

Blue Letter Bible: www.blueletterbible.com

CBC.ca. *7 Deadly Sins*: www.cbc.ca/7deadly/index.html

Christian Classics Ethereal Library. *Early Church Fathers*: www.ccel.org/fathers2

Early Christian Writings: www.earlychristianwritings.com

Evangelical Trinity Lutheran Church. *Crucifixion in the Ancient World*, by Richard P. Bucher: http://users.rcn.com/tlclcms/crucify.htm

FutureChurch: www.futurechurch.org

Gnosis Archive: www.gnosis.org

Magdalene.org: www.magdalene.org

Mary Magdalene: Author of the Fourth Gospel? (by Ramon K. Jusino): www.beloveddisciple.org

Mary Magdalene Chaplet: http://gigibeads.net/prayerbeads/saints/marymagdalene.html

Mary Magdalene icon by Robert Lentz: www.bridgebuilding.com/narr/gmm.html

Mary Magdalene lithograph by Richard Stodart: www.crosslink.net/~stodart/

Nag Hammadi Library: www.nag-hammadi.com/history.html

New Advent: www.newadvent.org

New Testament Gateway: www.ntgateway.com

Novena to St. Mary Magdalene: www.magdalene.org/novena.htm

Sacred Source (they carry a lovely Mary Magdalene statue): www.sacredsource.com

St. Mary of Magdala icon by Lu Bro: www.bridgebuilding.com/narr/lbmam.html

Videos

Biography—Mary Magdalene: The Hidden Apostle. A&E Home Video, 2000.

Mary Magdalen: An Intimate Portrait. View Video, 1995.

ReDiscovering Mary Magdalene: The Making of a Mythic Drama. CANCOM, 2001.

Chronology

Rather than giving you specific dates to remember, I'm presenting you
with a chronology that is mostly based on the century in which something
occurred. The only exceptions are the first century and our own twentieth
and twenty-first centuries.

Year(s)	Event(s)
c. 50–150	*Gospel of Thomas*
c. 70	Gospel of Mark
c. 80	Gospel of Matthew
c. 80–90	Gospel of Luke
c. 100	Gospel of Matthew
c. 125	*Gospel of Mary*
c. 150	*Gospel of Philip*
2nd century	Easter is celebrated
	Celsus refers to Mary Magdalene as a "half-frantic woman"
	Gnostic Christianity is very active
3rd century	*First Apocalypse of James*
	Baptistery with Mary Magdalene as myrrhophore is built at Dura-Europos
	Hippolytus composes his commentary on *Song of Songs*
4th century	*Acts of Philip*
	Pistis Sophia
	Manichaean Psalm-Book
	Christianity is legalized by Constantine
	Council of Nicaea
	Queen Helena's pilgrimage to the Holy Land
	Nag Hammadi texts are buried
5th century	Jerome refers to Mary Magdalene's name as an epithet
	One of the earliest crucifixion images
	Gnostic Christianity is almost completely wiped out by now
6th century	Pope Gregory the Great delivers his homily
	Pope Gregory organizes the seven deadly sins
	Mary Magdalene's grave is believed to be in Ephesus
7th century	Modestus refers to Mary Magdalene's martyrdom in Ephesus
8th century	Earliest mention of Mary Magdalene's feast day, July 22

Year(s)	Event(s)
9th century	Anglo-Saxon martyrology says Mary Magdalene went to live in the desert as a hermit out of sorrow
	Italian Vita eremitica suggests Mary Magdalene became a hermit out of penitence
	Church at Vézelay is founded and dedicated to the Virgin Mary
	Mary Magdalene's remains are transferred from Ephesus to Constantinople
10th century	Monks start acting out Passion plays
11th century	Guidelines in place for making people into saints
	Crusades begin
	Gesta episcoporum Cameracensum says Mary Magdalene's remains were transferred from Jerusalem to France
	Vita apostolica says that Mary Magdalene traveled in a boat with others to Marseilles
	Mary Magdalene's remains are believed to be at Vézelay
12th century	The Cathars are very active in France
	First Grail romance is written by Chrétien de Troyes
13th century	Evidence of Mary Magdalene's demons being associated with the seven deadly sins
	Jacobus de Voragine writes the *Golden Legend*
	Mary Magdalene's remains are "discovered" at St. Maximin
	Wolfram von Eschenbach writes his Holy Grail romance
	Albigensian Crusade is formed to wipe out Cathar heresy
14th century	The Knights Templar are dissolved
	Monastic orders begin to grow
	Mary Magdalene is depicted at the foot of the cross regularly
	Leonardo da Vinci paints *The Last Supper*
	Thomas Malory applies Holy Grail legend to Jesus' blood
16th century	Gregorian calendar reform
17th century	Stations of the Cross become a popular devotion

continues

continued

Year(s)	Event(s)
19th century	Victorian era
	Earnest Renan and other "naturalists" begin to speculate about Jesus' marital status
	A folklorist suggests that the Knights Templar were in possession of Gnostic wisdom and secret teachings about Christianity
	Gospel of Mary is discovered
1945	Nag Hammadi texts are discovered
1956	Pierre Plantard starts the Priory of Sion
1970	William Phipps suggests that Jesus and Mary Magdalene were married
1977	Nag Hammadi library and *Gospel of Mary* are published in English
1983	*Holy Blood, Holy Grail* is published in the United States
1988	*The Last Temptation of Christ* arrives in theaters, followed by a violent response
1993	*The Woman with the Alabaster Jar* is published
1998	Magdalene.org is premiered on the World Wide Web
2002	Foremost experts on Mary Magdalene gather with laypersons at St. Bartholomew's Church in New York for a conference, "Mary Magdalen: Prophet and Apostle in the Miriamic Tradition"
2003	*The Da Vinci Code* is published
2004	*The Passion of the Christ* opens in theaters, amid controversy over its graphic depictions of violence

Glossary

absolution   When a person confesses his or her sins to a priest in the Roman Catholic tradition, the priest then sets the person free of those sins. This act is called absolution.

alchemy   Alchemy usually refers to the practice of trying to turn one substance into another substance; you've probably heard about Renaissance alchemists trying to turn metal into gold. The term "alchemy" is now used loosely to indicate all kinds of transformative processes, particularly those that are spiritual, emotional, or psychological in nature.

anoint   The act of putting oil or ointment onto someone to indicate their consecration to a purpose; in this case, it was done for Jesus as the Messiah before his crucifixion. Kings of Israel were anointed in a ritual act of sanctification to the people and to God.

apocryphal   Something that's apocryphal often refers to a writing of questionable origin; in Christianity, however, the Apocrypha refers to texts that were included in the Greek version of the Old Testament but not in the Hebrew Bible. The Roman Catholic Bible includes the apocryphal texts but calls them "deuterocanonical," which means "books added to the canon." The Protestant Bible excludes all the apocryphal texts.

Aramaic   The language that was spoken by Jews in first-century Palestine was Aramaic. This is the language that Mary Magdalene would have spoken.

338   Appendix D

basilica   Originally, a basilica wasn't a church but a Roman public building where business was conducted. It is the architecture that defines a basilica—a tall, long hall lined by a row of columns on either side which separates the main aisle from aisles on either side. In the fourth century, after Christianity was legalized, basilicas started to be constructed as places of worship.

Book of Life   In the New Testament, the "book of life" is a book in which all of the righteous have their names inscribed. At the end of time, it says in *Revelation* (otherwise known as the *Apocalypse of John*), every person will be judged, and only those with their names in the book of life will enter paradise.

co-redemptrix   A "redemptrix" is a female redeemer. A "co"-redemptrix is a female who shares the role of redeemer with someone else; in this case, Jesus.

contemplative   A person who devotes his or her life to living in contemplation, or deep thought on a matter; in Mary Magdalene's case, she contemplates Jesus' sacrifice for humankind, her own penitence, and redemption.

Coptic   A late-Egyptian language written mostly in Greek characters. Today the Coptic language only survives as a liturgical language in the Coptic Orthodox Church.

cosmology   Refers to the theories of the way the universe and all of creation works.

crucifixion   A method of execution used by the Romans (though developed earlier) in which a victim was tied or nailed to a pole or cross and allowed to slowly die from exposure and exhaustion. Crucifixion was meant to be as much a warning to the public of the dire consequences of rebellion as a punishment for the victim.

cult   A group of people or a community that honors a particular deity or saint with religious observances. Today the term "cult" generally refers to a dangerous religious sect that isolates people from their communities and takes their money.

Danza de los Zancos   The name of this Spanish tradition literally reflects the nature of the event—"dance of the stilts," or "stilt dance."

deposition   The removal of Jesus from the cross.

docetic   Beliefs that describe the crucifixion and resurrection as events that only *appeared* to be what they were, and describe Jesus to have only *appeared* to be a real man are docetic. It comes from the Greek word *dokein*, which means "to seem."

Ecclesia   Greek for "church" or "assembly." This term refers to the entire body of believers in a given religion, particularly Judaism and Christianity. In Christianity, Ecclesia is another word for the collective term "the Church."

evangelist   Someone who spreads the gospel, as in missionary work. Matthew, Mark, Luke, and John are often referred to as "The Four Evangelists."

exorcism   A ritual that is performed to remove a demon from a person, place, or thing. Usually an exorcism is performed by a priest, but in some communities any Christian is thought to be capable of casting out demons.

gall   A bitter herb that was probably mixed with wine vinegar and offered to Jesus to ease his pain on the cross.

Gentile   A non-Jewish person.

Gnosticism/Gnostic/Gnosis   *Gnosis* is a Greek term for "knowledge." Gnosticism refers to an early sect of Christianity that flourished for several hundred years before finally being squeezed out by orthodox Christianity. There were many different schools of Gnostic thought, but they all shared a common theme of salvation through personal spiritual revelation and knowledge.

grotto   A small cave or carved-out impression from stone. Mary Magdalene is often depicted in art in a cavelike setting; these are references to her life in the grotto.

Hedonism   An overwhelming love of and desire for sumptuous comfort and pleasure. Mary Magdalene has often been portrayed as a hedonistic individual, wanton in her craving for carnal delights.

henna   An herb that is crushed and mixed into a paste, and then applied in artistic designs on the hands and feet of brides in some Middle Eastern countries, as well as India. The henna stains the skin a reddish color for about two weeks. This art is often called mendhi. Some Hebrew brides in first-century Palestine would have used henna to stain their hands and feet.

Hermetic   Around the first century, a new school of religious and philosophical thought called Hermetism grew up around the mythical figure of Hermes Trismegistus. Hermetism and its modern descendent, Hermeticism, have much in common with Gnostic thought.

Ketubah   A Jewish marriage contract. One of the purposes of this legal document was to specify a dowry that could revert to a woman in the event of divorce or widowhood.

Kosovo Polje   The location where Sultan Murad and Prince Lazar met in battle means "field of the blackbirds."

La Pyramide Inversée   At the Louvre Museum in Paris, France, there is a modern pyramid structure built of glass and steel in front of the main building. When you go into the Louvre, though, beneath the courtyard there is another pyramid of glass and steel hanging from the ceiling. *La pyramide inversée* is French for "the inverted pyramid." In the book *The Da Vinci Code*, we're led to believe that Mary Magdalene's bones are buried under a third tiny pyramid that stands beneath the point of *la pyramide inversée*.

liturgical   Having to do with liturgy, or the public expression of faith, prayer, and worship. The Christian *liturgical year* and *liturgical calendar* refer to when the major events of the faith are to be observed.

logos   In its most simple definition, logos is Greek for "word." It has more complex connotations, though, associated with "reason," both as humans experience it as a drive to know the Divine and as a universal principle that could describe "the mind of God."

martyrology   A text that records details about the lives and deaths of people who died for their faith, which in our case is Christianity. Martyrs usually went on to become saints.

mendicant   An order that depends on the alms and charity of others, with its members often begging for their sustenance rather than owning property and earning money.

Merovingian   The name of the first royal dynasty of Gaul, which would become France. The Merovingian kings ruled from the fifth to eighth centuries C.E. They were replaced by the Carolingians, the dynasty that included Charlemagne.

mystic   Someone who engages in contemplation or other religious and spiritual activities with the goal of developing a personal knowledge of, or some kind of spiritual union with, God is known as a mystic. Medieval mysticism rose in practice as a result of what many felt was an impersonal approach to Christianity by the Church.

Noli Me Tangere   Latin for "touch me not." This is the name by which the scene in which Mary Magdalene discovers the risen Christ outside the tomb has been known for centuries. There are countless paintings and sculptures depicting that specific moment.

novena   A type of candle in a tall, slender glass that you can find in many places, including some grocery stores. Often novena candles are associated with special novena prayers or readings, which are recited over the space of nine days.

pagan   A rather complicated term, *pagani* was invented by Christians in the fourth century and applied retroactively to describe non-Christians. It meant, more or less, "civilian," or "rustic." Pagans were those who followed Roman religions; those who sacrificed to the Roman gods and belonged to mystery cults. It was later applied more widely to refer to non-Christians in other areas of the world who followed their local religions.

Paraclete   In the New Testament, mention is made of the Paraclete, or "helper" that will come to comfort and aid believers after Jesus departs. Mainstream Christianity thinks of the Paraclete as the Holy Spirit based on what is written in the Gospel of John, and considers it part of a triune God. Manichaeans interpreted it differently.

Pascha   In Eastern Orthodox Christianity, Pascha refers to the Passover, or the time when Easter occurs. It is used in the way that other Christian traditions use the term "Easter."

Passion, The   The period of time in Jesus' life following the Last Supper, culminating with the crucifixion. It refers to the events during the last day of his life, with an understanding of the suffering he endured for the benefit of humankind.

patriarchal   A culture or institution that is governed by men is called patriarchal. Many people believe that patriarchal cultures place less value on women than on men.

penitent   One who feels sorrow or guilt for his or her sins or mistakes, and who may have sincerely set about on a new path in life to make amends for what he or she has done. Penitents may perform *penance*, spiritual or moral deeds to make amends for their past errors.

Pharisee   One of the powerful sects of Judaism at the time of Christ. They taught strict adherence to the written and oral laws.

Pistis Sophia   The literal translation of the Greek words *pistis sophia* is "faith-wisdom." *Pistis Sophia* is the collective title for a group of four Gnostic books probably written in the third century, in which Mary Magdalene is the disciple who understands Jesus' message best.

Platonic philosophy   Philosophy is the "love of wisdom." Plato was a philosopher who lived in Greece in the fourth century B.C.E. Philosophy based on his ideas is called *Platonic*.

polemic   An argument for or against something. As used in this book, a polemic is a document written to refute Gnosticism, such as Irenaeus of Lyon's *Against All Heresies*, written in the second century C.E.

pre-Raphaelite   In 1848, a society of painters broke away from producing the typical art of their day, determined to present their subjects with more beauty, realism, and depth than dictated by the prominent art school of the time. Mary Magdalene was one of the subjects Pre-Raphaelite artists were interested in exploring.

Rabboni   An honorific title that means "my teacher" or "master."

relic   Usually the corpse (or a piece of the corpse) of a holy person, but it could also refer to something associated with a holy person. For example, Mary Magdalene's alabaster jar was considered a relic, as was the cross and Jesus' crown of thorns.

reliquary   A container built to contain a relic; it may be as small as a pillbox or as large and elaborate as a sarcophagus. It may be meant for personal use only or for public display. Some were very simple, made of wood, and others were encrusted with precious metals and jewels.

resurrection   The raising of a person from the dead. In Jewish theology the resurrection of the dead was believed to occur at the end of time, when the bodies of the righteous arose to enter the presence of God and the wicked were judged. Jesus' resurrection is viewed by New Testament writers as the beginning of this end-time resurrection.

romance   A medieval romance is a long tale, written as an epic poem or a narrative, of the heroic adventures of a particular figure.

Sadducee   One of the other powerful sects of Judaism at the time of Christ. They taught strict adherence only to the written Mosaic law.

sepulchre   A burial chamber, or tomb.

stigmata   The phenomenon wherein a person manifests the wounds of Christ on his or her body. Francis of Assisi was the first stigmatist, developing the wounds after a period of prolonged isolation in the wilderness while following Mary Magdalene's example of a contemplative, hermitic existence.

Tarot   Tarot (pronounced *ta*-roh) cards are often associated with fortune telling and the occult now, but when they were first appeared around the fifteenth century in Italy, they were apparently just playing cards. The Tarot "trumps," are a subset of the 78-card Tarot deck that bear highly symbolic images. Among them are The Lovers, The Chariot, The Hermit, The Hanged Man, and The Tower.

Theotokos   Meaning "god-bearer" or "mother of god," this is a title used to refer to the Virgin Mary in Eastern Orthodox churches.

Torah When Christians refer to the Torah, they are usually referring to the first five books of the Old Testament—Genesis, Exodus, Leviticus, Numbers, and Deuteronomy. For Jews, however, the Torah is a much broader category. It can apply to the Books of Moses (the five books already mentioned), or to the Written Torah (the whole of Jewish scripture), as well as to the Oral Torah (the interpretation of the scriptures and how to apply the laws), or to all of these combined.

triptych A painting that's done on three separate panels. Usually the center panel is larger and contains the main subject, such as the crucifixion. Often patron saints are painted on the side panels.

unity theory A term by which we refer to the idea that Mary Magdalene was also Mary of Bethany and the anonymous sinner of Luke.

Vulgate A very popular translation of the Bible, from Hebrew and Aramaic, into Latin by the Christian "Church Father" Jerome in the late fourth century C.E. The Vulgate was the most commonly used version of the Bible for 1,500 years. The name comes from *versio vulgate*, which means, simply, "common translation."

Index

G

N